Core Concepts of Financial Accounting: A Study Guide

Merle W. Hopkins Ph.D.

Copyright © 2002 by Merle W. Hopkins, Ph.D.
All rights reserved.

This book, or parts thereof, may not be further reproduced by any means, electronic or mechanical including photocopying and recording, or by any information storage or retrieval system, without permission of the publisher and copyright holder.

Printed in the United States of America

ISBN 1-58692-441-9

Erudition Books
Courier Custom Publishing, Inc.
15 Wellman Avenue
North Chelmsford, MA 01863
877-408-5027

Please visit our website at www.eruditionbooks.com

Introduction to BUAD 250a
Topic 1
This topic ties to chapters 1 and 2 in the SSD text.

Accounting has been called the language of business. The most relevant interpretation is that business managers must have the ability to think and communicate in the accounting medium if the businesses and their managers are to prosper. Managers need the ability to ask relevant questions and fully understand answers to those questions as well as the implications of those answers. Communication in accounting involves speaking, listening, writing and reading. Managers must be able to communicate in accounting terms through all of these media.

Managers do not have to be accountants but they must have the ability to ask relevant questions being able to recognize 'bad' answers. If the manager does not have enough information about the topic under discussion, there is not much chance the manager will be able to differentiate between good and bad answers or good and bad advice. These comments are true at every management level where decision-making occurs. A former CEO of a publicly traded company told me that within his former firm, if he discovered a promotion candidate was unable to think and communicate in the accounting medium that the decision was always *not* to promote the individual. Another, more recent, situation involved a senior executive who had engaged me to develop his accounting and finance skills for his possible promotion to become the CEO of his firm [one of the Dow Jones Industrial 30].

Financial accounting represents the common basis for record keeping in firms whether there is a profit motive or not. Managers must make decisions involving allocation of scarce resources within a firm. These decisions reflect expected *future* results of the decisions. A manager's performance is usually evaluated on achieved results that have been measured in an accounting framework. Common uses of accounting information by managers might include some or all of these: finding a suitable mix of debt and equity when forming the firm, deciding which operating assets to acquire, selecting managers deserving of promotion, deciding how to better provide for the firm's liquidity needs, deciding how to evaluate operating results of the entity and its component parts, deciding how to budget better, evaluating actual results compared to budgeted results, and making proper decisions about dividends payments to shareholders. There are countless other uses of accounting information.

Your ability to learn accounting information in this course will be largely cumulative. As you progress through this class you are expected to learn new information in relation to material previously covered. You should develop a focused approach to this course starting now to make your work more productive during the semester. You should seek to understand not memorize. An understanding will allow you to think and communicate in accounting terms during this semester and beyond.

Accounting exists on two planes. Record keeping is the more basic of the two and can be thought of as 'bookkeeping'. Most firms engage in countless transactions that need to be recorded, summarized, and presented as financial statements that users will analyze to evaluate the firm's performance. Top management will evaluate the performance of the managers at various levels in the firm using financial statement information. Managers with the ability to engage in decision-making while using financial statement information have the capability of adding immense value to the firms they manage. Financial statement information is only meaningful when managers understand what the information implies.

My objective in this course is to develop your ability to add immense value to the firms you will manage. The accounting information you will need to use is both quantitative and qualitative. Financial statements are released to the public unless the firm is privately held. Private lenders usually require financial statement information but this data usually does not become public knowledge.

To develop the capability of making better decisions based on accounting information and concepts, managers need knowledge of the record keeping function to grasp financial statement subtleties. For example, with little knowledge of accounting, financial analysts may fail to observe important parts of the firm's operating results or condition. Accounting information does not give the whole story but does add an important part of any manager's knowledge base when making decisions to increase shareholder values.

Financial accounting seeks to provide useful information when making decisions. Published financial statements are 'general-purpose', and users need skills to obtain accounting information that has a bearing on the decision(s) being made.

The basic financial statements include the balance sheet (B/S), the income statement (I/S) and the statement of cash flows (Sof$F).

Balance Sheet
The B/S contains information about resources (**assets**) that are owned or controlled by the firm. Assets have probable future economic value usually through use or sale, are controlled by the firm and are related to a prior transaction. The balance sheet also contains information about the firm's obligations (**liabilities**). Liabilities involve probable future economic sacrifices, are unavoidable and are related to a prior transaction. The last part of the balance sheet is **owners' equity** representing the aggregate investment by owners. Owners' equity is often called 'net assets' because it equals assets less liabilities.

The **basic accounting equation** is
$$\text{Assets} = \text{Liabilities} + \text{Owners' Equity}$$

The basic accounting equation could be rewritten as
$$\text{Assets} - \text{Liabilities} = \text{Owners' Equity}$$
making it apparent why owners' equity and 'net assets' are the same.

Income Statement

The **income statement** (I/S) basically contains revenues, expenses and net income. Net income occurs when revenues exceed expenses. A net loss occurs when expenses exceed revenues.

Revenues generally must be earned. Revenues are 'good' things. If I could show you how to increase your revenues, you would likely be eager to learn how to accomplish this ☺. Later in this topic and in the course, I will refine this basic definition of revenues.

Expenses typically result from using up resources in the process of earning revenues. If I could show you how to reduce your expenses, you would likely be eager to learn more about what might be involved ☺. Later in this topic and in the course, I will refine this basic definition of expenses.

Net income is what remains of the revenues after covering the expenses. Net income is a 'good' thing and generally more is better than less. Would you rather have more or less income, if all other things were equal? [You knew the answer to that question at a 'tender' age.☺]

Statement of Cash Flows

The statement of cash flows (Sof$F) provides information about the firm's cash flows from three basic sources: operating, investing and financing activities. Sof$F information is prepared on a different basis than the I/S and the B/S, and often provides savvy financial statement users with a convenient summary of the cash flow activity.

Who Are These Financial Statement Users?

There are many groups using financial statements. All financial statement users are assumed to be aware of accounting principles used to prepare financial statements. Just as with so many areas in our lives, without an adequate grasp of the area we cannot absorb our desired meaning of the information being communicated to us. For example, assume any financial statement user makes a decision based on information contained in a set of financial statements and the decision turns out to be wrong because the decision-maker *misunderstood* the financial statements. The financial statement user has no excuse because he/she did not understand information that was properly reported. If the financial statements were not properly prepared and were audited by an accounting firm, there may be some legal recourse available to the user for losses traceable to the misstatement(s) in the financial statements and/or the accounting firm's failure to follow the standards of the accounting (auditing) profession. [The recent Enron experience provides a valuable example. Worldcom may provide another example depending on how the current situation plays out.]

How many of you want to obtain a position after graduations from which you will be promoted at least once? Upwardly mobile managers must have sufficient accounting skills to cause proper financial statements to be prepared. As importantly, managers need accounting skills to understand information contained in the financial statements prepared by firms with which they do business.

Representative user groups include: lenders, investors, potential investors, managers, employees, labor unions, customers, suppliers, competitors and governments. User groups must identify good ways to extract valuable information from the general-purpose financial statements.

Why Do We Need Accounting Standards (Rules)?
Can you imagine how entertaining football would be if each referee made up his own rules for the game? Maybe you think that would be entertaining, but the football teams would find it irritating. In the previous century there was a movement toward the development of a standardized set of accounting rules referred to as **generally accepted accounting principles [GAAP]**. Entities are free to choose specific accounting methods from GAAP. Users must have some basic knowledge of GAAP in order to understand what is meant by information in published financial statements.

Within GAAP there is a continuing trend limiting the range of acceptable choices. Originally, the range of choice was broader than at the present time. Another trend emerged in the last two decades of the twentieth century, reporting or disclosing fair market value information in the financial statements. The movement toward fair market value information has numerous supporters in high places and will probably continue. Historic cost data tends to be highly reliable but lacking the relevance of current but estimated market values. The tradeoff between elements of relevance and reliability will continue to 'bug' the accounting profession. Two important topics in this course have undergone significant changes in the last twelve months.

The Financial Accounting Standards Board [FASB] has been the senior private sector accounting rule-setting body since the 1970's. Most pronouncements involving GAAP are traceable to continuing deliberations of FASB. The Securities and Exchange Commission [SEC] has the ultimate legal responsibility for the accounting rules in the country. When the SEC has felt some improvement in GAAP has been desirable, it has demonstrated a willingness to exercise its legal authority to set accounting standards. Sometimes, accounting rules have resulted from actual or threatened federal legislation. Accounting rules reflect our social, legal, political and economic environments. Naturally, there have been considerable differences in accounting rules across national boundaries.

Let's Take a Look at the Basic Three Financial Statements
The basic three financial statements present information highly summarized information reflecting countless transactions. Properly prepared summaries are sufficient for mangers' use in decision-making.

The B/S contains assets, liabilities and owners' equity all measured at the 'balance sheet date'. You should think of the B/S as a *snapshot* of the firm's account balances at that moment in time. When a checking account statement summarizes all the deposits and checks that have cleared through the account in a time period. The ending balance is a 'snapshot' summary of all of that activity. The deposits and checks represent the activity *during* the period.

Assets
Assets are probable future economic resources that must be controlled by the firm resulting from some previous transaction. Probable future economic benefits may not be as certain as you think. Would a lottery ticket be an asset *before* the drawing? The assets need not be owned. For example, a leased car is an asset to its user although it is not owned.

If you sign a contract to occupy an apartment at a *future* date and you agree to make *future* payments to the landlord, you have no asset at this time because of the agreement. There would be no 'past transaction' between you and the landlord in this case. Attorneys describe the relationship between you and the landlord as an *executory* agreement.

Think of yourself as a 'business' instead of a student. What are some of your assets?

Liabilities
Liabilities are probable future economic sacrifices that the firm cannot avoid resulting from some previous transaction. The probable future economic sacrifices do not have to be 'sure things'. Estimated future economic sacrifices frequently appear as liabilities.

If you signed a contract to occupy an apartment starting at a *future* date and to make *future* payments to the landlord, you have no current basis to record a liability as a result of the contract. There would be no 'past transaction' and attorneys describe the relationship between you and your landlord as an *executory* agreement.

Can you name some things that would be liabilities in your balance sheet if you were a company instead of a person?

Owners' Equity
Owners' equity [OE] represents the owners' residual interest in the firm and is the difference between assets and liabilities, or net assets.

OE has two basic parts: **contributed capital** and retained capital. Some contributed capital **(CC)** was invested by the owners at the inception of the firm and could have been increased subsequently by additional investments by them. Original and subsequent investments by owners are indistinguishable within OE. Retained capital is called **retained earnings (RE)** if the firm is a corporation. For convenience, RE will be commonly used in this course. RE represents net income that has been earned and retained. Alternatively, net income could have been distributed to the owners in the form of dividends. [OE can be more complex than described here in Topic 11 we will cover added details.]

Financial statements are intended to be useful in decision-making and the relationship between CC and RE can provide insight into the firm's success to date. Consider two firms each having $100,000 in OE. The first has only $1,000 of that amount as CC and the other $99,000 is RE, while the second has 99% of the value in CC while only 1% is in RE. If both firms were founded five years ago and neither has paid out any dividends, which would you rather have founded? Hopefully, the answer is obvious to all. I am assuming that all of us are motivated, in part, by monetary rewards and the things we can do with them.

There are several concepts that help us fit all the pieces together into a coherent framework. The **entity concept** reminds us that separate entities should have separate financial statements [as well as underlying accounting records] in order that users can have a better sense of accountability regarding the economic results of each firm. The **historic cost convention** is a basic building block for much of the financial accounting model. The historic cost convention involves reporting assets and liabilities at their original amounts. Logical variations will be developed as we move through these topics. Accountants like to use historic cost for assets and liabilities because these numerical values are more reliable and easily traceable to source documents. The **going concern assumption** deals with a number of issues including asset valuation. Assets and liabilities are normally carried at their historic costs unless the accountants feel the firm has serious problems making it unlikely it will survive for another year. When a firm fails the going concern assumption, assets and liabilities may be revalued reflecting their current value in the balance sheet. For example, a piece of land might be revalued to fair market value if the going concern assumption has not been met.

Income Statement

The I/S contains revenues, expenses, gains and losses for the period. I/S are dated at the end of a specified time period and summarize the period's transactions. I/S are like a 'movie' of the period while B/S are more like a snapshot taken at the end of the period.

Financial statement **recognition** means the item will appear in the appropriate financial statement. For example, recognized revenues will appear in an I/S and an account receivable will appear in the B/S.

Revenues are recognized when they have been earned and realized. Revenues are earned when all of the work necessary to complete the task has been expended. [There are some exceptions to be developed later in these topics.] Revenue realization means the entity has collected the cash or there is a claim to cash.

Can you name some things that would be revenues for you, if you were a company instead of a person?

Expenses are recognized when something has been 'used up' in association with generating revenues. Ideally, there is some association between the recognition of revenues and expenses. Normally, we match revenues and expenses in the same time period in order to better measure income for that period. If a consulting firm has recognized some revenues, all of the expenses incurred in generating the revenues should be recognized in the same period in order to properly measure the profit or loss on the consulting engagement.

Can you name some things that would be expenses, if you were a company instead of a person?

Revenues and expenses occur in the entity's primary and recurring commercial activities. Ford Motor Corporation has the biggest auto finance subsidiary in the United States. That would be part of its primary activities as well as auto manufacturing and sales. There are likely other activities at Ford producing revenues and expenses since they are part of the entity's 'primary' activities. I often tell people that 'primary activities' are the things the entity does for a 'living'.

When other events occur outside the primary recurring commercial activities, we call them gains or losses in the income statement. Revenues and gains increase income (a 'good' thing). Revenues are recurring while gains are not. If a consulting firm performs work on a consulting contract with a client, revenues are recognized. If the same consulting firm sells a piece of equipment that had been used in the business, the consulting firm would recognize a **gain** if the equipment is sold for more than its cost when new. Gains make net income larger. [Selling used equipment would *not* be part of the *consulting* firm's primary commercial activities.]

Conversely, if the consulting firm had sold land for *less* than the price paid for the land when buying it, the consulting firm would recognize a loss for the difference. Losses make net income smaller. [Land would *not* be part of a *consulting* firm's primary commercial activities.]

What transactions might generate gains and losses for *you* if you were a company instead of a person?

Net income is the excess of the 'good guys'(revenues and gains) over the 'bad guys' (expenses and losses). Revenues and expenses are recurring and related to the entity's primary activities, while gains and losses and non-recurring and not related to the entity's primary activities. Gains and losses are peripheral to the entity's recurring commercial activities.

Would you prefer $1,000,000 in revenues or a gain of the same size?

No matter what your answer is, the correct *economic* answer depends on your value system. The revenue for $1,000,000 would be matched against all related expenses to obtain an income figure. On the other hand, the revenue would stem from a *recurring* activity. The gain would not be matched against any expenses and would all go to the bottom line. However, gains are non-recurring. Most companies with revenues of $1,000,000 want future revenues particularly if they were able to an adequate income from the effort. A gain of $1,000,000 would be a non-recurring event. I may have the 'luck' to win $1,000,000 in a poker game [gain] but not the skill to earn $1,000,000 per evening in a poker game [revenue].

Statement of Cash Flows
Cash flows come in three categories: operating, investing and financing. **Operating cash flows** are created in the firm's normal, recurring commercial activity. *Cash flows* from sales activities are operating cash flows regardless of when the revenue is *earned*. The cash might have been *earned* [revenue] in an earlier period but would be a cash flow only when *collected*. Similarly, a cash outflow for salaries would be an operating cash outflow when paid. The cash for salary might be paid out in the current year but might have been earned by the employee in an earlier year. Total operating cash flow will tell us if the firm's regular activities are currently generating positive or negative cash flows. Unless the firm is new, a firm should be producing *positive* operating cash flows from its operations. Occasionally, a firm might experience unusual business conditions and its cash flows from operating activities would be negative for a while.

If you were a company instead of a student, what would be some of your operating cash flows?

Investing cash flows result from purchases or sales of items that are not consumed in regular recurring commercial activities. If a financial consulting firm purchased investments with temporary surplus cash, we would treat the cash paid out as an *investing* use of cash. Buying or selling property, plant and equipment is an investing activity. Most of the time, buying and selling an investment is treated as an *investing* cash flow. If you were to make a loan to a friend, you would treat it as an investing activity. [I am assuming that you are not a bank. ☺] Net investing cash *outflows* might indicate firm is expanding if the biggest investing cash outflows are for purchases of property, plant and equipment.

If you were a company instead of a student, what would be some of your investing cash flows?

Financing cash flows are cash transactions between the entity and its debt-holders or owners. Transactions with debt-holders refer only to the *principal* amounts borrowed or repaid. [Interest portion is treated as part of operating activities.] Financing activities with owners include issuing equity securities paying dividends to them. Buying or selling treasury shares are financing cash flows, too. [When a corporation buys back shares from shareholders, these shares become 'treasury shares' until sold or retired by the corporation.]

Helpful Hint:
In general, all cash flows tied to dividends and interest are operating cash flows, *except for* dividends paid to shareholders [financing activities].

If you were a company instead of a student, what would be some of your financing cash flows?

Financial Statement Relationships:
For each of the independent fact situations below determine the effects on each of the financial statement elements shown in the following grid. Show increases with a '+' and decreases with a '-'. For this exercise, we will ignore the statement of cash flows. The purpose of this exercise is to expand your familiarity with the basic elements that comprise the financial statements. Additionally, it is important to begin to see how the financial statements reflect the results of countless transactions that meet the requirements to be included in the financial statements.

1. The firm received cash for work that will be performed next year.
2. The firm signed a lease on office space for a one-year period starting today. Half of the cash for the entire year was paid today. The remainder will be paid at the end of the lease term.
3. The firm leased a computer for one-year *starting next month* and will not have to pay any cash until the computer has been in use for three months.
4. One month of the one-year office rental has expired.
5. The owners invested some cash and other assets in the firm.
6. The firm invested some of its surplus cash in office supplies for later use.
7. The firm's employees were paid for one month's work except for one employee who specifically requested that the month's salary be paid to him at a later date.
8. The firm repaid money to its bank. For simplicity, assume there was no interest.
9. The firm performed consulting services for a client and collected 75% of the cash immediately. The remainder will be received at a later date as agreed upon.

	Balance Sheet			Income Statement		
	Assets	Liabilities	Owners' Equity	Revenues	Expenses	Income
1.	+ C	+ R				
2.	−	+	−			
3.						
4.	Pre Paid −		−		+	−
5.	+		+			

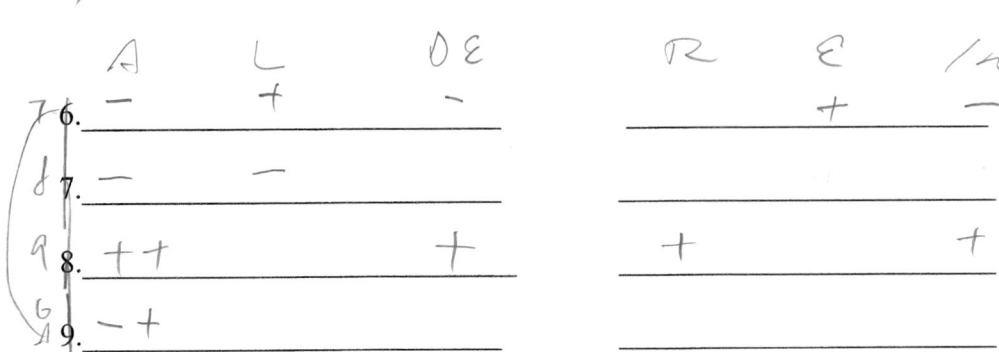

Answers:
1. Assets and liabilities would both increase for the full amount of the cash received. The firm has more cash [an asset] and owes the service [liability]. Revenues, expenses and net income would be unaffected.
2. Cash, an asset, would decrease and Prepaid Rent, an asset, would increase. The changes in these accounts would be only for the amount of cash that was paid at the inception of the lease. The remainder of the cash would not be recognized at the start of the lease because the unpaid portion of the lease would be executory [and not related to a past transaction]. Total assets would not change, but the composition of the assets would change.
3. Nothing would be recorded. The firm does not have the computer now and does not currently owe any amount. Nether party has performed at this time. The contract is fully executory. Later, when the computer is received, the liability will have to be recorded.
4. Decrease assets [Prepaid Rent] for the portion used up [one sixth of the balance in that account] and increase expenses [Rent Expense] for one sixth of the previous balance in the Prepaid Rent account. Inside the I/S note that when expenses increase that net income decreases. When net income decreases, there is a simultaneous decrease in the RE portion of OE. Thus the B/S equation stays in balance. Assets down and OE down by the same portion.
5. Assets [Cash] increases and OE [Contributed Capital] increases. Nothing in the I/S is changed and the B/S equation still is in balance.
6. One asset [Cash] decreases and another asset [Office Supplies] increases. These offsetting changes would be for the same amounts if dollar values were given. Note that there are no expenses associated with the mere purchase of supplies even though those supplies are intended for later use. Expenses are associated with the 'using up' of things in the process of try to generate revenues exceeding the expenses.
7. Expenses [Salaries Expense] would increase for the value of *all* employees' time consumed in the month and this would decrease income for the month. In turn, this would result in lower OE. Remember that part of OE is the cumulative result of income earned less dividends made available to the owners. The amount still owed to the one employee who requested to be paid at a later date would cause liabilities to increase [Salaries Payable]. Assets [Cash] would decrease by the amount paid to the employees. Net result is that changes in the B/S equation would, themselves, balance.

8. Liabilities [Notes Payable] and Assets [Cash] would both decrease with this transaction. For simplicity, interest on the loan was omitted.
9. Revenues would increase by the value of the services performed and this would increase income and OE, in turn. Assets [Cash] would increase by the portion received immediately and assets [Accounts Receivable] would also increase by the amount that is to be received later as agreed upon.

Related exercises can be found in the accompanying work Adding Value with Financial Accounting Exercises by Merle W. Hopkins.

Financial Statement Relationships:
Directions: Respond to each of the requirements below. The questions are independent unless otherwise noted. This exercise emphasizes the algebraic relationships between the components of the financial statements and further develops skill in using the basic elements of financial statements. Caution: some requirements may include unnecessary information that must not be utilized when correctly working those requirements.

1. $ __550__ A firm's liabilities were $900 at the start of a year. These liabilities are 90% of the firm's starting assets. If the firm's equity increased during the year by $450, what would be the ending OE?

2. $ __2500__ A firm's ending OE totaled $3,000 and this amount was 4 times as large as beginning assets. If the firm's beginning liabilities were $550 and liabilities decreased by $50 during the year, what were the firm's ending assets?

3. $ __15,000__ The owners of a firm contributed $2,500 to their firm during a year and the firm had net income of $800 during the same year. The owners made no withdrawals during the year. The firm's beginning OE was $3,000 and that amount was 25% of the firm's beginning liabilities. What were the firm's beginning assets?

4. $ __9600__ The owners withdrew $500 from their firm during the year for personal use. The firm's net income had been $1,200 for that same year. If the ending OE was $3,200 and this was half the ending liabilities, what would the firm's ending assets have been?

5. $ __2500__ In the previous problem [#4], what would have been the beginning OE?

6. $ __900__ A firm's assets doubled during a particular year while the firm's liabilities tripled in the same year. If the beginning assets had been $1,500 and this amount had been 125% of the beginning OE, what were the ending liabilities?

7. $ ~~3500~~ A firm was founded by three owners who each contributed $500 to the firm. Two of the owners each loaned $1,000 to the firm at the time the firm was formed. What were the beginning assets of the firm?

8. $ ~~2000~~ In the previous item [#7], if the assets increased by $500 *more than the liabilities* during the firm's first year of operations, what was the firm's ending OE?

9. $ ~~100,000~~ + If a firm bought a truck paying $50,000 down and financing the rest with a two-year note payable for $100,000, what was the *change* in the firm's *total assets* as a result of this transaction?

10. $ ~~50,000~~ In the previous item [#9], when the firm paid off half of the note payable, what would have been the *change* on the firm's *total assets* as a result of this 'pay off' transaction? You may ignore depreciation on the truck and interest on the note.

Answers:
1. $550
2. $2,500
3. $15,000
4. $9,600
5. $2,500
6. $900
7. $3,500
8. $2,000
9. $100,000 increase
10. $50,000 decrease

Financial Statement Elements:
For each of these independent situations, identify *which* financial statement elements are impacted. The elements are: assets, liabilities, and OE. OE is comprised of contributions by owners, revenues, expenses, gains and losses. I expect that you will show only the *net* change in each of the three elements. Indicate whether each of the elements you identify is increasing or decreasing by using an arrow pointing in the appropriate direction. In all cases, the firm is a consulting firm rendering financial advice to its clients.

$A = L + OE \qquad R - E = In$

1. The firm sold an investment for more than had been paid to purchase the investment. Show the effects of the sale transaction.

2. The firm collected some cash from a client for work the firm had done previously. The correct accounting had been done at the time the services were rendered. Show the effects of the collection transaction.

   No Change.

$A = L + OE \qquad R - E = I/L$

3. The firm paid for some supplies which had been purchased on account last month. The accounting had been done correctly when these supplies had been purchased. Show the effects of the payment transaction.

4. The firm provided some consulting services for a client and agreed that the client could pay for the services in two months. Show the effects of rendering the services.

5. The firm borrowed some money from a 'loan shark.' A loan shark is not a traditional lender. Show the effects of the borrowing transaction.

6. The firm repaid the principal of the amount borrowed from the 'loan shark' and the interest on the principal. Show the effects of the repayment.

7. The firm paid its employees for the work they performed during the month ending on the day the salaries were paid. Show the effects of this payment of salaries.

8. The owners contributed some cash to permit the firm to accomplish its expansion plans. Show the effect of this investment.

9. The firm's profits seemed to be larger than the managers had expected and the firm simultaneously declared and paid a dividend to its owners. A dividend involves distributing an asset to the firm's owners and reduces OE in the firm. Show the impact of the simultaneous declaration and payment of the dividend.

10. The city gave a piece of land to the firm with these conditions: (1) the firm could not move from the city and (2) the firm would employ at least 100 people for the next 4 years. The firm's managers had already decided that they would keep the firm in the city and that the firm's payroll would have been increased to 500 people for the next 5 years. Current accounting rules (GAAP) require that donations received be accounted for as gains. Show the effects of the donation on the accounting records of the firm.

Answers
1. Assets increase and OE increases. [Cash goes up by more than the investments decrease. OE increases because of the gain.]
2. Total assets do not change. [Cash increases and Accounts Receivable decreases. These changes are offsetting and total assets remain unchanged. In the accounting that would have previously recorded, assets (Accounts Receivable) would have increased when the OE increased because the revenue had been earned.]
3. Assets would decrease and liabilities would decrease. [Cash decreases and Accounts Payable decreases. When the Supplies had been purchased previously, the Supplies inventory account would have increased and Accounts Payable would have increased also.]
4. Assets and OE increase equally. [Accounts Receivable increases and Revenues cause an increase in owners' equity.]

5. Assets and liabilities both increase. [Cash and Notes Payable both increase. The reference to a 'loan shark' does not change the basics of the accounting implications.]
6. Assets [Cash] decrease by the amount of principal plus interest. Liabilities decrease only by the amount of principal repaid. OE decreases (due to the increase in Interest Expense).
7. Assets decrease and OE decreases. [Cash decreases and Salaries Expense increases. Expenses decrease OE.]
8. Assets and OE both increase. [Cash and Contributed Capital increase.]
9. Assets decrease and OE decreases. [Both Cash and RE decrease. The accounting implications are streamlined when the firm declares and pays dividends simultaneously as in this case. We will learn more about this later in topic 12.]
10. Assets would increase by the fair market value of the land contributed to the firm. If there were any conditions imposed by the donor beyond those the firm would have done absent the donation, then a liability for the excess would need to be recognized. In this case, all of the city's conditions are less than what the firm was already planning to do and, thus, no liability would need to be recognized in these circumstances. A gain for the full fair market value of the land would be recognized and this would cause OE to increase. [Cash and Gain would both increase.]

Overview of Financial Statements and the Balance Sheet

Topic 2
This topic ties to chapter 4 in the SSD text.

The **balance sheet equation** governs most accounting relationships.

$$\text{Assets} = \text{Liabilities} + \text{OE}$$

As in Lecture 1, OE includes the effects of revenues, expenses, gains and losses. As the sum of all of these income statement elements, net income is known as the 'bottom line.' Net Income flows into Retained Earnings and becomes part of OE. Because of this connection between the 'bottom line' and RE, the I/S becomes part of the B/S.

The B/S is usually shown as a **classified balance sheet**. Within the subdivisions, **current assets** and **non-current assets,** we will discuss several important account names expanding your 'vocabulary' of important accounting terms. Within these categories, the accounts are presented in descending order of liquidity. Current assets usually consist of Cash or other assets converting to cash within one year or the firm's operating cycle, whichever is longer. Current assets also include accounts intended for *consumption* within one year. Sometimes, immaterial assets are shown as current assets too.

Cash is a current asset if it is unrestricted and intended for use as needed. Cash would include currency and checking account balances. If management had agreed in a contract to some restrictions on the use of Cash or if management intended to restrict Cash for some future use, restricted amounts would be shown as non-current assets.

Cash equivalents are not Cash but are treated is if they were Cash. Cash equivalents must have maturity dates of three months or less when purchased. Thus, cash equivalents must be debt securities. Investments in money market securities are cash equivalents. While not Cash, cash equivalents are 'close enough' to Cash to be treated as Cash for financial statement purposes. [If a firm purchased a debt security maturing in *six* months, the security would not be a cash equivalent when purchased. If the firm were preparing a balance sheet four months after buying the debt security, would the debt security be a cash equivalent? No. The cash equivalent requirements have to be met *when buying* the security.]

Accounts receivable are current assets containing amounts *earned* by the entity but not yet collected. Accounts receivable [A/R] occur when firms provide goods and/or services to customers agreeing to be paid later. In some business this is a routine occurrence. Revenue must be recognized when earned and realized. Realization means the seller has the cash or a claim to cash. The claim to cash is most commonly called an A/R if it arose in the course of ordinary business by providing goods or services to customers. If a receivable is created in a *lending* transaction accountants are likely to call it a Note Receivable [N/R]. [The most basic difference between a N/R and an A/R depends upon the formality of the relationship between the parties. If the receivable is documented by a written, signed document it more likely will be called a N/R. If the receivable from a business relationship between the parties, it will more commonly be called an A/R.]

Prepaid items are usually current assets because they are intended for consumption within one year or are immaterial. Common examples include Prepaid Insurance, Office Supplies, Prepaid Rent and Prepaid Salaries. Assume the firm pays an employee for one year's salary in advance on August 31 of Year 1. At the end of Year 1, if a classified B/S must be prepared, how much of the Prepaid Salary will appear as a current asset? [Answer: 7/12 of the amount paid to the employee. 5/12 of the year's salary has been used up becoming an expense, while the remainder of the year's salary continues to be an asset.]

Short-term investments are made for a many business reasons and these will be developed at length in Topic 9. For now, we will take a look at the basic motives for holding investments in other firms. A firm might have temporary surplus cash and wish to make investments for the purpose of earning some interest, dividends or price appreciation until the cash might needed later. These investments might be classified as a current or non-current assets as discussed earlier. Typical investments include certificates of deposit, debt securities [original maturity exceeding three months], or equity securities such as shares of stock in another entity.

Non-current assets include all other assets controlled or owned by the firm.

Non-current investments might be made for a variety of reasons including strengthening business relationships.

Property, Plant and Equipment [PPE] represents a broad range of assets to be *used* over several accounting periods in the firm's operations including land, buildings and equipment. PPE collectively comprise a major portion of the assets owned or controlled by a firm. These assets are 'used' [not 'used up'] in the firm's operating activities. The costs of these assets are not expensed in one year (if at all). Rather, expenses from the use of these assets result from a systematic and rational process called depreciation. Suppose you buy a car paying $40,000 thinking you will use the car for four years. Further, you estimate that the car will be worth $8,000 to you when you sell it or trade it in after four years. While using the car you will experience a decline in value of $32,000 [$40,000 - $8,000]. The depreciation method we'll use for now is the 'straight-line' method because $8,000 of the total expense will be recognized in each year over the four-year life. As depreciation is recognized over the asset's life, a related account related to the PPE 'accumulates' deprecation on the car. Unimaginatively, this account is called **Accumulated Depreciation** and its balance is offset against the PPE account to produce an amount usually referred to as the **book value or carrying value** of PPE.

Intangible assets are non-current assets referring to assets that lack physical substance. Important intangible assets include copyrights, patents, leasehold improvements, goodwill and trademarks. These assets usually have lives spanning multiple accounting periods providing benefits to the firm.

Total liabilities are sub-divided into **current liabilities** and **non-current liabilities** depending upon when the liabilities will be paid or otherwise stop being economic obligations. Within these categories, the accounts are presented in descending order of liquidity.

Current liabilities include **accounts payable [A/P]** and other **accrued liabilities** such as salaries payable, interest payable and rent payable. These liabilities result from buying on account something that will be used in the operations of the firm. The supplier might offer credit terms giving a stated period of time before the payment is due. Accrued liabilities result from having 'used up' something in operations *prior* to paying for it. Identify a liability you could create by using something up before you pay for it. [If you use a credit card to pay for something you consume right away, you are left with an 'accrued liability.' In general, when things are 'used up' before they are paid for, the 'consumer' has an accrued liability.]

Another current liability results when reclassifying part of a long-term liability as a current liability to show that part of the total liability will be paid within one year. A **Note Payable** [N/P] could have a due date in less than one year and be shown in a classified balance sheet as a current liability. Financial statement users normally interpret current liabilities as requiring the use of current assets or to be otherwise settled within one year. If a firm has received assets from a customer prior to providing services to that customer, the liability to the customer is commonly called Unearned Revenues or a Deferred Revenues. This liability will be settled by performing services.

Examples of non-current liabilities include **N/P**, **deferred income tax liabilities**, some lease obligations and other debt arrangements requiring payments in future accounting periods.

OE is usually broken down into two major components: **contributed capital** [CC] and **Retained Earnings** [RE]. CC reflects investments by owners and involved no revenues when the investment occurred. CC can be capital stock and preferred stock if the firm is a corporation. RE generally represent income earned by the firm and not paid out in the form of **dividends**. Later this semester, we will see that there are other things that impact OE.

When a firm has positive Net Income, this amount will increase RE in a procedure to be explained in Topic three.

The **accrual basis** of accounting involves recognizing revenues and expenses based on economic events without necessarily waiting for the related cash flows to occur. Accrual **revenues** are recognized when they have been earned and realized. Accrual **expenses** are recognized when resources have been consumed or 'used up'. The **cash basis** is notably

17

less sophisticated in that it recognizes revenues when they are received [without regard to whether they have been earned or not]. Cash basis expenses are recognized when payments are made.

If a person works for a month, the person will have earned some Salary Revenue and need not have been paid yet. With accrual accounting the earning revenues and being paid are different economic events. Alternatively, suppose a new employee started working for an employer and received a cash advance [prepayment] on the first work day to help the employee settle some personal obligations. The employee would treat the cash advance as an asset (cash) and as a liability. The main point of this example is that the employee would recognize a liability rather than revenue because the value has not yet been. By receiving the cash advance, the employee has a liability to provide services for the employer. Later, as the employee provides services to the employer, the liability decreases and the employee's Salaries Revenue increases.

B/S and I/S are prepared using the accrual basis of accounting. While the cash basis is rarely used for financial statement [F/S] preparation, F/S users should be aware of how the cash basis works to avoid making careless mistakes about F/S information.

Cash and Accrual Basis of Accounting:
This exercise will help you understand the basic differences between and the implications of the cash basis and accrual basis. The Frank Company was formed on January 1 in Year 1. My real motive in this exercise becomes apparent when working requirements 3 and 4.

Revenues:
1. During Year 1, the firm earned $5,000 providing services to its only client while collecting $5,600 from that client.
2. During Year 2, the firm earned $4,700 providing services to its client while collecting only $3,600.
3. In Year 3, the firm earned $5,000 while collecting $6,100.

Expenses:
1. The firm paid $3,100 in Year 1 for salaries and other things related to producing revenues while using up things having a value of $3,700.
2. In Year 2, the firm had total expenses of $3,100 while making total payments of $4,500.
3. In Year 3, cash payments for salaries and other things totaled $3,400 while total expenses were $3,600.

Required:
1. Determine income for Year 1, Year 2, and Year 3 using the ***accrual basis*** of accounting. 1300   1600   1400

2. Determine income for Year 1, Year 2, and Year 3 using the *cash* basis of accounting.   2500   900   2700

3. Related to revenues on the accrual basis, determine the net balance in A/R or in Unearned Revenues at the ends of Year 1, Year 2, and Year 3. A/R and Unearned Revenues would not appear in a cash basis B/S.

UR 600   AR 500   UR 600

4. Related to expenses on the accrual basis, determine the net balance in Accounts Payable or in Prepaid Items at the ends of Year 1, Year 2, and Year 3. Accounts Payable and Prepaid Items would not appear in a cash basis B/S.

AP 600   PPI 800   PPI 600

Requirement 1:

In Year 1 on accrual basis, the revenues (earned) are $5,000 while the expenses (used up) are $3,700. Thus, accrual income for Year 1 is $1,300.

In Year 2 on accrual basis, the revenues (earned) are $4,700 while the expenses (used up) are $3,100. Thus, accrual income for Year 2 is $1,600.

In Year 3 on accrual basis, the revenues (earned) are $5,000 while the expenses (used up) are $3,600. Thus, accrual income for Year 3 is $1,400.

Requirement 2:

In Year 1 on cash basis, the revenues (collected) are $5,600 while the expenses (paid for) are $3,100. Thus, cash basis income for Year 1 is $1,500.

In Year 2 on cash basis, the revenues (collected) are $3,600 while the expenses (paid for) are $4,500. Thus, cash basis loss for Year 2 is ($900).

In Year 3 on cash basis, the revenues (collected) are $6,100 while the expenses (paid for) are $3,400. Thus, cash basis income for Year 3 is $2,700.

Requirement 3:
At the end of Year 1, there is a $600 balance in Unearned Revenues because the firm has collected more from its client that the value of the services provided to that client. The firm owes the client some future services and the most appropriate account title to describe this relationship is Unearned Revenues.

At the end of Year 2, there is a $500 balance in A/R because the firm has collected less from its client that the value of the services provided to that client. The client owes the firm the excess of the services it has received over what it has paid to the Frank Company over the two years combined. Services provided to the client over the two years totals $9,700 and the total amount received from the client over the same two years is $9,200. Thus, the client owes Frank Company $500.

At the end of Year 3, there is a $600 balance in **Unearned Revenues** because the firm has collected more from its client that the value of the services provided to that client. Frank Company owes the client the excess of the payments it has received over the value of the services provided to the client over the three years combined. Services provided to the client over the two years totals $14,700 and the total amount received from the client over the same two years is $15,300. Thus, Frank Company owes $600 in services to the client.

Requirement 4:
At the end of Year 1, there is a $600 balance in **A/P** because the firm has consumed things of more value than it has paid to its suppliers. This A/P or $600 is a liability representing what the firm owes to its suppliers.

At the end of Year 2, there is an $800 balance in **Prepaid Items** because the firm has paid more to its suppliers than the value of the things it has consumed. For the two years combined, the firm has consumed resources worth $6,800 and has paid out $7,600.

At the end of Year 3, there is a $600 balance in **Prepaid Items** because the firm has paid more to its suppliers than the value of the things it has consumed. For the three years combined, the firm has consumed resources worth $10,400 and has paid out $11,000.

B/S accounts carry over from year to year. This is unfortunate in the case of liabilities where we would prefer to let 'bygones' be forgotten. For assets, we are happy they carry over from year to year. Imagine your frustration if you were to learn that your biggest assets would be 'reset' to zero at the end of every year. The only offsetting benefit might come from learning that your liabilities would be 'zeroed out' at the end of each year. If this were how business worked, there would be a big effect on our saving and spending patterns. ☺

A/P, Prepaid Items, A/R and Unearned Revenues are important accounts for keeping an accurate record of the economic assets and liabilities of firms. Despite its ease of use, the cash basis does not carry these items in the B/S. Cash basis F/S can be very misleading and are rarely encountered in the real world. The last time I saw cash basis F/S in a real world setting, the accountants' letter preceding the F/S was longer than the F/S themselves.

Financial Statement Elements:
For each of the following situations, determine which F/S elements are involved. Identify which of the following elements are involved: Assets, Liabilities, OE, Revenues, Expenses, Dividends, Gains and Losses. The last five of these are special OE accounts. Additionally, indicate whether the *dollar amount* of these elements will increase or decrease as a result of the transaction that is described. Whenever possible, after identifying which F/S elements are involved, attempt to name the *specific* involved element. This firm provides financial consulting services for clients.

July 15

$$A = L + OE \qquad R - E = In$$

1. A firm was formed when its six owners each invested $6,000 in cash on July 15 of Year 1.

   36000   36000

2. On August 1 of Year 1, the firm bought two computers for $3,000 each paying 30% of the price at the time of the purchase.

   Comp + Cash
   6000 -1800   4200

3. The firm moved into an office on August 1 of Year 1 and paid $4,000 covering the first four months. The monthly rate was $1,000.

   Cash + Prepaid Rent
   -4000   +4000

4. The month of August has ended. Consider the impact on the elements created in item #3.

   Prepaid Rent
   -1000   -1000   +Rent 1000   -1000

5. The firm completed consulting services for a client on September 10 of Year 1. The services were valued at $30,000. 20% of this amount was collected at the time the services were completed. The remainder will be collected later and no interest will be charged on the portion not collected now.

   Cash   AR
   +6000 +24000   30,000   +30,000   +30000

6. The firm consumed consultants' labor valued at $11,000 in completing the services described in #5. The consultants will not be paid until a later date.

   +11,000   +Sal 11000

7. The firm paid its secretary $2,500 for the month of August on the last day of August.

   -2500   -2500   +2,500   -2500

8. On September 1 of Year 1, the firm paid another $1,800 of the purchase price of the computer [item #2 above] and paid $100 dollars in interest.

   -1800   -1800   +100   +100   -100

9. On September 30 of Year 1, a consulting client paid the firm $20,000 for work that was set to begin in Year 2. No part of this amount will be earned in Year 1.

   +20,000   +20,000

10. On August 31 of Year 1, the firm received a phone bill in the amount of $600 for services rendered by the phone company. No payment was made immediately, but the firm did record the amount in its accounting records.

    +600   -600   +600   -600

11. On September 15 of Year 1, the firm paid for the phone bill as the due date drew near.

    -600   -600

12. The firm paid its secretary for the months of September and October. The secretary received this payment at the end of September. September's salary was paid early to facilitate the secretary's purchase of a new laptop computer.

    -5000 + 2500   -2500   +2500   -2500

13. The month of October has ended. Consider the impact on the elements involved in #12.

    PP Sal
    -2500   -2500   +2500   -2500

14. On November 1 of Year 1, the remainder of the payment for the services provided [item #5] was collected in full.

    AR   Cash
    -24000 +24000

15. On October 10 of Year 1, the firm paid the consultants for their services [item #6].

    -11000   -11000

$A = L + OE \qquad R - E = In.$

16. On November 2 of Year 1, the firm purchased some land for $13,000 paying 60% down and signing a note for the remainder.

    +13000 -7800 +5200

17. On December 6 of Year 1, the firm sold the land purchased in #16 for $15,000. [For simplicity, pay off the related liability in item 18 below.]

    -13000 +15,000   2000   2000   2000

18. On December 6 of Year 1, the firm paid off the amount owed from the purchase of the land in item #16 above. The interest was $75 on the amount that was owed.

    -5275   -5200 -75   +75   -75

19. On December 20 of Year 1, the firm purchased some shares in another firm for $1,800.

    Cash   Fin
    -1800 +1800

20. On December 20 of Year 1, the firm sold the shares for $1,700.

    Cash   Fin
    +1700 -1800   -100   +100   -100

Answers:

1. Increase both assets and OE by $36,000. Specific names of accounts are Cash (asset) and CC (OE).
2. Increase assets for $4,200 (net) and increase liabilities for the same amount. Changes in specific accounts include Cash (assets decreasing by $1,800 and Computers (asset) increasing by $6,000. N/P (liability) would increase by $4,200 reflecting the amount still owed for the computer.
3. Total assets would not change. One asset, Cash, would decrease by $4,000 and another asset, Prepaid Rent, would increase by $4,000.
4. At the end of August of Year 1, expenses would increase and assets would decrease each by $1,000. Rent Expense (expense) would increase by $1,000 and this would have a 'domino effect' decreasing income and decreasing OE by the same amounts. [Is it intuitive that more expense means less income and less OE?] Prepaid Rent (asset) would decrease by $1,000, the amount of value 'used up' in September. Importantly, note the changes in the balance sheet equation components actually do balance: assets decrease and OE decreases ☺.
5. Assets would increase by $30,000 and revenues would increase by $30,000. Two assets accounts are involved here. Cash (asset) would increase by $6,000 and A/R (asset) would increase by $24,000. Consulting Revenue (revenue) would increase by $30,000. Revenues increase producing a 'domino effect' increasing income and OE by the same amounts. [Is it intuitive that more revenues means more income and more OE?] Importantly, note the changes in the B/S equation components actually do balance: assets increase and OE increases. ☺
6. Increase expenses and increase liabilities. Specifically, Salaries Payable (liability) increases by $11,000 and Salaries Expenses (expense) increases by $11,000. More expenses means less income and less OE. The impacts on the B/S equations are balanced: OE has decreased and liabilities have increased. ☺
7. Assets decrease and expenses increase both by $2,500. Salaries Expenses (expense) and Cash (asset) are the specific accounts involved. Increasing expenses means less income and less OE. The impacts on the B/S equation components are balanced. ☺

8. Assets decrease by $1,900. Liabilities decrease by $1,800. Expenses increase by $100. Specifically, Cash (asset) decreases by $1,900, the amount of cash payment required. N/P (liability) decreases by the amount of principal being repaid. Interest Expense (expense) increases by $100 the value 'used up' in the form of interest. More expenses mean less income and less OE. The changes on the B/S components balance: assets down $1,900, liabilities down $1,800 and OE down $100. ☺
9. Assets increase by $20,000 and liabilities increase by the same amount. Specifically, Cash (asset) increases by $20,000 and Unearned Revenues (liability) increase by $20,000. There is no I/S involvement because no revenues have been earned yet. ☺
10. Liabilities increase by $600 and OE increases by the same amount. Specifically, Utilities Payable (liability) increase by $600 and Utilities Expense (expense) increase by $600. More expense means less income and less OE. The changes in the B/S components do still balance. ☺
11. Assets and liabilities both decrease by $600. Specifically, Cash (asset) and Utilities Payable (liability) both decrease by $600. The changes in the B/S components balance. ☺ Why is there no I/S involvement here? [Answer: because the expense associated with the phone bill was recognized when the bill was *received* (step 10 above).]
12. Assets decrease by $2,500 (net) and expenses increase by $2,500. Specifically, Cash (asset) decreases by $5,000 and Prepaid Salaries (asset) increases by $2,500. Salaries Expense (expense) increases by $2,500. The increase in expenses decreases income and decreases OE. The changes in the B/S components *balance*. This is a good thing. ☺
13. Assets decrease and expenses increase both by $2,500. Prepaid Salaries (asset) decrease and Salaries Expense (expense) increase. More expense means less income and less OE. The changes in the B/S components are in balance.
14. Total assets do not change. Specifically, Cash (asset) increases by $24,000 and AR (assets decreases by $24,000. Total assets were unaffected. Why was there no I/S involvement here? [Answer: because the revenues associated with the cash collected now had been properly and previously recognized when earned (step 5 above).]
15. Assets and liabilities both decrease by $11,000. Specifically, Salaries Payable (liability) decreases and Cash (asset) decreases. The changes in the B/S components are in balance. ☺ There is no I/S involvement because the proper expense had been previously recognized.
16. Assets increase by $5,200 (net) and liabilities increase by the same amount. Specifically, Cash (asset) decreases by $7,800 and Land (asset) increases by $13,000. N/P (liability) increase by $5,200. The changes in the B/S components are in balance. None of the I/S elements are involved.
17. Assets increase by $2,000 and gain increases by the same amount. Specifically, Cash (asset) increases by $15,000 and Land (asset) decreases by $13,000. Gain on Sale of Land increases income and OE by $2,000. The changes in the B/S components are in balance. [For simplicity, pay off of the related liability in item 18 below.]

18. Decrease assets by $5,275, decrease liabilities by $5,200 and increase expenses by $75. Specifically, decrease Cash (asset) by $5,275. N/P (liability) decreases by $5,200. Interest Expense (expense) increases by $75. More expense means less income and less OE. The changes in the B/S components are in balance. ☺
19. Assets are unchanged. Specifically, Cash (asset) decreases $1,800 and Investments (asset) increase for the same amount. No I/S elements are involved in this transaction.
20. Assets decrease by $100 and loss increases by $100. Specifically, Cash (asset) increases $1,700, Investments (asset) decrease $1,800 and Loss on Sale of Investments increases $100. The loss decreases income and OE.

Income Statements and the Accounting Cycle: Tying Things Together

Topic 3

This topic ties to chapters 5 and 7 in the SSD text.

In this lecture we will first cover the **income statement** and the accounts used to report the results of operations. Until this point, we have emphasized the B/S impacts resulting from I/S accounts. I/S and B/S both reflect the accrual basis.

A multiple-step I/S for a firm that might sell services might have these important components:

The Merle Consulting Company
Income Statement
For the Year Ended December 31, Year 1

Sales Revenue	$19,000
Operating Expenses:	
Salaries	6,000
Occupancy	5,500
Depreciation	1,500
Utilities	600
Operating Expenses	$13,600
Operating Income	$4,400
Other Revenue (Expense)	
Interest Revenue	20
Interest Expense	(120)
Gain on Sale of PPE	300
Loss on Sale of Land	(100)
Other Revenue net	$100
Income Before Taxes Expense	$4,500
Income Tax Expense	1,400
Net Income	$3,100

I want to focus on some basics issues before progressing to some of the topics you found in the reading. The I/S contains revenues, expenses, gains and losses for an accounting period. Revenues and expenses come from the firm's primary line(s) of business and recur. Gains are losses are peripheral to the entity's primary line(s) of business and are not recurring. The same gain or loss cannot occur again. Similar gains and losses may occur from time to time. A consulting firm is not in the real estate business and the sale of land would cause likely cause a gain or loss unless it was sold for exactly the same price that had been paid to buy it. Likewise, the sale of PPE by a consulting firm would likely cause a gain or loss because sales of PPE would not be part of the firm's on-going activity.

Interest revenue (expense) is treated differently than other revenues and expenses because lending (borrowing) is incidental to the primary business activity. The incidental nature of these items in relation to the primary business activity is adequately important to require that primary and incidental activities be presented in different locations in the I/S. I/S allow users to readily determine how the firm is faring in its primary business activities and the impacts of what peripheral activities the firm might engage in.

Sales Revenue comes from the sale of inventory. Examples of inventory include petroleum products (ExxonMobil), food products (Ralph's), textbooks (USC's bookstore) and hamburgers (McDonalds').

Service Revenue comes from performing services instead of products. Consultants and attorneys likely derive most of their revenues from performing services. If an attorney sold relatively insignificant amounts of software to clients, those product sales revenues would likely be reported as part of other revenue and expense in an I/S.

What similarities and differences exist when comparing sales revenues and service revenues?

Interest Revenue is earned over time as a result of having invested or lent money to another and where there is an interest rate involved.

Other Revenues can include any amounts earned by the firm from various activities other than the primary activities. These might include interest revenue, dividend revenue, rent revenue, royalty revenue among others. When grouped as Other Revenues, a user would interpret the components as peripheral to the firm's main line of activities. If any of these might be *individually* significant, it could be reported as a separate line item in the 'other revenue' area or be included in the total for 'other revenues' and the specific dollar amount shown in the footnotes to the I/S.

Cost of Goods Sold (CGS) is the *expense* that occurs when tangible merchandise is sold to customers. It summarizes the merchant's costs of buying or building the inventory that is sold to the customer. The spread between CGS and Sales Revenue expresses the seller's ability to sell the product in the competitive marketplace.

Selling, General and Administrative Expense is a collection of expenses that might include Depreciation Expense (on *administrative* facilities), Salaries Expense, Rent Expense, Selling Expense, Research and Development Expense, Bad Debts Expense among others. Sometimes, these expenses are grouped together in published FS. Usually management of a firm will have access to all of these.

Interest Expense is the 'economic rent' charged for borrowing from other entities. Interest is the cost of postponing payments and is an expense to the borrower.

Income Tax Expense summarizes income taxes levied at various levels and determined using financial accounting (FA) rules and not according to tax accounting (TA) rules. The extensive differences between FA and TA rules create the complexity. FA goals strive to deliver information useful in decision-making. TA goals center on governments' need to generate tax revenues to the governments. If differences between TA and FA rules are temporary, there are future tax consequences when they reverse. Alternatively, some differences between TA and FA never reverse and have no future ax consequences as a result. Income Tax Expense in the income statement [FA] is made up of two sub-components: current tax expense and deferred tax expense. The deferred tax expense results from presently recognizing the future effects that result when the temporary differences reverse. Current tax expense aggregates all of the income taxes that are currently payable at the various levels of government.

Comprehensive Income consists of net income adjusted for all of the items affecting OE other than transactions with owners. In various accounting topics in the FA part of this course, there are some situations where proper accounting treatment requires adjustments to OE but not having an effect on net income. The changes in OE are added to or subtracted from net income to arrive at comprehensive income (unless they resulted from transactions with the owners). Comprehensive income is a relatively new concept in FA and is a required disclosures associated with income statements. [We will visit this issue again in Topic 12.]

There are three special items that appear near the bottom of the I/S when certain circumstances have occurred. When the entity has made a decision to dispose of or discontinue a line of business, a **Discontinued Operations** item may appear in the I/S below the Income Tax Expense caption indicating the effects resulting from the decision to discontinue this line of business. The Discontinued Operations item is presented net of its tax effects. An **Extraordinary Item** is reported when the entity has a material gain/loss not related to normal operating activities and not expected to occur again in the foreseeable future. Accountants usually use the terms 'unusual' and 'infrequent' to describe these conditions. By reporting them in a special way and net of tax near the bottom of the I/S, FS users are on notice of the special nature of the events giving rise to this gain/loss. Extraordinary items, by definition, are not expected to be recurring and should be properly interpreted by FS users. **Cumulative Effects** of changes in accounting methods are the third of the three special items that appear near the bottom of the I/S when they occur. The Cumulative Effects item summarizes the aggregate changes in net incomes for all of the years *prior* to the year when the method was changed. The FS for those prior years are *not* restated using the new method but the income effects that *would have* resulted from restatement are shown as Cumulative Effects in the I/S for the year when the entity *did* change accounting methods. The end result is that the aggregate income for all of the firm's life is as if the new method had been in continuous use. [There are changes in accounting methods that are treated fundamentally as if they were actually corrections of errors. Their Cumulative Effects item appears as an adjustment to beginning RE and the previous *are restated* unlike the more ordinary treatment described above. Except for these brief comments here, these special changes in accounting methods are beyond the scope of this class.]

There is another 'special' item not appearing in the I/S but having an effect on it and the B/S. **Prior period adjustments** are required when a *material* error is discovered in *previously* published financials. The previously published financials have to be restated. The appropriate adjustment is made to the beginning RE balance in the period the error is discovered. The financial community is on notice that when prior period adjustments occur, the financials have been restated from those that were previously available. Do not confuse corrections of errors with changes in estimates. **Changes in estimates** involve normally recurring revisions in the estimates and are inherently part of the accounting cycle. Changes in estimates do not result in restatement of previously published financials.

Earnings Per Share (EPS) is a widely watched measure of financial performance. EPS results from dividing the net income available to common shareholders by the weighted average number of common shares outstanding for the period. More simply, EPS is income available to common shareholders scaled by the number of common shares outstanding so financial statement users can make easier comparisons between firms. EPS data are required disclosures. [We will visit this issue again in Topic 12.]

Sometimes we find it sufficient to think in terms of total assets. Other times, we will want to think in terms of specific assets. For this latter purpose, knowledge of specific accounts titles will help us communicate better. In general, we should have a separate account for each different thing we wish to monitor. Different assets, liabilities, OE, revenues, expenses, gains, and losses will provide more useful information to FS users when kept in separate accounts.

Accounting is based upon the double-entry system. This permits FS to keep track of the assets controlled and to have summary information regarding the source of those assets. Consider this simple (smart?) example: A firm has $1,000,000 in cash. What are possible sources of that money?

Do you think that knowledge of the money's source adds much valuable information to anyone interested in the firm's FS? The same example extends to our personal lives. If a person you are seriously dating has $1,000,000, would you have an interest in knowing something about where the cash came from? FS users usually will not be able to trace the $1,000,000 to a *specific* source, but will have information enabling informed judgments about its origins. This simple (smart?) example illustrates the power of **double-entry accounting**. People have tried to improve upon it and have been unsuccessful.

Let's revisit our 'old' friend, the basic accounting equation:

$$\text{Assets} = \text{Liabilities} + \text{OE}$$

We have recently seen that it is desirable to keep information about different assets and liabilities in *separate* accounts for ease of understanding what we have. For example, we would keep our credit card liabilities separate from any liability we might have for a student loan or a car loan. The concept of an account is merely a 'place' to keep information about something that is of interest to management of the firm. For example, would it make sense to keep Salaries Expense in a different account than Rent Expense? [Yes.] Managers have an interest in monitoring many expenses as they attempt to better manage the firm and hold appropriate people accountable.

Conceptually, accounts are shown in the form of a 'T'. What's really important for us at this point is that there is a 'right side' and a 'left side'. A 'T' account does that for us quite nicely.

Pacioli, an Italian monk in the late 1400's, is given credit for creating the accounting system we still use today: the double entry system. In the aggregate, the double entry system of accounting allows us to track what we have and where it came from. Recall the exercise you read about a while ago. [It was the exercise where we speculated on the possible sources of $1,000,000 in the possession of a person and then in the possession of a firm.] **Pacioli arbitrarily decided assets show balances on the left. Alternatively, liabilities and OE accounts would show balances on the right.** This causes the basic accounting equation *and* the 'left' and the 'right' balances to be simultaneously in balance. As we work through some exercises in this topic and later in the course, when the balances on the 'left' do not equal the balances on the 'right', you'll have a signal that something has been recorded on the 'wrong' side.

When you need to *increase* an asset account, you must add something on *left* side of that specific account. The balance before the *current* transaction would be on the left side, that balance would be *increased* by whatever you add on the left side. On the other hand, if you had wanted to decrease an asset account, you would have to put something on the right hand side to reduce the balance in the account.

Consider this 'T' account. I have put a $10 balance on the left side. If you want to *increase* the *balance* in that account by $6, must you place the $6 on the left or the right side? [Left] Now, see that the account balance would be $16 *after* placing the $6 on the left side.

Consider another 'T' account with a $20 starting balance on the *right* side. Suppose you want to *increase* the balance in the account to $32. *What amount* do you have to place on *which* side? [$12 on the *right* side.] Now, see that the account balance would be $32 *after* placing the $12 on the right side.

Consider another 'T' account with a $40 starting balance on the right side. What could you do to the account to make the balance *decrease* by $15? [Place $15 on the left side.] See that the $40 starting balance on the right side would be reduced by the $15 on the left to produce a $25 ending balance *after* the transaction has been recorded.

Let's try one more example. Consider a new 'T' account with a $50 starting balance on the left side. Suppose you wish to cause the account balance to be $28. What do you have to do to the account to change the account balance to $28? [Put $22 on the right side.] See that the $50 opening balance would *reduced* by the $22 to $28, the desired ending balance.

As mentioned above liabilities also have left and right sides, but their normal balances would be on the right. Increasing a liability can be accomplished by adding something in the account on the right. Decreasing a liability can be accomplished by placing something in the account on the left.

I want you to do a little 'art' work here to cement your understanding of the key concepts to this point.
1. Write out the basic accounting equation.
2. For each element in the basic accounting equation, create a 'T' account and place these balances on the correct side. Assets $100, Liabilities $60 and OE $40.
3. In each 'T' account, place arrows 'up' and 'down' indicating the correct side for making the account balance move in that direction.
4. Does the basic accounting equation balance for you?
5. Do the left hand balances equal the right hand balances?
6. Are you ☺?

Answers:
1. The basic accounting equation: Assets = Liabilities + OE
2. Assets $100 on the left. Liabilities $60 on the right. OE $40 on the right.
3. In the assets 'T' account, the up arrow is on the left and the 'down' arrow is on the right. In the liabilities 'T' account, the up arrow is on the right and the 'down'

arrow is on the left. In the OE 'T' account, the up arrow is on the right and the 'down' arrow is on the left.
4. Yes. ☺
5. Yes. ☺
6. You are.

There are two general OE types of accounts: CC and RE. Both of them keep their normal balances on the right. Their balances increase on the right and decrease on the left.

Debits and Credits
The names for the left and right sides are **debit** and **credit**, respectively. These names have no meaning beyond left and right. Do not associate any meaning with these names, especially if you have worked previously with these terms.

You may recall that net income increases OE. The implicit implication for us now is that all of the revenues, expenses, gains, and losses are really OE accounts serving a special purpose. These special purpose OE accounts exist to organize information so management can better monitor the firm's operating results. It would be more useful to know which expenses were up and down compared to a year ago if you were the manager of the firm.

Revenues increase OE and carry normal balances on the right (credit) as do the OE accounts. Decreases in revenues are recorded with debits (left). Gains increase OE and increase or decrease exactly as revenues do. Expenses decrease OE and carry their normal balances on the debit (left) side. A credit (right) to an expense will decrease the expense and ultimately increase OE. Losses decrease OE just as expenses do.

Is the Accounting Cycle a New Type of Exercise Machine?
Not exactly. Firms engage in countless transactions during a year and these have to be analyzed, recorded and summarized before becoming information appearing in FS. This process of producing FS is on the bookkeeping plane. When the bookkeeping functions smoothly it is almost invisible. However, when bookkeeping is not working smoothly, the firm experiences frustration at lack of available or reliable data. Many important decisions cannot wait for the FS to be prepared.

One situation that I am personally familiar with involved a firm with liquidity concerns. The owner requested daily reports on the cash balance. The bookkeeper began marking in pencil deposits waiting to be made in her accounting records *prior* to the actual deposit of the funds into the checking account. The actual deposits were bunched and actually made every two or three days. The bookkeeper then absent-mindedly recorded the actual deposit as if it were *another* deposit. As a result, the deposits were effectively double-counted. The owner was receiving reports of cash balances that came close to the expected balances. Thus, the owner did not suspect any mistake was in the making and did not question the numbers he was receiving. This inadvertent 'double-counting' went on for about three weeks and masked the firm's true cash shortage. The owner of the business was in Europe when the bank contacted him about the overdrawn condition of the firm's checking account. Initially fearing that an employee theft had occurred in his absence, he discovered the 'double counting' of deposits described above. The business ceased to exist within seven days.

As an accounting period draws to a close, some accountants need to review the accounting records identifying any account balances to be adjusted before FS are prepared. These adjustments are **adjusting journal entries** and ensure that all account balances are correct before FS are prepared.

At the end of the period, **closing journal entries** are recorded to zero out all of the income statement accounts transferring their balances into the RE account. This is how net income mechanically is transferred into the RE account. Closing journal entries 'zero out' revenues, expenses, gains, and losses. The amount needed to balance the closing journal entry is 'miraculously' equal to the net income figure. Can you establish why this is not a miracle? [I'll put the answer at the end of the exercise that starts below. ☺]

Recording Transactions and Adjusting Journal Entries:
The USC Company [the firm] was formed on April 30, Year 1 when three owners each invested $20,000. One of the owners also lent the firm $15,000 at 12% per year. The principal and interest are both due on April 30, Year 2.

During Year 1, the firm purchased supplies inventory on account at a cost of $1,200. At the end of the year there were supplies on hand totaling $100.

During Year 1, the firm paid its suppliers $1,000 for supplies that had been previously purchased on account.

Early in Year 1, the firm collected $28,000 from its clients properly crediting Unearned Revenue for this entire amount since none of it had been earned yet.

During the remainder of Year 1, the USC Company provided $36,000 services to its clients. The clients had already paid for all but $10,000 of the $36,000 as part of the $28,000 that had been previously received from the clients. The remaining $10,000 will be paid to USC later.

The USC Company hired four consultants at a monthly salary of $600 each. These four consultants worked for the firm from May 1, Year 1 until the end of the year. The firm pays its employees on the last day of each month for services rendered during that month. One of the consultants asked for and was granted a $700 advance against his salary for the following year. Another consultant asked the firm to postpone paying her for the last month of Year 1. This postponement was for some special tax purpose and the postponed amount will be paid in February of Year 2.

During Year 1, the firm used up utilities with a value of $1,200. However, the firm had to pay $1,300 to the utilities firms during Year 1.

The firm rented an office space on May 1, Year 1, at a monthly cost of $1,500. The contract with the landlord required that the rent be paid on May 1 and November 1 for six-month periods beginning on those dates. The first payment was required on May 1, Year 1, the day the firm occupied the office space. The second payment was made on November 1 of Year 1 as required by the agreement.

Required: Determine the proper amounts that the firm would report in the FS prepared at December 31, Year 1 for each of the accounts listed below. Assume all the accounting was done correctly and that the accounts were properly adjusted at the end of Year 1. Calculations not required.

Account	Amount	Account	Amount
Cash	$ 63,400	Consulting Revenues	$ 36,000
Prepaid Rent	6,000	Salaries Expense	19,200
Supplies Inventory	100	Rent Expense	12,000
Accounts Receivable	10,000	Supplies Expense	1,100
Prepaid Utilities	100	Utilities Expense	1,200
Prepaid Salaries	700	Interest Expense	1,200
Accounts Payable	200		
Notes Payable	15,000		
Interest Payable	1,200		
Unearned Revenues	60,000		
Salaries Payable	600		

Solution: Create separate accounts as needed in solving this problem. An account exists to meet the needs of the users of the financial system.

Debit Cash and credit Contributed Capital for $60,000 each. Debit Cash and credit N/P for $15,000 each. At the end of Year 1, it would be necessary to debit Interest Expense and credit Interest Payable for $1,200 each [$15,000 x 12% x 8/12 = $1,200].

Debit Supplies Inventory and credit A/P for $1,200 each. At the end of Year 1, debit Supplies Expense and credit Supplies Inventory for $1,10 each. This would reflect that

$1,100 of the supplies had been used up in the year. Note that the *ending* balance in Supplies Inventory equals $100, the proper year-end balance.

Debit A/P and credit Cash for $1,000 each. Note the *ending* balance in A/P equals $200, the amount still owed to the suppliers.

Debit Cash and credit Unearned Consulting Revenues for $28,000 each.

Debit Unearned Revenues for $26,000 and debit A/R for $10,000. Credit Consulting Revenues for $36,000. The portion that already been paid to USC must be taken out of Unearned Consulting Revenues. The portion that is still owed to USC [$10,000] is in A/R. Note: the ending balance in Unearned Revenues is $2,000 [$28,000 credited earlier and $26,000 debited here = $2,000 ending balance.]

The summary entry for the entire year involves debits to Salaries Expense for $19,200 and to Prepaid Salaries for $700. Credit Salaries Payable for $600 and Cash for $19,300. The $700 is the advance of the salary to one consultant and the $600 represents the amount owed to another consultant who asked for her last month's salary to be paid in February of Year 2.

Debit Utilities Expense for $1,200 and debit Prepaid Utilities for $100. Credit Cash for $1,300.

Debit Prepaid Office Rent for $6,000 and Office Rent Expense for $12,000. Credit Cash for $18,000.

Final Account Balances:
Cash $63,400, Prepaid Rent $6,000, Supplies Inventory $100, AR $10,000, Prepaid Utilities $100, Prepaid Salaries $700, A/P $200, N/P $15,000, Unearned Consulting Revenues $2,000, Salaries Payable $600, Interest Payable $1,200, Contributed Capital $60,000, Consulting Revenues $36,000, Interest Expense $1,200, Office Rent Expense $12,000, Supplies Expense $1,100, Salaries Expense $19,200, and Utilities Expense $1,200.

The USC Company has Net Income in Year 1 of $1,300. Total OE at the end of Year 1 after all accounts have been closed out would be $61,300. $60,000 contributed by the owners plus RE of $1,300.

[The answer to the question at the end of the text before starting the example above: Closing journal entries balance when you put a credit into RE equaling net income because of bookkeeping 'mechanics'. Debiting Revenues and Gains to 'zero' out their balances and crediting Expenses and Losses to 'zero out' their balances, leaves the closing journal temporarily *entry out of balance* by the difference between those debits and credits. That difference equals Net Income if a *credit* is needed to balance the entry [or Net Loss if a *debit* is needed to balance the entry]. Since Net Income 'flows' into RE, if we need a credit to balance the entry we credit RE. If a debit is needed, then we debit RE. Remember, Net Income increases RE and a Net Loss would decrease RE.]

Accounting Cycle:

Prepare the appropriate journal entries based on this information for Year 1.

1. The Magic Company [the firm] was formed on August 1, Year 1 when four people each invested $1,000 in the firm. One investor lent $800 to the firm that is to be repaid on August 1, Year 2 along with $72 of interest.

2. The firm leased an office space for one year on August 1, Year 1 and moved in that same day. The monthly rate was $40 and the rent for the entire year had to be paid on January 31, Year 2.

3. On August 1, Year 1, the firm rented some office furniture and computers for two years. The firm paid $240 at the time of signing the rental agreement. The contract calls for the second rental payment in exactly one year. [Assume the full amount of each payment is debited into Prepaid Equipment Rent at the time each payment is made.]

4. On August 15, Year 1, the firm purchased some supplies for use in the business at a cost of $700. This amount was charged to the firm's account.

5. On August 16, Year 1, the firm returned 30% of the supplies it had purchased because they were defective.

6. On August 15, Year 1, the firm hired four employees at a monthly salary of $50 each. These employees are to be paid at the end of each month for the period ending on that day. Their first payday will be on August 31, Year 1.

7. On September 30, Year 1, the firm purchased some securities at a cost of $1,000 paying cash.

8. On September 30, Year 1, the firm paid the amount owed for the supplies it had purchased earlier.

9. On October 1, Year 1, the firm completed its first consulting project for a client. The project was valued at $5,000 and the client paid 70% immediately and promised to pay the remainder on February 28, Year 2. Merlin promised not to charge interest on the unpaid amount.

10. Record the paydays for August, September, October, November and December. Remember that paydays occur on the last day of each month for the period then ended. Refer to item 6 above.

11. On November 1, Year 1, the firm received $3,500 for a consulting project to be started late in Year 1.

12. During the last month of Year 1, Magic completed $2,000 of the project discussed in the previous item.

13. On November 30, Year 1, the firm sold its investments for $700 cash.

As of December 31, Year 1, identify accounts where the balances need to be adjusted prior to the preparation of the financial statements at the end of the year. Supplies on hand at the end of the year were $200 by actual count.

Prepare a balance sheet at December 31, Year 1 and income statement for the five months ended December 31, Year 1. Show the account titles and the correct balances in the accounts as they would appear in each of these FS. There is no need to prepare a SofSF.

In Year 2, the following events occurred.
1. On January 16, Year 2, the firm hired one more employee at a monthly salary of $60 each. The firm also increased the salaries of the continuing employees to $70 per month each.

2. The firm finished the remainder of the project described in items 11 and 12 from Year 1.

3. The firm collected the amount that was owed from the client for the project described in item 9 from Year 1

4. The firm obtained a very large client. The firm provided $6,000 in services for this client through the remainder of Year 2. Of this amount 40% was still owed to Merlin at the end of Year 2.

5. The firm paid its employees the proper amounts on each of the paydays in Year 2.

6. The firm bought supplies on account at a cost of $1,100.

7. The firm made the appropriate office rent payment of $480 on January 31, Year 2.

8. The firm purchased some shares at a cost of $1,500 on June 1, Year 2.

9. On August 1, Year 2, the firm repaid the investor that had lent it $800 plus the interest that was due.

10. On August 1, Year 2, the firm moved to larger office space signing a one-year lease for the year beginning on that day. The monthly rent on the new office space was $70. This rental agreement required the year's rent to be paid at the time the firm moved into the new offices.

11. On August 1, Year 2, the firm made its second payment of $240 for the annual rental of office equipment and computers.

12. The firm received $50 in dividends on October 15, Year 2.

13. The shares were sold on November 23, Year 2, for $1,900.

At the end of Year 2, identify the accounts that need to be adjusted in order that their ending balances are correct for the preparation of FS. Supplies on hand at the end of Year 2 by actual count were $300.

Prepare a B/S at December 31, Year 2 and I/S for the year ended December 31, Year 2. Show the account titles and the correct balances in the accounts as they would appear in each of these FS. There is no need to prepare a SofSF.

Solution to Accounting Cycle:
1. Debit Cash for a total of $4,800. Credits to CC for $4,000 and N/P for $800. On August 1, Year 1, there would be no interest yet since no time has passed since the borrowing date. At the end of Year 1, an adjustment would need to be made to reflect the 'using up' of interest since the borrowing date. That adjustment would include a debit to Interest Expense and a credit to Interest Payable for $30 each. [$72 times 5/12 = $30. Five months out of twelve have passed since the borrowing date. 5/12 of the interest has been accrued as an expense and as a liability.]

2. No journal entry can properly be made on August 1, Year 1, since no elements of FS exist on this date. The contract is executory on this date. By the end of Year 1, however, it is necessary to record an adjustment to reflect the expense and the liability related to the passage of five months' time. Debit Office Rent Expense and credit Office Rent Payable, both for $200. Magic has used up five months time in the office space and economically owes the landlord for that use [even though no amount is to be paid at the end of Year 1].

3. Debit Prepaid Equipment Rent and credit Cash both for $240 on August 1, Year 1. By the end of Year 1, an adjusting journal entry related to this entry is required to make the accounting records correct at that point in time. The adjusting entry involves a debit to Equipment Rent Expense and a credit to Prepaid Equipment Rent both for $100.

4. Debit Supplies Inventory and credit A/P both for $700.

5. Debit A/P and credit Supplies Inventory both for $210.

6. On August 15, Year 1, no journal is appropriate since no one has performed any part of the obligations yet. The requirement to record the paydays is in step 10 below.

7. Debit Investments and credit Cash both for $1,000.

8. Debit A/P and credit Cash both for $490.

9. Debits to Cash for $3,500 and to A/R for $1,500. Credit Consulting Revenues for $5,000 since the full amount has been earned by this date.

10. The August payday will involve a debit to Salaries Expense and credit to Cash for $100 [4 times $50 per month times 50% = $100]. The September through December paydays will each have debits to Salaries Expense for $200 and a credit to Cash for the same amount. Thus, the total debits to Salary Expense through and including the December 31, Year 1, payday will be $900 and total credits to Cash will be the same amount.

11. Debit Cash and credit Unearned Consulting Revenues for $3,500 each.

12. Debit Unearned Consulting Revenues and credit Consulting Revenues for $2,000 each.

13. Debit Cash for $700 and Loss for $300. Credits to Investments for $1,000 to zero that account out (you have sold all of your Investments and that account balance should be zero. Credit Gain on Sale of Investments for $150.

14. At the end of Year 1 there are two more account to be adjusted, Supplies Expense and Supplies Inventory. Debit Supplies Expense and credit Supplies Inventory both for $200.

The Magic Company
Balance Sheet
December 31, Year 1

Assets:
Cash	$9,870
Accounts Receivable	1,500
Prepaid Equipment Rental	140
Supplies Inventory	100
Total Assets	$11,610

Liabilities:
Unearned Revenues	$1,500	
Office Rent Payable	200	
Interest Payable	30	
Notes Payable	800	
Total Liabilities		$2,530

Owners' Equity:
Contributed Capital	$4,000	
Retained Earnings	5,080	
Total Owners' Equity		$9,080

Total Liabilities and Owners' Equity $11,610

The Magic Company
Income Statement
For the Five Months Ended December 31, Year 1

Consulting Revenues		$7,000
Expenses & Loss:		
Salaries	$900	
Supplies	390	
Office Rent	200	
Equipment Rent	100	
Interest	30	
Loss	300	
		1,920
Net Income		$5,080

Year 2:

1. No journal entry is required based upon this information. The payday journal entries for Year 2 are requested in item 5 below.

2. Debit Unearned Revenue for $1,500 and credit Consulting Revenue for the same amount.

3. Debit Cash for $1,500 and credit A/R for the same amount.

4. Debits to Cash and A/R for $3,600 and $2,400, respectively. Credit Consulting Revenues for $6,000.

5. For the January 31, Year 2, payday, debits to Salaries Expense for $270* and a credit Cash for $270. The other eleven paydays in Year 2, each involve debits to Salaries Expense for $340* and credits to Cash for the same amount. [*(4x$50x1/2) + (1x$60x1/2) + (4x$70x1/2) = $270] [**(1x$60) + (4x$70) = $340]

6. Debit Supplies Inventory and credit A/P for $1,100 each.

7. Debit Office Rent Payable for $200 to remove the liability carried over from Year 1. Debit Office Rent Expense for $40 to record the cost of using the office space for the first month of Year 2. Debit Prepaid Office Rent for $240, recording the value of rent paid in advance. Credit Cash for $480. [There are other ways this entry could be recorded on January 31, Year 2. If you have recorded the entry differently and you adjust it properly in Year 2, you can still get correct financial statements at the end of Year 2. There are proper alternative ways to obtain correct FS.]

8. Debit Investments $1,500 and credit Cash for the same amount.

9. Debits to Interest Payable for $30, Interest Expense for $42 and N/P for $800. Credit Cash for $872.

10. There are many ways to explain the accounting associated with this information. I will explain this in this in what I believe is the most transparent manner. Step 1: On August 1, Year 2, the previously recorded prepayment of office rent ($240 from item 7 above) has fully expired. Let's record that expiration with a debit to Office Rent Expense and a credit to Prepaid Office Rent both for $240. Step 2: debit Prepaid Office Rent and credit Cash for $840 each. Step 3: the year-end adjustment is a debit to Office Rent Expense and a credit Prepaid Office Rent each for $350*. [*5x$70 = $350]

11. There are many ways to explain the accounting associated with this information. I will explain this in this in what I believe is the most transparent manner. Step 1: record the expiration of the Prepaid Equipment Rent balance carried over form the previous year ($140). Debit Equipment Rent Expense and credit Prepaid Equipment Rent each for $120. Step 2: Debit Prepaid Equipment Rent and credit Cash both for $240. Step 3: Debit Equipment Rent Expense and credit Prepaid Equipment Rent both for $100 as the year-end adjustment to those two accounts.

12. Debit Cash and credit Dividend Revenue* both for $50. [* Dividend Income]

13. Debit Cash for $1,900. Credits to Investments and Gain on Sale of Investments for $1,500 and $400 respectively.

14. An adjustment to Supplies Inventory is needed at the end of Year 2. Debit Supplies Expense and credit Supplies Inventory for $1,000 each.

The Magic Company
Balance Sheet
December 31, Year 2

Assets:
Cash	$8,978
Accounts Receivable	2,400
Prepaid Office Rent	490
Prepaid Equipment Rental	140
Supplies Inventory	200
Total Assets	$12,208

Liabilities:
Accounts Payable	1,100
Total Liabilities	$1,100

Owners' Equity:
Contributed Capital	$4,000
Retained Earnings	7,108
Total Owners' Equity	$11,108

Total Liabilities and Owners' Equity $12,208

The Magic Company
Income Statement
For the Year Ended December 31, Year 2

Consulting Revenues		$7,500
Dividend Revenue		50
Gain on Sale of Investments		400
		$7,950
Expenses and Loss:		
Salaries	$4,010	
Supplies	1,000	
Office Rent	630	
Equipment Rent	240	
Interest	42	5,922
Net Income		$2,028

Financial Statement Analysis

Topic 4
This topic ties to Chapter 3 in the SSD text.

FS analysis essentially involves investigating the relationships among data chiefly drawn from the FS themselves. The objective is to find whether those relationships conform to or differ from their past values. Comparisons may also be made to current or previously computed values for other firms or to the industry group to which the firm belongs.

Whenever we compute ratios, it is important to understand what the ratio is trying to measure. Memorizing the components of ratios will not allow any analyst to really understand what the ratio is expressing or what implications might result if a ratio is higher (smaller) than previous values or in comparison to the industry.

Advice for you in your career: Never use a ratio in a presentation or conversation unless you know how to compute it and what it means intuitively. People who know how to compute the ratio and what it means can spot someone's attempt to appear knowledgeable 'a mile off' and this is not flattering for the 'pretender'.

With ratios, their **trends** can be a source of valuable information. A single year's ratio can be much more useful if seen in comparison to the same ratio for the same firm one or two periods earlier. Alternatively, contemporary comparisons between the ratios for the firm under analysis against firms in the same industry can be valuable too. Either type of comparison can add an important dimension to your ability to interpret a ratio.

Debt Ratio:
Total Liabilities/Total Assets
This ratio indicates the percentage of the assets that were supplied by debt holders and other creditors of the firm. If the ratio equaled zero, all of the assets would have supplied by the owners. If the ratio were 1.0, all of the assets have been supplied by debt holders and other creditors.

In general, a lower debt ratio means that less reliance on borrowed capital has occurred. There can be important exceptions to this general rule however, and knowledge of the particular industry can be particularly helpful. Public utilities and some real estate development enterprises achieve their desirable rates of return for equity holders by using generous amounts of debt in their capital structures.

Current Ratio:
Current Assets/Current Liabilities
This ratio is a liquidity measure scaling the available assets by existing claims on those assets. A current ratio larger that one generally indicates the firm should have little trouble meeting its current obligations with assets currently on hand.

In general, a higher current ratio is preferred to a smaller current ratio. The composition of the current assets and current liabilities can be important. Some current assets may be much more liquid that other current assets. Similarly, some current liabilities may not require outlays of assets for elimination (example: unearned revenues).

Return on Sales:
Net Income/Sales
This ratio expresses the portion of total sales that is not consumed by expenses. Net income is available for the owners of the firm as a reward for having made an investment in this firm. Net income can be influenced by accounting methods. Later, in this course we will learn more about the potential impacts resulting from accounting method choice.

Knowledge of the accounting methods used by the firm can add much to the analysis.

A higher return on sales measure is preferred to a smaller measure. This is easy to grasp when you consider that net income is in the numerator.

Asset Turnover:
Sales/Total Assets
This ratio expresses the firm's sales scaled by the firm's total assets. The result is that we have a valuable sense of how much 'business' the firm generated in relation to the assets the firm has employed. The denominator can be influenced significantly by accounting methods and care should be used to identify whether this has been a material factor. To a lesser extent, the numerator (sales) can be influenced by accounting methods and the analyst should consider whether accounting methods have the potential to distort this ratio.

A higher asset turnover measure is preferred to a smaller measure. This is easy to grasp when you consider that sales are in the numerator.

Return on Equity:
Net Income/Stockholders' Equity
This ratio scales the firm's net income by the owners' equity [OE]. Otherwise, it can be difficult to compare firms on their net incomes. Net income is a much more useful number when compared to the investment required to generate it.

A higher return on equity measure is preferred to a smaller measure. This is easy to grasp when you consider that net income is in the numerator.

Knowledge of the accounting methods used by the firm can add much to the analysis.

Price/Earnings Ratio:
Fair Market Value of a Share/Earnings Per Share
This ratio compares the market value of the firm to the firm's net income. EPS is the net income on a per share basis. Share prices represent the fair market value of the firm on a per share basis also.

The DuPont Framework
This analysis breaks return on equity into two components for easier analysis and to provide better insight into the firm's results. In math, you can preserve the value of a fraction if separating the

numerator and denominator into two separate fractions and providing an identical value for the 'missing' elements. Let me show you what I mean:

Original Fraction: 1/8

1/8 = 1/A   x   A/B   x   B/8

The value of the original fraction will be preserved if we replace identical values in for the unknowns, A and B.

The value of this analysis can be clear if you start with the return on equity ratio and decompose it by inserting sales in for the A and assets in for the B in my example above.

Return on Equity:
Net income/ OE   =   Net Income/Sales   x   Sales/Assets   x   Assets/OE

The three fractions at the right are familiar to us. The first is the profit on sales ratio. The second is the asset turnover ratio. The third ratio scales the firm's assets by OE and is intuitively influenced by the firm's use of financial leverage (debt).

Cash Flow Ratios:
These ratios can be useful because they incorporate the use of cash flow measures and are less subject to distortion by choices of accounting methods.

Advice to Users of Ratios:
No one ratio 'tells it all'. Knowledge of accounting methods, experience and the willingness to make comparisons across time and across firms will all contribute significantly to your skill in this area.

There are many more ratios that various sources have developed. One source has identified over 300 ratios that can be calculated. I think it is better for a skilled analyst to interpret ten ratios correctly than for a novice to interpret 100 ratios when analyzing a particular firm.

The Statement of Cash Flows
Topic 5
This topic ties to Chapter 6 in the SSD text.

The statement of cash flows (Sof$F) gives knowledgeable users of FS a detailed summary of cash flows for the period. These cash flows are divided into the three main categories: operating, investing and financing.

1. **Operating Activities**: The cash flows generated by the firm's main line(s) of business. Users can easily tell whether the firm is succeeding or failing in its main line(s) of business by reviewing this section. The main line(s) of business should be a 'cash pump' supplying enough cash to drive the firm's growth and fuel its future survival.
2. **Investment Activities**: The cash flows related to purchases or sales of 'investments' in a broad sense. Investments include: operating assets (PPE), investments in non-operating assets (shares and bonds of other firms, certificates of deposit) and lending activities (Notes Receivable).
3. **Financing Activities**: The cash flows resulting from principal transactions with debt holders and transactions with owners of the firm. Transactions with the owners fall into three categories: investments in the firm by owners, paying owners some cash dividends and transactions involving 'Treasury Shares'. Treasury shares are shares repurchased from the owners of the firm

Through cash flows of a firm, skillful users of FS can learn much information about the firm without having to rely upon knowledge of accounting methods.

The B/S and the I/S reflect the accrual basis. Recall, revenues are recognized when earned and realized. Revenues can be recognized in the I/S before the related cash is collected. Expenses are recognized when things are 'used up'. Expense recognition will often occur prior to the actual payment (AP) or after the actual payment (prepaid items).

In contrast to the accrual basis B/S and I/S, the Sof$F provides a valuable perspective of the firm from a different perspective. Without relying on the accounting methods, estimates and assumptions inherent in accrual accounting FS, the Sof$F looks at the *actual* cash flows for the period. Just as one can better appreciate a statue when viewing it from different angles, the firm can better be understood when viewed from the accrual accounting *and* the cash flow perspectives. If cash flows from *operating* transactions and net income are materially different, the FS user should pay particularly close attention to the accounting methods, estimates and assumptions. Keep in mind, operating cash flows result from the firm's recurring activities as *most* of the components of the I/S. [For example, gains (losses) are not from the operating activities but are in the I/S.]

Cash and cash equivalents are treated as cash. **Cash equivalents** consist of debt securities acquired when their maturity date was three months or less. When the security is purchased it is classified as a debt security or not. Cash equivalent status does not change during the holding period through the passage of time. Let me explain an example and three questions to reinforce the key points about cash equivalents.

A debt security was acquired on May 31, Year 1. Its maturity date is March 1, Year 2. The answers are in [brackets].

1. Is this debt security a cash equivalent in the owner's B/S dated June 30, Year 1? [No]
2. Is this debt security a cash equivalent in the owner's B/S dated December 31, Year 1? [No]
3. On January 2, Year 2, this security was sold to another firm. Would the second investor properly classify this security as a cash equivalent in its B/S dated January 31, Year 2? [Yes]

To provide more complete information, disclosure is required of material transactions not involving the use of cash. Without disclosure of these items, users would suspect that some transactions occurred but were omitted from the Sof$F.
Here are some examples of non-cash transactions:

1. A firm bought some PPE paying nothing down and signing a note payable for the purchase price. [Debit PPE and credit Notes Payable.]
2. A firm issued some common stock to acquire land for future development. [Debit Land and credit CC.]
3. A firm gave up some investments in partial payment on a N/P. Ignore interest for convenience. [Debit N/P and credit Investments. Assume the fair market value of the Investments equaled their carrying value.]

There are two broadly used methods for preparing Sof$F: the indirect and the direct methods. These methods only involve differences in the presentation of the cash flows from operations. We will only cover the indirect method. You will not be responsible for the direct method. The investing and financing activities are *identical* under both methods.

The **indirect method** is emphasized in this course and chiefly reconciles net income to operating cash flows. We must adjust net income for non-cash revenues and expenses included in the I/S. [Examples include: Depreciation Expense on PPE does not involve cash outflows but lowers net income. Amortization Expense from expiration of part of an intangible asset reduces net income but does not consume any cash in the current period. If an amount had been received prior to earning it in the current period, it would have been accounted for previously as an Unearned Revenues. Earning this amount in the current period would *increase* net income but would *not* increase cash in the current period.]

The **direct method** for the Sof$F does not start with net income. Instead, this method requires that all I/S items from operating activities be converted to the 'cash basis'. Sales Revenue is converted to 'Amounts Collected from Customers (or Clients)'. Salaries Expense is converted to 'Amounts Paid to Employees'. Tax Expense is converted to be 'Amounts Paid for Taxes'. Depreciation Expense and Amortization Expense do not appear in the direct method Sof$F because they are *non-cash expenses*. Gains and losses from the I/S do not appear in the direct method operations section because they result from *non-operating* activities. The direct method requires reconciliation between net income and cash flows provided (used) by operations appear in a supplementary schedule. [This is the same reconciliation as in the operating section when using the indirect method. I will later work through an exercise with you that accomplishes most of the work for the direct method but with much less effort required of you ☺.]

To begin to acquaint you with the skills needed to understand various pieces of information related to the Sof$F, let's work through this exercise together. I will have to explain some new accounting 'tricks' as we work through this exercise. Briefly review the exercise before reading my comments following item 6 below.

Statement of Cash Flows
Selected Requirements

Listed below are selected account balances for the Ross Corporation at December 31, Years 1 and 2. Also available for you is selected information from the B/S for the Ross Corporation for the year ended December 31, Year 2. All numbers in 000's for ease of presentation.

Selected Balance Sheet Accounts

	Year 2	Year 1
Assets:		
Accounts Receivable	$32	$17
Prepaid Salaries	1	4
Property, Plant & Equip.	415	210
(Accumulated Depreciation)	(119)	(69)
Investments	82	96
Liabilities & Owners' Equity:		
Salaries Payable	$39	$21
Notes Payable	79	45
Dividends Payable	11	14
Contributed Capital	31	22
Retained Earnings	54	24

Selected income statement information for the year ended December 31, Year 2:

Sales revenue	$252
Depreciation	63
Salaries Expense	146
Loss on sale of equipment	49
Gain on sale of investments	41
Net Income	56

Additional information:
1. During Year 2, PPE costing $160 was sold for cash.
2. During Year 2, an $80 N/P was issued in exchange for PPE.
3. During Year 2, the firm sold Investments for $98 cash.

Required: Determine the correct dollar amounts for each of the following items.

1. Cash paid for salaries in Year 2. $ 125
2. Payments for the purchase of Investments in Year 2. $ 42
3. Notes Payable paid off in Year 2. $ 46
4. Cash dividends paid in Year 2 $ 29
5. Cash received from the sale of PPE in Year 2 $ 90
6. Cash paid for PPE in Year 2 $ _____

All of the account titles in the B/S and I/S data above should seem familiar to you. If not, you might wish to review parts of previous lectures and exercises before continuing with this exercise. These selected pieces of information do not constitute complete sets of any FS. The B/S and I/S data above are not complete presentations of either FS. Thus, no totals are required, nor would they be meaningful, if presented.

We will first focus on the additional information and attempt to construct journal entries for each piece of that additional information summarizing all of the data available to us.

During Year 2, PPE costing $160 was sold for cash. This tells us that PPE was reduced during the year because equipment that had cost us $160 when acquired was sold [credit PPE $160]. PPE would have to be credited for $160. There would have to be a debit to Cash for an amount not known yet to us. There would be a debit to Accumulated Depreciation reflecting that an asset upon which some depreciation had been accumulated has now been sold. Just as it makes sense to take the sold asset out of the books, it makes sense to remove from the books as well all of the depreciation that had accumulated on that asset. When an asset is sold, a gain or loss might result. The gain or the loss is difference between the book value of the asset and its sales price. The **book value of a piece of PPE** equals the price originally paid for the asset less any Accumulated Depreciation on that asset up to the date of sale. Losses are debits and gains are credits in the journal entry we are constructing. [In the I/S information that is given we can see there is a Loss on Sale of Equipment for $49.] Summarizing to this point, the journal entry will contain debits to Cash, Accumulated Depreciation and Loss on Sale of Equipment. There will be one credit to PPE for the original cost of the PPE being sold now.

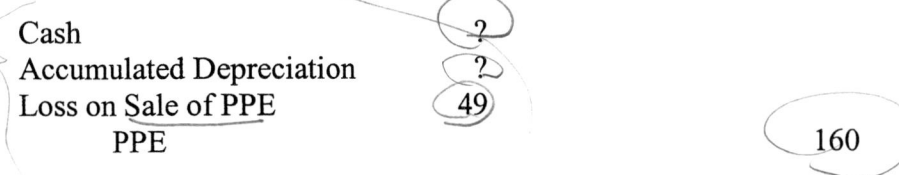

```
Cash                            ?
Accumulated Depreciation        ?
Loss on Sale of PPE            49
     PPE                              160
```

If we can determine the amount debited to Accumulated Depreciation in the entry above, we could obtain the cash received from the sale of the equipment and know answer to the fifth requirement in the exercise.

Let us examine the Accumulated Depreciation account to squeeze out of it the necessary debit in the journal entry above. The Accumulated Depreciation account started the year with a $69 balance and ended the year with a balance of $119. [The parentheses in the B/S information merely indicate that both of these balances were credits and since these accounts are included under the assets heading something must be done to indicate the 'contra' nature of these accounts.] The journal entry made when recording depreciation involved a debit to Depreciation Expense and a credit to Accumulated Depreciation for the appropriate dollar amount. The I/S information tells us that Depreciation Expense was $63, thus Accumulated Depreciation would have been credited for $63 in Year 2. If Accumulated Depreciation started the year with $69 credit balance *and* was credited for $63 during the year, then something must have been taken out of the account during the year. Recall the need to remove Accumulated Depreciation from the accounts when disposing of some PPE? Using logic, the amount removed from that account must have been $13.

Draw out a T account for Accumulated Depreciation and put the numbers in the proper places. Start with a credit balance of $69. Then credit the account for $63. Then debit the account for ?. The ending balance in the account is $119 as a credit. How much is the unknown debit? [$13 ☺]

Now, back to the journal entry above, we can determine the cash sales price of the PPE sold in Year 2 must have been $98. After all, the journal has to balance. ☺ Note that this is cash received from the sale of PPE in Year 2 (required item 5 in the exercise above).

During Year 2, an $80 Note Payable was issued in exchange for PPE. This is the second piece of additional information in the exercise. This transaction was a non-cash transaction debiting PPE and crediting N/P each by $80. We will need to utilize this information later as we work through this exercise.

PPE $80
    Notes Payable   80

We can now fairly easily see how to derive the answer to required item six in the exercise above by piecing together information discussed recently. The PPE account started the year with a balance of $210 and we have identified two changes in that account's balance: an *increase* of $80 and a *decrease* of $160. Since the account's ending balance is known to be $415 from the B/S information in the exercise, additional PPE must have been acquired at a cost of $285. [$210 + $80 - $160 + $285 = $415]

Draw out a T account for PPE and put the numbers in the proper places. Start with a debit balance of $210. Then debit the account for $80. Then credit the account for $160. The PPE account was debited for an unknown amount when PPE was purchased. The ending balance in the account must be $415 debit. How much is the unknown debit? [$285 ☺]

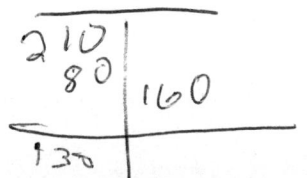

During Year 2, the firm sold Investments for $98 cash. This is the third piece of additional information in the exercise above. The journal entry to record this transaction would have a debit to Cash for $98 and a credit to Investments reducing that account for the *original* cost of the investments that are now being sold. When investments are sold, there may be a gain or loss as a result of whether the cash proceeds of the sale are greater or smaller than the cost basis of the investments being sold. In the I/S information, we see there is a Gain on Sale of Investments for $41. Gains are credits in journal entries.

The journal entry made to record the sale of investments would have included these accounts and amounts:

Cash	$98	
Gain		41
Investments		?

The credit to Investments would be for $57 in order to balance the journal entry. ☺ Note, the Investments account started the year with a $96 balance and ended the year with an $82 balance. In addition to the sale of investments with an original cost of $57 identified through the journal entry above, something else must have happened in the year to produce the ending balance as shown. Logic indicates that additional investments must have been *purchased* at a cost of $43. [$96 -$57 + $43 = $82]

Draw out a T account for Investments and put the numbers in the proper places. Start with a debit balance of $96. Then credit the account for $57. Then debit the account for $? The Investment account was debited for an unknown amount when an Investment was made. The ending balance in the account must be an $82 debit. How much is the unknown debit? [$43 ☺] $43 represents the answer to item two in the exercise above.

Cash paid for salaries in Year 2 can be determined easily with the use of a journal entry. Salaries Expense is known to be $146 from the I/S information provided. From the B/S information available to us we can see that there are two accounts bearing some connection to Salaries Expense: Prepaid Salaries and Salaries Payable. Prepaid Salaries decreased during the year from $4 to $1. This decrease could be explained with a *credit* to the Prepaid Salaries account for $3. Salaries Payable increased during Year 2 by $18. This increase could be explained by a *credit* to Salaries Payable during Year 2 for $18.

Salaries Expense	$146	
Prepaid Salaries		3
Salaries Payable		18
Cash		?

Cash paid for salaries in Year 2 must have been $125. This is the answer to item 1 in the exercise above.

N/P started Year 2 with a $45 balance and we have discovered that this account balance was increased by $80 as a result of the second piece of additional information in the exercise. Notes Payable paid off in Year 2 must be $46 determined as follows. [$45 + $80 - ? = $79]

Draw out a T account for N/P and put the numbers in the proper places. Start with a credit balance of $45. Then credit the account for $80. Then debit the account for $? The N/P account was debited for an unknown amount when some N/P was repaid. The ending balance in the account must be a $79 credit. How much is the unknown debit? [$46 ☺] $46 represents the answer to item three in the exercise above.

To find cash paid for dividends in Year 2, we need to cover some of the basic relationships involving Net Income, RE, Dividends Payable and payments of cash for dividends. As we have seen earlier in this course, net income increases RE. When dividends are declared, RE is debited and Dividends Payable is credited. In short, net income increases RE and declaring dividends decreases RE. RE at the start of Year 2 was $24. Net income for Year 2 was $56. Since ending RE were $54, dividends of $26 must have been declared in Year 2. [$24 + $56 - ? = $54]

Draw out a T account for RE and put the numbers in the proper places. Start with a credit balance of $24. Then credit the account for $56. Then, debit the account for $? The RE account was debited for an unknown amount when dividends were declared. The ending balance in the account must be a $54 credit. How much is the unknown debit? [$26 ☺] $26 is a credit to Dividends Payable in the item that follows.

The journal entry when declaring dividends in Year 2:

Retained Earnings $26
    Dividends Payable   26

Dividends Payable was $14 at the start of the year and increased by $26 as a result of the declaration of dividends in the journal entry immediately above. Since ending Dividends Payable were $11, dividends of $29 must have been paid in Year 2. [$14 + $26 - ? = $11]

Draw out a T account for Dividends Payable and put the numbers in the proper places. Start with a credit balance of $14. Then credit the account for $26. Then debit the account for $? The ending balance in the account must be $11 credit. How much is the unknown debit? [$29 ☺] $29 represents the answer to item four in the exercise above.

In this next exercise, we'll actually put together a Sof$F using two complete B/S an I/S and some additional data. This comprehensive exercise will provide a solution that 'balances' because the *change in cash* during the year is the check figure.

Statement of Cash Flows:

Balance Sheets	Starting	Ending
Cash	$1,000	$13,300
Accounts Receivable	2,000	4,000
Supplies Inventory	1,000	3,000
Prepaid Rent	2,000	1,000
Property, Plant and Equipment	8,000	21,000
(Acc. Depr.)	(3,000)	(4,000)
Investments	6,000	2,000
Total Assets	$17,000	$40,300
Accounts Payable	$1,000	$5,000
Interest Payable	1,000	800
Unearned Revenues	2,000	1,000
Current Notes Payable	1,000	500
Taxes Payable	2,000	4,000
Salaries Payable	2,000	5,000
Non-current Notes Payable	5,000	15,000
Total Liabilities	$14,000	$31,300
Contributed Capital	$1,000	$5,000
Retained Earnings	2,000	4,000
Total Owners' Equity	$3,000	$9,000
Total Liab. & Owners' Equity	$17,000	$40,300

Income Statement for the Year Ended December 31:

Sales	$30,000
Gain on Sale of Investment	6,000
	$36,000

Expenses and Loss:
Salaries Expense	$14,000	
Supplies Expense	3,000	
Rent Expense	6,000	
Depreciation	3,000	
Interest Expense	1,500	
Loss on Sale of PPE	1,000	$28,500
Income Before Income Taxes		$7,500
Tax Expense (40%)		3,000
Net Income		$4,500

Additional Information:
1. The firm sold PPE for $1,000 less than the carrying value of the PPE at the date of sale. The original cost of the PPE had been $4,000. Accumulated Depreciation was $2,000 at the date of sale.
2. The firm sold an investment for $10,000. The investment's original cost was $4,000.
3. The firm declared and paid a cash dividend of $2,500.

Required: Determine the proper sources or uses of cash from each of these three activities: Operating, Investing and Financing.

Creating your solution:

[On a separate sheet of paper, create a framework into which we can insert pieces of the solution as we work through this together, one step at a time. Let's build the framework vertically, starting with the heading. As I add a new element of the solution, let's add it to the framework. Leave plenty of room for the operating activities portion. It always takes up the most space. Merle]

Statement of Cash Flows
For the Year Ending December 31, Year 2

Cash Provided (Used) by Operating Activities:
 Net income

Cash Provided (Used) by Investing Activities:
 1000   PPE
 10000   Invest.

Cash Provided (Used) by Financing Activities:

Let's start by inserting Net Income at the top of the operations section as a 'source' of Cash. With the indirect method, Net Income is assumed to be an **operating** source of Cash. This assumption forces many adjustments to correct for yet-to-be-discovered deficiencies in the assumption.

Make yourself familiar with the account titles in the B/S and in the I/S. These titles are probably familiar to you now. Then review the additional information and build journal entries summarizing the information contained there. The journal entries were are building are not to record the events themselves, rather to let us 'see' the implications of journal entries that would have been recorded in the period to produce the financial statements presented. If you do not have sufficient information provided, we will have to examine the B/S and the I/S to complete the journal entries.

As we recall from our earlier work, Net Income results in an *increase* in RE. Since RE started the year with a $2,000 balance and was increased by $4,500, then something must have been *deducted* because the ending balance in RE is only $4,000.

$$RE: \$2,000 + \$4,500 - ? = \$4,000$$

The unknown is $2,500 and represents dividends *declared*. When dividends are *declared* there is a debit (decrease) to RE and a credit (increase) to Dividends Payable. When dividends are *paid*, there is a debit (decrease) to Dividends Payable and a credit to cash.

While we have the information in our minds, let's figure out cash paid for dividends. Dividends Payable started and ended the year without a balance. Thus, dividends paid in the year must have been $2,500 to cancel out the credit to Dividends Payable from declaring dividends.

From the first item of additional information, we can determine there was a Loss on Sale of PPE. When anything is sold for *less* than its carrying value (book value) the difference is recognized as a loss. In this case the Loss on Sales of PPE is $1,000. By looking in the I/S, we can confirm the accuracy of our conclusion. Debit Loss on Sale of PPE for $1,000. We must debit Accumulated Depreciation for $2,000 to remove depreciation previously taken on the PPE being sold now. PPE must be credited for $4,000 to remove the PPE being sold. To balance the entry, we must debit Cash for $1,000.

Loss on Sale of PPE	$1,000	
Accumulated Depreciation	2,000	
Cash	1,000	
PPE		4,000

Before moving on to the second piece of additional information, let's extract the valuable implications of this journal entry for purposes of building the S$F. Is there any Cash involved in the journal entry? [Yes, $1,000. The Cash results from an **Investing** activity.]

The $1,000 debit to Cash will result in a $1,000 Investing source of Cash and will need to be placed into the Investing section in the Sof$F we are building.

The Loss in this journal entry reduces net income but does *not* reduce cash flow from *operating* activities. This requires that the loss be 'added back' to offset the decrease in Net Income but not associated with a decrease in Cash Flow from **Operating** Activities. See the connection. The Loss was already included implicitly in the Net Income figure that was placed at the top of the operations activities ($4,500). However, the loss did not result from an operating activity and must be adjusted out. Adding back the $1,000 for the loss accomplishes just that.]

'Update' the Accumulated Depreciation and Property, Plant and Equipment accounts for the changes in their balances caused by the journal entry shown above. The debit to Accumulated Depreciation decreases that account's balance and the credit to PPE also decreases that account's balance. Record these two decreases <u>between</u> the starting and ending balances in both accounts. For now, note that neither 'update' explains fully the change from the starting to the ending balances. We will discover the remaining information later.

Note that we have done 'something' with each component of the journal entry summarizing the sale of PPE at a loss. The Loss has been added in the Operations section, Cash has been added in the Investing section, Accumulated Depreciation and PPE have been treated as 'updates' to their respective account balances in the balance sheet.

From the second item of additional information, we can 'build' a journal entry summarizing the data presented there. Debit Cash for $10,000 and credit Investment for its original cost of $4,000. Logically, the Gain on Sale of Investment must have been $6,000 since we sold the investment for $6,000 *more* than its original cost.

Cash	$10,000	
Gain on Sale of Investment		6,000
Investments		4,000

Before moving on to the third piece of additional information, let's extract the valuable implications of this journal entry for purposes of building the Sof$F. Is there any Cash involved in the journal entry? [Yes. $10,000 of Cash was received from the sale of Investments. This source of Cash results from an **Investing** activity and must be placed in that section.]

The Gain in this journal entry increases net income but does not increase cash flow from operating activities. This requires that the gain be 'deducted from' Net Income in the **Operations** section to offset the increase in Net Income but *not* associated with an increase in Cash Flow from Operating Activities. Subtracting the gain in the operating activities section offsets the effects having previously included it in the I/S *increasing* net income.

Finally, treat the credit to Investments in the journal entry as a subtraction from the beginning balance in that account. Note carefully, this $4,000 decrease *does* explain the movement in that account's balance from $6,000 at the start of the year to $2,000 at the end of the year. I recommend you place a check mark by the $2,000 ending balance to reflect that we have reconciled the beginning and ending balances in this account.

Note that we have done 'something' with each component of the journal entry summarizing the sale of Investments at a gain. The Gain has been deducted in the Operations section, Cash has been added in the Investing section and the credit to Investments has been subtracted as an 'update' to its account balance in the B/S.

From the third item of additional information, we are reminded of journal entries we created earlier involving Net Income, RE and Dividends Payable.

Declaring a Dividend:
Retained Earnings $2,500
    Dividends Payable   2,500

Paying a Dividend:
Dividends Payable $2,500
    Cash   2,500

The third item of information was unnecessary to analyze the changes in the RE account. This piece of additional information does serve to confirm the accuracy of our earlier work involving these accounts. We do need to extract the valuable implications of these journal entries for purposes of building the SofSF.

The debit to RE was and is the reconciling item to explain the change in that account's balance between the start and the end of the year. Place a 'check' mark to the right of the ending $4,000 balance in RE to indicate the reconciliation is complete.

In our solution to this point we have reconciled changes in Investments and RE. The change in Cash provides our final check figure to the entire statement of cash flows. For each unreconciled account in the B/S other than Cash, we must assume the change involved Cash unless it becomes clear there is another explanation. Let us start with the first account below Cash in the B/S: A/R.

HELPFUL GENERAL RULE: All interest and dividends are operating items *except for* dividends paid to owners. Dividends paid to owners are *financing* activities.

Accounts Receivable (A/R) increased by $2,000. Would this increase in A/R be associated with a source or use of Cash? An increase in A/R means we generated more revenues than cash collections from customers. The larger revenues were recognized in the I/S, increasing Net Income but cash collected from customers had to be *less* than the revenues by $2,000. Hence, A/R increased by $2,000. The $2,000 must be treated as a *deduction* in the **Operations** sections to adjust for the extent to which Net Income does not accurately reflect the change in the Cash for the year (related to Revenues and A/R).

Fortunately, there is faster way to work through most of the accounts that need reconciliation. Build a hypothetical journal involving the account being reconciled and Cash. In this case, A/R went up in the year. Debit A/R and credit Cash both for $2,000. This more succinctly reflects that the increase in A/R is associated with a use of Cash.

This hypothetical journal entry is shown here:
Accounts Receivable $2,000
    Cash   2,000

Supplies Inventory increased by $2,000. We can more efficiently see the effect on Cash by using a hypothetical journal entry as just explained. If Supplies Inventory increased by $2,000, that implies a debit to Supplies Inventory and we can easily imagine a credit to Cash. The credit to Cash for $2,000 represents a use of Cash in the **Operations** section since supplies are purchased for use in operating activities.

Supplies Inventory $2,000
    Cash   2,000

Prepaid Rent decreased during the year by $1,000. We can analyze the effect on operating cash flow using the hypothetical journal entry approach.

Cash $1,000
    Prepaid Rent   1,000

The decrease in Prepaid Rent is associated with an operating source of Cash because all of the Rent Expense in the I/S (and hence in Net Income) is not related to a current use of Cash. To the extent of $1,000, the Rent Expense had been paid in a previous period. Treat the debit to Cash in this hypothetical journal entry as an operating *source* of cash.

PPE *increased* by a total of $13,000 during the year. However, we have previously identified a *decrease* in this account during the year for $4,000. Thus, the presently *unexplained* change is for $17,000 (not the $13,000 that would otherwise seem so apparent). Using the hypothetical journal entry approach to indicate the source of use of Cash:

PPE $17,000
    Cash   17,000

This use of $17,000 Cash would belong in the Investing section and we would place it there under the Cash from Sale of Investments item.

Accumulated Depreciation increased in the year from $3,000 to $4,000. We have already isolated a $2,000 **decrease** in that account balance during the current year from the sale of PPE analyzed earlier. Thus, the presently *unexplained* change is for $3,000:

Accumulated Depreciation

Care must be used to correctly interpret the parenthetical values here. These values are credits, not negatives. Recall the normal balance of the Accumulated Depreciation account is a credit. The $2,000 shown above as a *reduction* (minus sign) causes a $1,000 credit balance. *If* the parentheses meant 'negative', there would be a $5,000 negative balance in that account. To avoid all confusion, let us see this in the form of a T account:

Start with a $3,000 credit balance in Accumulated Depreciation. Debit $2,000 from the sale of PPE discussed earlier in this exercise. The ending balance is this account is known to be $4,000 credit. How much must have been added to this account and why? The only other item effecting Accumulated Depreciation is Depreciation Expense. When we record Depreciation Expense there is a debit to the expense and a credit to Accumulated Depreciation. From the I/S we can see that the expense was $3,000. This would result in a $3,000 credit to the Accumulated Depreciation account and provides the 'missing' piece of information. ☺

The credit to Accumulated Depreciation enables us to 'check off' that account as we move through the balance sheet.

There is another important observation related to the journal entry recording Depreciation Expense. This entry reduces Net Income, but has no effect on Cash Flows from Operating Activities. Depreciation Expense does not involve the use of any Cash. We will need to *add* $3,000 for Depreciation Expense in the operations section to offset the reduction in net income that occurred when included the *non-cash* Depreciation Expense of $3,000.

Accounts Payable increased in the period from $1,000 to $5,000. Is the increase in A/P associated with a sources or use of Cash? Using the 'short-cut' approach, we can think of a journal entry involving a credit to A/P for $4,000 and a debit to Cash for the same amount. The increase in A/P must be associated with an operating increase in Cash. More logically, the increase in A/P occurred when the firm purchased goods and services on account *but saved* Cash by not paying off as much as had been acquired on account.

Interest Payable decreased in the period from $1,000 to $800. Is this decrease in Interest Payable associated with a source or use of Cash? Using the 'short-cut' approach, we can think of a debit to Interest Payable and a credit to Cash. The decrease in Interest Payable must be associated with an operating use of Cash. More logically, the decrease in Interest Payable occurred as a result of paying more interest than was 'used up' in the period. Interest Expense had been $1,500 and the firm must have paid interest of $1,700 in order for the liability to *decrease* by $200.

Unearned Revenues decreased from $2,000 to $1,000 in the period. Is this decrease in Unearned Revenues associated with a source or use of Cash? Using the 'short-cut' approach, we can think of a debit to Unearned Revenues and a credit to Cash for $1,000. More logically, the decrease in Unearned Revenues means that Revenues earned in the period exceeded Cash received in advance. Thus, Net Income was $1,000 larger than was the cash collected from customers (when isolating on Unearned Revenues). We must subtract the decrease in Unearned Revenues in the operations section.

Current Notes Payable decreased from $1,000 to $500. Is this decrease associated with a source or use of Cash? Using the 'short-cut' approach, we can think of a debit to Current N/P and a credit to Cash both for $500. More logically, the decrease in Current N/P resulted from paying off part of the principal. This use of $500 cash belongs in the financing section of the Sof$F because it is a payment to debt-holders.

Taxes Payable increased from $2,000 to $4,000. Is this increased associated with a source or use of Cash? Using the 'short-cut' approach, we can think of a debit to Cash and a credit to Taxes Payable both for $2,000. More logically, the increase in Taxes Payable means payments for taxes were not as large as was the Tax Expense for the period, and thus, the liability increased. We must treat this as an operating source of cash for $2,000.

Salaries Payable increased from $2,000 to $5,000 in the period. Is this increase associated with a source or use of Cash? Using the 'short-cut' approach, we can think of a debit to Cash and a credit to Salaries Payable both for $3,000. More logically, the increase in Salaries Payable means payments for salaries were *not as large* as was the Salaries Expense for the period, and thus, the liability increased. We must treat this as an operating source of cash for $3,000.

Non-current Notes Payable increased from $5,000 to $15,000 in the period. Is this increase associated with a source or use of Cash? Using the 'short-cut' approach, we can think of a debit to Cash and a credit to Non-current N/P both for $10,000. More logically, the increase in Non-current N/P means the firm borrowed an additional $10,000 in the period. We must treat this as a financing source of cash in the Sof$F for $10,000.

Contributed Capital increased from $1,000 to $5,000 in the period. Is this increase associated with a source or use of Cash? Using the 'short-cut' approach, we can think of a debit to Cash and a credit to CC both for $4,000. More logically, the increase in CC means the firm received an additional $4,000 from some investors in the period. We must treat this as a financing source of cash for $4,000.

We are now ready to 'wrap-up' this exercise. Subtotaling the cash flows and their adjustments for each of the three sections, we obtain these values:

Cash Provided from Operating Activities	$7,300
Cash Used in Investing Activities	($6,000)
Cash Provided from Financing Activities	$11,000
Total Cash Provided During the Year	$12,300

This total change in cash during the year, $12,300, equals the increase in Cash during the year. One activity required to complete the Sof$F involves adding beginning cash to total cash provided in the year to yield the firm's ending cash.

It might look something like this:

Cash Provided from Operating Activities	$7,300
Cash Used in Investing Activities	(6,000)
Cash Provided from Financing Activities	11,000
Total Cash Provided During the Year	$12,300
Add: Beginning Cash	1,000
Equals: Ending Cash	$13,300

This next exercise is presented to provide another opportunity to understand more about the interaction of the three financial statements.

Financial Statement Articulation:
Selected I/S and B/S accounts are presented below for your use in meeting the requirements of this problem. Use the relationships between revenues, expenses, assets, liabilities and OE to figure out the numerical values for the unknowns.

Selected I/S Account Balances for the Year Ended December 31, Year 2:

	Year 2
Consulting Revenues	AA
Rent Revenues	LL
Salaries Expense	$80
Utilities Expense	40
Insurance Expense	25
Rent Expense	35

Selected B/S Account Balances at December 31, Year 2 and Year 1:

	Year 2	Year 1
Accounts Receivable	$110	$70
Rent Receivable	60	50
Prepaid Salaries	20	40
Prepaid Insurance	GG	5
Prepaid Rent	50	10
Salaries Payable	$40	$30
Utilities Payable	FF	15
Rent Payable	15	JJ
Unearned Rent Revenue	50	20

Selected Additional Information Related to Cash Flows for the Year Ended December 31, Year 2:

	Year 2
Cash collected from clients	$200
Cash collected from tenants	100
Cash paid for salaries	CC
Cash paid for utilities	25
Cash paid for insurance	35
Cash paid for rent	60

Year 2 Consulting Revenues   AA = 240

Year 2 Cash Paid for Salaries   CC = 50

December 31, Year 2 Utilities Payable   FF = 30

December 31, Year 2 Prepaid Insurance   GG = 15

December 31, Year 1 Rent Payable   JJ = 0

Year 2 Rent Revenues   LL =

Consulting Revenues for Year 2 is 'related' to A/R and cash collected from clients in this exercise. Let's use journal entry relationships to isolate on the unknown. Cash collected from clients would be a debit in a journal entry. A/R increased by $40 during Year 2 and that would a debit also in the journal entry. No other B/S accounts are 'related' to Consulting Revenues. Thus, Consulting Revenues for Year 2 would have to $240. This would 'balance' the journal entry.

Cash	$200	
A/R	40	
Consulting Revenue		240

Cash Paid for Salaries in Year 2 is 'related' to Prepaid Salaries and Salaries Payable in the B/S data provided. Cash Paid for Salaries is also related to Salaries Expense from the I/S provided. Let's use journal entry relationships to isolate on the unknown. Debit Salaries Expense for $80. Credit Prepaid Salaries for the *decrease* in that account's balance. Credit Salaries Payable for the *increase* in that account's balance. Cash Paid for Salaries in Year 2 is the balancing value.

Salaries Expense	$80	
Prepaid Salaries		20
Salaries Payable		10
Cash		50

Utilities Payable at December 31, Year 2 is 'related' to Utilities Expense in the I/S and cash paid for utilities. Let's use journal entry relationships to isolate on the unknown. Debit Utilities Expense for $40. Credit Cash (paid for utilities) $25. Utilities Payable would have to have been credited for $15 to 'balance' the journal entry.

Utilities Expense	$40	
Cash		25
Utilities Payable		15

Thus, the December 31, Year 2 balance in Utilities Payable would have been $30.

Let's take a look at the T account representation of these Utilities Payable relationships.

The opening balance in Utilities Payable is $15 (credit). This balance increased by $15 during the year (in the journal entry above). Thus, the ending balance in this account would have been $30 (credit).

Prepaid Insurance at December 31, Year 2 is 'related' to Insurance Expense in the I/S and to cash paid for insurance. Let's use journal entry relationships to isolate on the unknown. Debit Insurance Expense for $25. Cash paid for insurance is a credit for $35. Thus, Prepaid Insurance would have to have been debited for $10 to balance the entry.

Insurance Expense	$25	
Prepaid Insurance	10	
Cash		35

Prepaid Insurance at the end of Year 2 would have to have been $15. The beginning debit balance in the account would have been $5 and this would have increased by $10 as a result of the journal entry shown above. The ending balance in Prepaid Insurance at the end of Year 2 would have been $15.

Rent Payable at December 31, Year 1 is 'related' to Rent Expense in the I/S and to Prepaid Rent in the B/S. Cash paid for rent is another piece of information that must be considered. Let's use journal entry relationships to isolate on the unknown. Debit Rent Expense for $35. Debit Prepaid Rent for $40. Credit Cash paid for rent $60. Rent Payable would have to have been credited for $15 in order to balance the entry.

Rent Expense	$35	
Prepaid Rent	40	
Cash		60
Rent Payable		15

Click here to see a T account representation of these Rent Payable relationships.

The opening balance in Rent Payable is an unknown credit $. During the year, Rent Payable would have been credited $15 as shown in the journal entry above. If the final account balance for the year was $15, then the beginning balance must have been zero.

Rent Revenues for Year 2 are 'related' to Cash received from tenants, Rent Receivable and Unearned Rent Revenue. Let's use journal entry relationships to isolate the unknown. Cash collected from tenants is a debit for $100. Rent Receivable will be a debit for $10. Unearned Rent Revenue will be a credit for $30. Rent Revenue is Year 2 must be a credit for $80 to 'balance' the entry. ☺ This is the value we need to finish the exercise.

Cash	$100	
Rent Receivable	10	
Unearned Rent Revenue		30
Rent Revenue ☺		80

Revenue Cycle
Topic 6
This topic ties to chapter 8 in the SSD text.

Revenue recognition criteria provide the conceptual framework for the revenue cycle. There are two criteria: revenues must be earned and realized before appearing in the I/S. While these criteria seem easy to apply, real-world economic activity creates countless complications requiring high-level judgment by management and their accountants.

Examples will help you to understand how the basic revenue recognition criteria are not always adequate when considering revenue recognition for a specific real world firm.

FRANCHISOR ACCOUNTING ISSUES
Franchisors receive resources for letting other entities (franchisees) perform the subject matter of the franchise. McDonald's Corporation sells franchises to franchisees allowing use of the McDonald's name for a specified time period. A franchisor's recognition of the initial franchise fee as revenue depends on the nature and timing of the duties required of the franchisor under the agreement's terms. If the agreement required that all of the 'work' be performed at the start of the franchise period, then recognizing all of the revenues at that time would be appropriate. Alternatively, if the agreement required that the franchisor continue providing substantial services during the franchise term, then revenues should be recognized relative to the work being done each period. Management and their accountants will exercise serious judgment determining what part of the initial franchise fee should be revenue for a specific year.

FRANCHISOR EXAMPLE:
Assume a franchisor sells a franchise to a franchisee operate a restaurant for ten years. The franchise term starts on January 1 of Year 1. The initial franchise fee is $200,000 and the franchisor will provide 40% of the required services divided equally over the first two years of the franchise term. The remaining services will be provided evenly over the remaining eight years of the franchise term. Additionally, the franchisor will receive 6% of the franchisee's sales. Sales will not begin until the initial year of the ten-year franchise term has *ended*. During the first year the franchisor will select the restaurant site, construct and equip the facility and, finally, train top-level franchisee management. During the second year, the franchisor will provide on-the-job training for franchisee management and train the franchisee's employees while the restaurant is in operation.

Assume the franchisee's gross revenues for Years 2 and 3 are $1,200,000 and $1,800,000, respectively.

Required: Determine the franchisor's revenues for the Years 1, 2 and 3.

Answers:
Year 1: $40,000. [$200,000 x 40% x ½]
Year 2: $112,000 [($200,000 x 40% x ½) + (6% x $1,200,000) = $40,000 + $72,000]

Year 3: $133,000 [($200,000 x 60% 1/8) + ($1,800,000 x 6%)]

SERVICE OR MEMBERSHIP CONTRACTS

Some firms sell memberships or service contracts requiring the firm to make specified services or facilities available to the member during the membership period. Some of you are familiar with this arrangement through memberships at health or fitness clubs. When should the club recognize the related revenues? Should the revenues be recognized in full when signing the agreement? Should the revenues be recognized when the membership period starts (if different than the signing date)? Should the revenues be recognized when the first payment is made? Should the revenues be recognized when more than half of the total payments have been made? Should the revenues be recognized when all of the payments have been made? Should the revenues be recognized when the membership period has ended? If recurring payments required, are they sufficiently large enough to cover the future marginal costs associated with servicing the extra member? [The revenues should be recognized in the same pattern as the necessary services are delivered to the members. The point is to illustrate judgmental complexities arising when applying revenue recognition criteria in everyday situations.]

EXAMPLE
A health club sells a one-year membership to an individual on May 31 of Year 1 for $540. The membership period starts right away. The $540 is to be paid in four unequal installments. 40% is due on signing, 30% is due three months after signing and two payments of 15% each at six months and none months.

How much *Unearned Membership Revenue* should the club report at these dates?
May 31 of Year 1   [$216 = $540 x 40%] Nothing has been earned yet.
December 31 of Year 1   [$144 = $216 + $162 + $81 – (7) ($45)]

How much *Membership Revenue* should the club report for this member for the year ended December 31 of Year 1?   [$315 = (7) x ($540/12)]

Percentage of Completion Method for Long-Term Construction Projects

Construction firms have special revenue recognition criteria when projects last more than one accounting period. There are two acceptable accounting methods for possible use with long-term construction projects: the **percentage of completion method** and the completed contract method. The percentage of completion method is preferred when reliable estimates are available. The rules make sense and reflect the economic substance between the construction firm and its customer. These rules implicitly incorporate changing estimates. Previous FS are not revised when estimates are revised.

The percentage of completion method requires reliable estimates of costs necessary to complete the project, or alternatively, the estimated costs of the completed project. At the end of each year a fraction must be constructed in which the numerator reflects the sum of costs incurred to date on the project. The numerator is a 'cumulative' concept reflecting the aggregate project costs to date. The denominator is the estimated *total* cost of the project. Deriving this from data given might require the estimated costs to complete be added to the costs incurred to date in order to develop the estimated total cost of the project. Alternatively, the estimated total costs of the project might be given directly and no further computations required. This fraction provides the project's percentage of completion.

The percentage of completion is multiplied by the 'contract price'. The contract price is the consideration the buyer has agreed to pay to the construction firm. The product of this multiplication represents *cumulative* revenues recognized to date. We must subtract all revenues previously recognized (if any) to obtain revenues for the current period. Expenses recognized for the current period equal the costs incurred in the current period. The annual journal entry recording the revenues and the expenses is made to balance by debiting or crediting an account representing the project during the construction phase, **Construction in Progress**. Construction in Progress [CIP] is an inventory-type account for the construction company and is a current asset.

The costs incurred each year are debited into the CIP account.

Conservatism requires that any expected losses be recognized immediately. In the percentage of completion method, this requires a loss be recognized equal to the total expected loss on the project *increased* be any profits previous recognized on the project.

EXAMPLE
Courtney Construction Company has a contract to construct a street for the City of Los Angeles at a total price of $9,000 [for convenience, all numbers are in thousands of dollars]. While negotiating the contract for the street, Courtney Company estimated the street might cost $6,000 to build. In Year 1 of the street project, Courtney incurred costs of $1,500. At the end of Year 1, Courtney estimates the street will require another $4,400 to complete. Courtney Construction Company uses the percentage of completion method.

During Year 2, Courtney spends another $1,500 on the street and estimates that the costs of the completed street will be $6,100.

Required:
For Year 1, what are the revenues and expenses recognized on this project? At the end of Year 1, what would be the ending balance in the CIP account?

For Year 2, what are the revenues and expenses recognized on this project? Round to the nearest dollar. At the end of Year 2, what would be the ending balance in the CIP account?

Year 1 Revenues are **$2,288**. [$1,500/($1,500 + $4,400)] ($9,000) = $2,288 - $0 = $2,288.

Year 1 Expenses are **$1,500**.

The Year 1 ending balance in CIP is **$2,288**. [$1,500 + $788*]

*It will be helpful to construct a journal entry: Debit Expense and CIP for $1,500 and $788, respectively. Credit Revenues for $2,288.

Year 2 Revenues are **$2,138** [$3,000/$6,100)] ($9,000) = $4,426 - $2,288= $2,138.

Year 2 Expenses are **$1,500**.

The Year 2 ending balance in CIP is **$4,426**. [$1,500 + $788 + $1,500 + $638**]

**It will be helpful to construct a journal entry: Debit Expense and CIP for $1,500 and $638, respectively. Credit Revenues for $2,138.

CREDIT TERMS

Selling on credit requires firms to establish **credit policies** that can range from 'tight' to 'loose'. Credit policies should be consistent with the firm's objectives. Increasing sales and/or increasing the 'bottom line' might be among the objectives. Deciding to offer credit terms involves more risk and should be accompanied by appropriate expected returns.

Consider a simple example and whether each firm should offer 'no', 'easy' or 'tight' credit terms. Assume three firms have only one product each. All three products sell for $100 per unit. Firm A's product costs $20 per unit to make. Firm B's product costs $60 per unit to make. Firm C's product costs $90 per unit to make. Which firm is most likely to offer 'easy' credit terms? Which firm is most likely to offer 'tight' credit terms?

An easy way to analyze this situation might be as follows. If all the firms sell 100 units on credit, what percentage of each firm's customers *must actually pay* for the goods in order for each firm to *break even*?

FIRM A: 20% of firm A's customers must actually pay in order for firm A to break even. If we have revenues of $2,000 we can cover the costs of selling 100 units. (100 units)($100 per unit)(20%) = $2,000. (100 units) (costs of $20 per unit) = total costs of $2,000. Collect $2,000 out of total sales of $10,000 yields 20%.

FIRM B: 20% of firm B's customers must actually pay in order for firm B to break even. If we have revenues of $6,000 we can cover the costs of selling 100 units. (100 units)($100 per unit)(26%) = $6,000. (100 units) (costs of $60 per unit) = total costs of $6,000. Collect $6,000 out of total sales of $10,000 yields 60%.

FIRM C: 20% of firm C's customers must actually pay in order for firm C to break even. If we have revenues of $9,000 we can cover the costs of selling 100 units. (100 units) ($100 per unit) (90%) = $9,000. (100 units) (costs of $90 per unit) = total costs of $9,000. Collect $9,000 out of total sales of $10,000 yields 90%.

This example illustrates the relationship between credit policies and the opportunities for profit from sales of units. Competitive pressures pose challenges when setting credit policies in real-world situations that cannot easily be incorporated into an example like this.

SALES DISCOUNTS

Sales discount terms encourage customers to pay for goods purchased on credit to make quicker payments. A common example of sales discount terms is '2/10, net 30'. [Read as: 'two ten net thirty'.] This authorizes a customer paying on the tenth day to deduct 2% of the invoice price and remit the remainder to the seller in full settlement. Alternatively, the seller expects to receive 100% of the invoice on the thirtieth day in full settlement.

There is a benefit to the seller far greater than quicker access to the cash from the customer. These terms represent an approximate simple interest annual rate of 36%* for paying early. This rate of return should be sufficient to induce all buyers with adequate liquidity to take advantage of those terms. That's my point, if the buyer does _not_ take advantage of these terms, then the buyer must have some liquidity problems. If sellers observe that a buyer does not pay early and earn the 36% rate of return, the _seller_ should question the wisdom of further sales on account to this _particular_ customer.

*(2% savings by paying 20 days early) times (the number of 20 day periods in a year: 360/20) = **36%**

Sales Discounts are contra revenues and result in reductions from the gross revenue amounts. Contra revenue accounts have debit balances and when offset against Sales Revenues cause net sales to be lower than gross sales.

TRANSACTIONS INVOLVING SHIPMENT OF GOODS

When buying or selling merchandise (goods) in the ordinary course of business, the timing of the purchase (sale) occurs at the point of the transaction when there is no need for shipment of the goods. If the buyer picks up the goods from the seller or if the seller itself delivers to the buyer, the transaction occurs when the buyer takes possession of the goods. However, when shipment involving a third party is involved, the timing of the purchase/sale depends upon the shipping terms established that are part of the sale contract. With **'FOB shipping point'** terms, the buyer becomes the owner when the shipper takes possession of the goods from the seller. With **'FOB destination'** terms, the buyer becomes the owner when the shipper delivers the goods to the proper location (usually the buyer's place of business). Shipping terms also establish responsibility for paying the shipping costs. With FOB shipping point, the buyer bears responsibility for paying the shipping costs and with FOB destination, the seller bears responsibility for paying the shipping costs.

EXAMPLES
On December 23 in Year 1 the Rick Company agreed to buy goods at a cost of $8,000 from the Stephanie Company on FOB shipping point terms. The goods were shipped on December 28 and arrived on January 3 in Year 2. The invoice (paperwork sent through the mail) arrived on January 2 of Year 2 and was recorded on that date by Rick Company. [Nothing had been recorded in Year 1 related to the purchase of these goods.]

Required:
In which year should Stephanie Company record the revenue? Year 1*

In which year should Rick Company record the purchase? Year 1**

Should Rick Company correct its accounting records for Year 1 to reflect the purchase in that year? Yes***

Should Rick Company correct its accounting records for Year 2 to avoid the purchase be 'double booked'? Yes****

*The goods were sold on a FOB shipping point basis and the goods were shipped in Year 1.

**The goods were purchased on a FOB shipping point basis and the goods were shipped in Year 1.

***The goods were purchased on a FOB shipping point basis and the goods were shipped in Year 1. The purchase correctly belongs to Year 1 and is not recorded in the books for that year. [The books for Year 2 will have to be adjusted to avoid 'double booking' the purchase.]

****The goods were purchased on a FOB shipping point basis and the goods were shipped in Year 1. The purchase correctly belongs to Year 1 and should not be recorded in the books for Year 2. [The books for Year 1 will have to be adjusted to record the purchase in the correct year.]

ACCOUNTING FOR UNCOLLECTIBLE ACCOUNTS RECEIVABLE
Sales on account create revenues and assets (A/R). Previously, we have side-stepped the issue of uncollectible A/R. In fact, uncollectible A/R are part of economic reality and accrual financial statements will reflect this. Knowing that some A/R will not be collected creates concern about overstating assets in the balance sheet, specifically the A/R. If you believe that some A/R will not be collected, then it would be optimistic to report the overstated receivables in the balance sheet and ignore that their economic value to the entity has been marginally reduced to the extent of expected uncollectibility.

At the time of sale or when preparing balance sheets later, entities do not know which specific customers will not pay. Proper accounting for uncollectible A/R involves use of a new account, Allowance for Uncollectible Acccounts. This is a contra asset account and carries a normal credit balance. A/R less the Allowance for Uncollectible Accounts [AUA] equalsl the 'carrying value' of A/R. **Carrying Value of A/R** is a commonly used term in the business community and it should not be confused with the recorded value of A/R.

There are two methods in widespread use related to uncollectible A/R. One is the **percentage of sales method** and is also known as the income statement method. The second is the **aging method** and is also known as the balance sheet method. The details of these methods will be explained shortly.

When adjusting the books at year-end and when using either method, Bad Debts Expense [BDE] is debited and AUA account is credited. The decreases total assets and increases expenses. [Increased expenses causes less income and less OE as we move through the accounting cycle.] The adjusting journal entry is recorded based on *estimates* generated according to the specific method selected for use in connection with its uncollectible A/R. The adjusting journal entry can look like this:

BDE   XXXXXX
    AUA   XXXXXX

Later, when the firm has additional knowledge about specific A/R that might not be collectible, the firm can 'write off' those accounts considered to be partly or wholly uncollectible. The write off entry is the same for both methods. The write off entry debits AUA account and credits A/R. The write off entry can look like this:

AUA   XXXXXX
    A/R   XXXXXX

The write off entry does change the legal relationship between the parties. The customer 'written off' still owes the full amount. The write off entry does not change the firm's *total* assets. By decreasing both of the accounts in the write off entry, total assets are unaffected.

Occasionally, a firm that was written off will partially or fully pay an amount that was owed. This comes as a pleasant surprise to the seller because it had previously concluded that the amount should be fully or partially written off due to expected uncollectibility. Two journal entries are usually recorded when these recoveries take place. The first entry 'restates' the A/R and the AUA to the books in implicit acknowledgement that the earlier write off has proven overly conservative. The second entry records the collection from the customer.

A/R   XXXXXX
    AUA   XXXXXX

```
Cash                              XXXXXX
    A/R                                XXXXXX
```

There are important benefits from recording both journal entries deriving from an accurate history of a specific customer's account. However, from a financial statement perspective, these entries can be condensed to better see the impacts on the balance sheet:

```
Cash                              XXXXXX
    AUA                                XXXXXX
```

PERCENTAGE OF SALES METHOD:
When recording the adjusting journal entry [AJE] using the percentage of sales method, the amount of the debit to BDE is calculated using management's estimated percentage of credit sales that will become uncollectible multiplied by the firm's credit sales for the period. Management's estimated percentage will reflect the firm's credit policies and other information influencing the customers' ability to pay for credit sales.

EXAMPLE
If a firm had credit sales in Year 1 of $3,000,000 and the firm's management estimated that 2% of credit sales would become uncollectible, the firm would debit BDE for $60,000 in that year and credit AUA for the same amount.

AGING METHOD
When recording the AJE using the aging method, the goal is to cause the carrying value of A/R to equal what management currently estimates to be 'collectible' from A/R. The A/R account is not adjusted. The balance in the AUA account is adjusted to equal what management estimates to be uncollectible. Recall, that the carrying value of A/R equals A/R less AUA. The relationships below will help you understand this.

A/R	$Total amount owed to the firm
-AUA	-$Amount estimated to be *uncollectible*
=Carrying value	=$Amount estimated to be *collectible*

EXAMPLE
Before recording AJE at the end of Year 1, assume a firm had a $3,000,000 balance in A/R and $90,000 credit balance in its AUA account. As a result of reviewing the balances in all A/R accounts, the management has estimated that the firm will likely collect $2,850,000 from its year-end A/R. The AJE will involve debiting BDE and crediting the AUA both for $60,000. Thus the ending balance in AUA that would appear in the B/S would be $150,000.

$3,000,000 $Total amount owed to the firm
-150,000   -$Amount estimated to be *uncollectible*
$2,850,000   =$Amount estimated to be *collectible*

COMPREHENSIVE EXAMPLE
Accounting for Uncollectible Accounts Receivable:
The Zachary Company was formed in Year 1 and sells goods only on account. The firm had proper balances in A/R and the AUA of $500 and $40, respectively, at the end of Year 2. Selected data related to uncollectible A/R are presented below for your use as appropriate.

	Year 3	Year 4	Year 5
Credit Sales	$800	$1,000	$1,100
Collections on Account	700	900	900
Write-Offs of A/R	50	70	100
Recoveries of Previous Write-Offs	10	20	30

When using the percentage of sales method, assume the firm has correctly estimated that the percentage of sales that will not be collected is 5% in Year 3. However, assume the firm increases this estimate to be 8% for Years 4 and 5.

When using the aging method of accounting for uncollectible accounts receivable, assume the firm properly estimated at the end of Year 3 that $490 of its AR would be collectible. At the end of Year 4, the firm has estimated that it will not be able to collect $60 of its A/R balance. At the end of Year 5, the firm has estimated that it will collect $890 of its A/R balance at that date.

Requirements:
Using the Percentage of Sales Method calculate the following values.

	Year 3	Year 4	Year 5
BDE	$ 40	$ 80	$ 88
Carrying value of A/R at December 31	510	510	592
AUA at December 31	40	70	88

Using the Aging Method calculate the following values and place your answer in the space provided.

BDE $ 60 ✓ $ 50 ✓ $ 100 ✓

Carrying Value of A/R at December 31 $ 490 ✓ $ 520 ✓ $ 590 ✓

AUA at December 31 $ 60 ✓ $ 60 ✓ $ 90

Answers for Percentage of Sales:

BDE for Year 3   (5%)($800) =   **$40**

Carrying value of A/R at December 31, Year 3 $550-$40=   **$510**

AUA at December 31, Year 3 $40 - $50 + $10 + $40 =   **$40**

BDE for Year 4   (8%)($1,000)   **$80**

Carrying value of A/R at December 31, Year 4 $580-$70=   **$510**

AUA at December 31, Year 4 $40 - $70 + $20 + $80 =   **$70**

BDE for Year 5   (8%)($1,100) =   **$88**

Carrying value of A/R at December 31, Year 5 $680-$88=   **$592**

AUA at December 31, Year 5 $70- $100 + $30 + $88 =   **$88**

Answers for Aging Method:

BDE for Year 3   **$60**
$60 is the necessary 'plug' in AUA to end up at $60, the estimated uncollectible A/R amount.

Carrying Value of A/R at December 31, Year 3 $550 AR - $60 AUA = **$490***
*The estimated collectible A/R.

AUA at December 31, Year 3 $40 - $50 + $10 + $60* = **$60**
*Plugged

BDE for Year 4 **$50**
$50 is the necessary 'plug' in AUA to end up at $60, the estimated uncollectible A/R amount.

Carrying Value of A/R at December 31, Year 4 $580 AR - $60 AUA = **$520***
*The estimated collectible amount of A/R.

AUA at December 31, Year 4 $60 - $70 + $20 + $50* = **$60**
*Plugged

BDE for Year 5 **$100**
$100 is the necessary 'plug' in AUA to end up at $90*. $90 equals the estimated uncollectible A/R amount.

Carrying Value of A/R at December 31, Year 5 $680 A/R - $90 AUA = **$590***
*The estimated collectible amount of A/R.

AUA at December 31, Year 5 $60 - $100 + $30 + $100* = **$90**
*Plugged

Inventories
Topic 7
This topic is related to Chapter 9 in the SSD text.

Inventories are assets owned be sold in the ordinary course of business. 'Ordinary course of business' refers to the primary business activities of a particular firm. Firms may produce a wide range of goods and services for their customers and clients. In this topic we will discuss accounting problems encountered by firms from the sale of goods (products) to customers. Inventories can be carried from period to period and present accounting problems not encountered when the firm's primary outputs is service-based. When sold, inventory costs become the expense, Cost of Goods Sold.

Inventories are important assets to the firm owning them. We will focus on the accounting methods associated with inventories. Managers must be skillful in other areas related to inventories too. [For example, sensing how much inventory and what type of inventory to hold.] Firms have developed practices that allow buyers and sellers to communicate clearly in ways that allow both to know who the owner of the goods might be at all times.. When the goods are harmed during shipment, the buyers and sellers must have a means of determining who has responsibility for the loss.

INVENTORY OWNERSHIP
The transfer of title to goods is easy to establish if the buyer obtains the goods from the seller without a 'middleman' being involved. Whether the goods have been paid for yet is irrelevant whether there is a 'middleman' or not. An independent third party observing the transaction between the buyer and the seller would know who had title to the goods at a moment in time. Unless the parties agree specifically to terms for each transaction, when there is a 'middleman' [common carrier] the situation requires these shipping terms: **FOB shipping point** and **FOB destination.**

SHIPPING TERMS
With FOB shipping point, the inventory's title shifts from the seller to the buyer when the inventory is given to the common carrier. When the common carrier gets possession, the seller and the buyer have consummated their transaction. Thus, during the shipment period, the buyer has title to the goods and would include them in its financial statements as a purchase/payable/inventory even though the goods might not arrive at the buyer's place of business prior to the end of the buyer's fiscal year. Ownership is the important characteristic regarding the goods.

With FOB destination, the title converts to the buyer when the inventory is given over to the buyer by the common carrier. When the buyer obtains possession, the seller and the buyer have consummated their transaction. Thus, during the shipment period, the seller has title to the goods and would include them in its financial statements as inventory. Once again, ownership is the important characteristic regarding the goods.

If buyers or sellers book inventory transactions in the wrong accounting periods, their F/S will look better or 'worse' than if the accounting was done correctly. Problems with 'cutoffs' need to be examined carefully with a keen grasp of the concepts.

CONSIGNED GOODS

Consignments occur when the owner of goods and another party agree that the owner (consignor) will ship goods to the other party (consignee) but keep the ownership of the goods. This is a fairly common event in business. If a manufacturer (or wholesaler) wants a retailer to sell the manufacturer's goods *without having to bear the economic risks of ownership,* the parties might agree to a consignment arrangement. Mere shipment to the consignee does not shift ownership to the consignee. The consignor should record no sale unless the consignee is successful in selling the goods to a third party. Normally, if the consignee cannot sell the goods, the goods would be returned to the consignor. The consignee would discard unsold perishable goods if the consignor agreed.

The key issue in consignments is that all the goods owned may not be in the physical possession of the owner. Appearance and reality may differ.

INVENTORY VALUATION

Current ownership of inventory requires that it be shown as an asset in the entity's B/S. Previous ownership of inventory requires that cost of goods sold be reported in the I/S. The value we associate with inventory owned includes all of the costs necessary to make the asset ready for its intended use. A separate issue arises when we determine the basis for **inventory valuation**. These inventory costs become cost of goods sold [CGS] after the goods have been sold.

Examples of necessary costs to make the inventory ready for its intended use would include:

Invoice amount
Shipping costs [if paid by buyer (FOB shipping point)]
Insurance costs if paid by buyer
Assembly costs after delivery to the buyer
Purchase discounts available to the buyer are <u>deducted</u> from the invoice costs because they make the inventory 'cheaper' to buy and place in service.

By including these costs in the cost basis of inventory, the firm can most easily 'match' inventory costs against sales revenue when the inventory is sold. Matching of sales revenue and cost of goods sold (expense) illustrates the matching principle as discussed earlier. The excess of sales revenue over CGS is **gross margin** and represents a valuable measure of the firm's ability to price and sell goods in the retail market relative to costs of making inventory ready to sell. Gross margin [GM] is widely used.

INVENTORY SYSTEMS

Enterprises choose a 'system' for keeping inventory costs organized. One system is the **perpetual system** because it 'perpetually' keeps the Inventory account updated for purchases and sales of inventories. Purchases of inventories will increase the Inventory account with a debit. The corresponding credit would be to A/P if the purchase had been on account or a credit to Cash if paid for at the time of the transaction. Similarly, the sale of any inventory will cause the Inventory account to be decreased (credited) to reflect the decline in the amount of inventory on hand with the corresponding debit to CGS (expense).

With the **periodic system** the Inventory account is *not* kept perpetually correct as purchases and sales occur. The periodic system uses a temporary special account, Purchases, when goods are acquired. Purchases is a debit balance account and holds the value of all the entity's acquisitions of inventory for the period. When using the periodic system, no CGS is recognized when goods are sold. CGS in the periodic system requires that a physical count of inventory be taken at the end of the accounting period. The physical count of inventory combined with an inventory method enables the firm to derive its CGS for the period.

It is estimated that half of inventory thefts are attributable to employees.

In the periodic system, CGS is determined by summing Beginning Inventory and Purchases to obtain Cost of Goods Available for Sale. Ending inventory is deducted from the Cost of Goods Available to yield CGS. Intuitively, this tells us that the costs of inventory we started with plus the costs of goods acquired this period all become CGS *except for* what we still have on hand at the end of the year.

Beginning Inventory	$1,500
Purchases	25,000
Cost of Goods Available	$26,500
Less: Ending Inventory	3,000
CGS	$23,500

When analyzing inventory transactions, I usually do not mention Cost of Goods Available because it is only a subtotal.

Ending Inventory from one year must be the Beginning Inventory for the next year.

AN EXERCISE INVOLVING INVENTORY CUT-OFFS
The Jason Company [the firm] counted inventory on December 31, Year 1. Assume the firm uses the periodic system. The inventory amounted to $340,000 as determined by the

physical count. In reviewing the accounting records of the Jason Company, you have established the following:

a. Included in the physical count were goods on the firm's shipping dock waiting to be shipped to a customer. The sales terms were FOB shipping point. The goods were picked up by Federal Express late in the afternoon of December 31, Year 1. The goods had a cost of $20,000 and a retail value of $35,000. The firm had mailed the sales invoice to the customer on January 3, Year 2, and recorded the sale on account on the same day in the books for Year 2.

Required:
What adjustments to the firm's physical inventory count and the firm's accounting records seem appropriate? [The answer can be found below.]

b. The firm purchased $60,000 of goods from a supplier. The purchase terms were FOB shipping point. The purchase invoice arrived on January 3, Year 2, and the purchase was recorded in the books for Year 2 on that day. The goods were shipped on December 24, Year 1 and arrived two weeks later.

Required:
What adjustments to the firm's physical inventory count and the firm's accounting records seem appropriate? [The answer can be found below.]

c. The firm ordered some inventory from a supplier on December 22, Year 1. The goods cost $70,000 and the purchase terms were FOB destination. The goods were shipped on December 23, Year 1 and arrived one week later. The goods were inadvertently overlooked when taking the physical count on December 31 because they had been temporarily stored with the goods waiting for shipment out to customers. The invoice arrived on January 6, Year 2, and the purchase was recorded in the books on that day.

Required:
What adjustments to the firm's physical inventory count and the firm's accounting records seem appropriate? [The answer can be found below.]

Here are the answers to the three requirements above:

a. The physical inventory needs to be adjusted downward. The goods belonged to the buyer at the end of December 31 and should not be included in the Jason Company's ending inventory on December 31, Year 1. The sale should be recorded in Year 1 and not in Year 2 as is now the case. Thus, the physical count must be adjusted downward by $20,000 and an adjusting journal entry in the books for Year 1 debiting A/R and crediting Sales both for $35,000 must be recorded at the end of Year 1. [A/R and Sales in Year 2 have to be credited and debited, respectively, to remove these from the books for Year 2.]

b. The purchased goods should be *added* to the physical count. These goods belonged to Jason on December 24, Year 1 since they had been shipped to the Jason on that date. The accounting records of the firm also need to be adjusted since the purchase is now recorded in the books for Year 2 and it properly a purchase in Year 1. In the books for Year 1, debit Purchases and credit A/P for $60,000 each. [In the books for Year 2, debit A/P and credit Purchases both for $60,000.]

c. The goods should be *added* to the physical count. At the end of Year 1, these goods belonged to Jason and should be reflected in the firm's ending inventory. In the books for Year 1, Purchases should be debited and A/P should be credited both for $70,000. [In the books for Year 2, A/P should be debited and Purchases should be credited both for $70,000 to remove the transaction from the books for that year.]

PURCHASE DISCOUNTS

When a seller offers a Sales Discount, the buyer will think of it as a Purchase Discount. These two ideas are the 'mirror image' of the other. Typical purchase discount terms might be 2/10, net 30. The buy can deduct 2% of the invoice if paying on the 10th day otherwise the entire invoice amount is due on the 30th day. We calculated the approximate (simple) annual rate of return associated with such terms [36%]. The important point to note here is that Purchase Discounts are subtracted from Purchases to yield Net Purchases. Purchase Discounts is a normal credit balance account since it is contra to Purchases. Frequently and for simplicity, Net Purchases is called merely 'Purchases'. Note that CGS is *decreased* if Purchase Discounts are taken.

Beginning Inventory		$8,500
Purchases	$42,000	
Less: Purchase Discounts	-1,000	
Net Purchases		$41,000
Cost of Goods Available		$49,500
Less: Ending Inventory		4,000
CGS		$45,500

What is the effect on Net Income caused by Purchase Discounts? [Net Income is made larger because CGS was made smaller.]

Similarly, there are other accounts that are 'contra' to Purchases for **Purchase Returns** and **Purchase Allowances**. Purchase Returns is credited when goods are returned to the supplier for various reasons including: buyer discovers the items are defective or that the buyer discovers it has an oversupply. Purchase Allowances is credited when price reductions are granted by the seller as an alternative to having the goods be returned by the buyer. The seller might grant price concessions to avoid return of the goods by the buyer because of some tolerable but undesirable defect. An example might be a small dent on the side of a refrigerator that had not been noted previously and for which the seller accepts responsibility. Both Purchase Returns and Purchases Allowances are credit balance accounts and are deducted from Purchases to obtain Net Purchases.

AN EXAMPLE INVOLVING PURCHASE DISCOUNTS, PURCHASE RETURNS AND ALLOWANCES

Accounting for Purchase Discounts and Purchase Returns & Allowances:

The June Company [the firm] buys merchandise for resale from a variety of suppliers that offer different discount terms. The June Company uses the periodic inventory system and debits Purchases when acquiring merchandise.

The following are selected transactions from the firm's accounting records for Year 1. Prepare journal entries for (a) the purchase, (b) the payment within the discount period [(c) or alternatively, the journal entry if the payment occurred on the due date].

The June Company purchased merchandise with an invoice amount of $4,000. The goods were purchased FOB shipping point and the sales terms offered were 2/10, net 30. The goods were shipped on May 1 and arrived 5 days later. 40% of these goods were returned immediately because they were the wrong colors. Show the three requested journal entries and the journal entry to record the return of the goods prior to making the payment.

The answer is shown below in italics.

(a) Debit Purchases $4,000 and credit A/P for the same amount. Debit A/P and credit Purchase Returns both for $1,600. (b) Debit A/P for $2,400. Credit Cash for $2,352 and Purchase Discounts for $48. (c) Debit A/P and credit Cash, both for $2,400.

The June Company made another purchase where the invoice amount was $9,000 and the sales terms offered were 3/10, net 30. The goods were purchased FOB destination and they arrived on August 1. The sizes of some of the goods were not exactly what had been ordered but the seller offered to deduct $1,000 from the invoice amount if June would agree to keep them. The June Company accepted the goods at the lower price before any payment was made to the seller. Show the three requested journal entries and the entry to record the purchase allowance prior to any payment being made.

The answer is shown below in italics.

(a) Debit Purchases and credit A/P both for $9,000. Debit A/P and credit Purchase Allowances both for $1,000. (b) Debit A/P $8,000. Credit Cash for $7,760 and Purchase Discounts for $240. (c) Debit A/P and credit Cash both for $8,000.

EFFECTS OF INVENTORY ERRORS

Whenever understatements or overstatements occur in connection with inventories, the result often affects B/S and I/S of the entity. CGS and GM can be important components in a firm's I/S. Recall, the basic format of the I/S through GM:

Sales Revenue		$240,000
Beginning Inventory	$20,000	
Purchases (or Net Purchases)	90,000	
Less: Ending Inventory	-25,000	
CGS		85,000
GM		$155,000

Over- or understatements in any of these components will produce errors in FS. These over- or understatements will result from any failure to account properly for inventory transactions. Sometimes, failures result from recording a transaction in the wrong accounting period [bad 'cut-offs']. Other times, the failures may stem from recording the transactions incorrectly or from errors made while taking the physical inventory.

If Sales Revenue is understated, GM would obviously be understated. If CGS is understated, GM is overstated. The more difficult relationships occur within the CGS components. If Beginning Inventory (or Purchases) is overstated, CGS would be overstated and GM would be understated. If Ending Inventory would be overstated, CGS would be understated and GM would be overstated.

A helpful way to organize these important relationships for easier use follows. Let the I/S elements that *increase* income be designated by 'plus' signs and elements that serve to *decrease* income be designated by 'minus' signs in this 'I/S'.

Sales Revenue	+
Beginning Inventory	−
Purchases (or Net Purchases)	−
Less: Ending Inventory	+
CGS	−
GM	+

When there is a logical cause-and-effect relationship between the elements _and_ the signs are the same, leave the 'prefixes' the same. If the signs are different, change the prefixes.

Examples: Sales are understated, what is the effect on GM? [GM is understated.]
Beginning Inventory is understated, what is the effect on CGS? [CGS is understated.]
Purchases are understated, what is the effect on GM? [GM is overstated.]

Inventory errors may have implications for I/S that may be shown comparatively. For example, Purchases that should be recorded in Year 1 might be unintentionally recorded in Year 2. While this mistake will reverse itself out over time, it will cause the I/S for Years 1 and 2 to be incorrect. Purchases in Year 1 will be understated and Purchases in Year 2 will be overstated. GM in Year 1 will be overstated and GM in Year 2 will be understated.

Another inventory related error with implications for comparative I/S results from under- or overstatement of ending inventory in the Year 1 I/S. This would cause CGS for Year 1 to be incorrectly stated. The under- or overstatement of ending inventory at the end of Year 1, would have the _same_ impact on Beginning Inventory at the start of Year 2. Overstated Ending Inventory at the end of Year 1 would cause overstated Beginning Inventory in the I/S for Year 2. The effects resulting from this error would be the same as we have seen previously.

Consider this 'stylized' I/S for two years comparatively.

Sales Revenue	+	+
Beginning Inventory	−	−
Purchases (or Net Purchases)	−	−
Less: Ending Inventory	+	+
CGS	−	−
GM	+	+

When Ending Inventory in Year 1 is overstated, the Beginning Inventory for Year 2 is also overstated. _Resist the temptation to change the prefixes because the signs are different._

Also, resist the temptation to interpret under- and overstatements between two components when there is no logical relationship between them. For example, if Sales in Year 1 are overstated, what is the affect on Purchases for Year 1? [There is no effect because there is no logical relationship.]

Assume Ending Inventory at the end of Year 1 is overstated. What is the effect on Year 1 net income? [Year 1 net income is overstated.] What is the effect on Year 2 net income? [Year 2 net income is understated.] What is the effect on OE at the end of Year 2? [OE at the end of Year 2 is correctly stated. The net incomes for Years 1 and 2 were over- and understated, respectively. Thus, OE at the end of Year 2 is correctly stated. ☺]

INVENTORY METHODS

Firms must choose an inventory method as well as an inventory system. While other inventory methods exist, we will confine ourselves to the First-in, First-out [FIFO] and Last-in, First-out methods [LIFO] methods in this course. These method names are very descriptive of the flow of *costs*. [Do not be distracted by the physical flow of *goods*.]

FIFO assigns costs to the units sold from the *oldest* costs of units on hand. The oldest costs come from the earliest purchase of goods on hand at the time of the sale. FIFO periodic and FIFO perpetual always will yield the same results for Ending Inventory. **When using the periodic system, it is assumed that all the purchases occur before the first sale.** This assumption makes the periodic system easier to apply in practice.

LIFO assigns costs to the units sold from the newest costs of units on hand. These newest costs come from the most recent purchase of goods that are on hand at the time of the sale. LIFO periodic and LIFO perpetual usually will yield different results for Ending Inventory. Recall, that when using the periodic system, it is assumed that all the purchases occur before the first sale.

An Example of Inventory Methods:

The basic data are presented below for the three years covered by the example: Year 1, Year 2 and Year 3. At the start of Year 1, the firm had 40 units on hand with a cost basis of $8 per unit. Remember that Ending Inventory from one year becomes Beginning Inventory of the subsequent year. All purchase costs and sales prices are stated on a per unit basis.

	Year 1	Year 2	Year 3
Purchases	Jan. 200@ $10	Feb. 250@$15	Jan. 200@$20
	Feb. 100@$12	May 160@$17	Aug. 100@$22
	Jun. 200@$14	Jun. 140@$19	
Sales	Mar. 150@$30	Apr. 180@$35	Jul. 260@$45
	May 180@$30	Jul. 150@$40	Nov. 50@$50
	Dec. 100@$35	Nov. 200@$40	

Sales figures for Years 1-3 are $13,400, $20,300 and $14,200, respectively. Purchases for the same three years, respectively, are $6,000, $9,130 and $6,200.

1. Ending Inventory at December 31, Year 1, using perpetual LIFO is valued at $1,480. The oldest of these units are 10 units at $8 left from the beginning inventory and 100 units left from the June Year 1 purchase at $14 per unit. It is helpful to ensure that the number of physical units at the end of the year is correct. The firm started with 40 units as indicated in the first paragraph. Total units purchased in Year 1 are 500. Total units sold in Year 1 are 430. [40 + 500 – 430 = 110 ending inventory units.]

2. GM for Year 2 using periodic FIFO is $12,100. Ending Inventory at the end of Year 1 using periodic FIFO is $1,540 (110 units at $14 per unit). This becomes Beginning Inventory at the start of Year 2. Purchases for Year 2 are given as $9,130 above. Ending Inventory at the end of Year 2 is 130 units at $19 per unit for $2,470. CGS for Year 2 is $8,200 and, when deducted from Year 2 Sales of $20,300, yields GM for Year 2 of $12,100. It is helpful to ensure that the number of units on hand at the end of the second year is correct. The firm started Year 2 with 100 units and purchased a total of 550 units. Units sold in Year 2 total 530. Thus, there should be 130 units on hand at the end of Year 2.

GM in Year 2:
Sales		$20,300
Beginning Inventory	$1,540	
Purchases	9,130	
Ending Inventory	-2,470	
CGS		$8,200
GM		$12,100

3. CGS for Year 3 using periodic LIFO is $6,350. Beginning Inventory for Year 3 is $1,320. Purchases for Year 3 are $6,200. Ending Inventory at the end of Year 3 is $1,170. Thus, CGS for Year 3 is $6,350. It is helpful to ensure that the number of units on hand at the end of each year is the correct quantity. For Year 3, the beginning units were 130, units purchased were 300 and the units sold were 310. Thus, Year 3 ending quantity should be 120 units.

Beginning Inventory	$1,320	
Purchases	6,200	
Ending Inventory	-1,170	
CGS		$6,350

LIFO LIQUIDATIONS

When inventory quantities decrease and a firm is using LIFO, older inventory costs *per unit* are matched against revenues reflecting current sales prices. This development often results in GM that are higher than normal as a result of matching older [presumably lower] costs with current revenues. If units purchased had been equal to units sold, GM would have been consistent with the usual LIFO results. However, when units purchased are less than units sold, the distortions described above may result. This possible result impairs the ability of external FS users to interpret changes in the GM percentage from year to year.

Declines in inventory quantities might result from unusual business conditions [such as a strike by the common carrier handling the deliveries] or result from management's decision to cut purchases and inventory levels.

LIFO provides management with more opportunities to 'manipulate' the financial statement results than FIFO.

Specific identification is a third inventory method that can be used when firms have the ability to specifically identify individual inventory units. A car dealership can uniquely identify automobiles with vehicle identification numbers. Such companies will use the specific identification method to more accurately determine inventory cost flows. Specific identification is usually associated with inventory units that are individually expensive. Ending Inventory will consist of the costs associated with the inventory units that remain on hand at year-end. No assumptions about cost flows are needed.

ESTIMATING INVENTORIES

When producing financial statements on an interim basis and when there have been stable relationships between inventory costs and selling prices, firms may decide to estimate the period's ending inventory rather than taking a physical inventory [counting all of the inventory on hand]. The advantage stems from avoiding the loss of production time while taking the physical inventory. This is usually described as the **gross margin method**. This is probably more of an approach than a method and it is rarely acceptable for producing annual FS because of the uncertainty about the true inventory level.

Consider this example for a firm that has a normal GM percentage of 30% from prior years and a stable relationship between inventory costs and inventory selling prices. Sales Revenue, Beginning Inventory and Purchases are available from the accounting records of the firm. GM should be $90,000 if Sales Revenue for the period is $300,000.

Sales Revenue		$300,000
Beginning Inventory	$70,000	
Purchases (or Net Purchases)	180,000	
Less: Ending Inventory	?	
CGS		?
GM		$90,000

What would CGS be in this example? [$210,000]

What would Ending Inventory be in the above example? [$40,000]

Insurance companies usually accept results from GM method calculations as a basis for settlements after thefts or fires. Very few thieves will leave a detailed account of the goods they've stolen and ashes are very hard to count. ☺

Other Operating Items in the Expenditure Cycle

Topic 8
This topic ties to Chapter 10 in the SSD text.

In this topic we will consider a wide variety of FS implications associated with employees and their compensation other than salaries and wages as was developed much earlier. Income taxes also play an important role in the FS of taxable entities and we will need to consider those FS consequences.

Employee Compensation Issues
Employees create FS implications well beyond the basic amounts paid for salaries and wages. Management should anticipate these FS implications when making operating decisions. Users of FS need adequate knowledge to understand disclosed information and to be aware of important economic information *not* contained in the FS.

Payroll Taxes
Payroll taxes are imposed by various governments and become part of the firm's FS. While numerous payroll taxes may be imposed, we will chiefly consider the Federal Insurance Contributions Act [FICA] and usually called social security. The details of the variety of payroll taxes an entity may face are unnecessary given our purposes in this course. However, it is important to grasp the basic means by which payroll taxes can be levied.

Social security tax is levied on the employees and the employers equally until some base level income per employee has been reached. This base level changes each year and is approximately $85,000 at this writing. Above that base level, only the employer has to pay a social security tax on payroll. There is a smaller, but related, tax referred to as Medicare. This tax is also paid equally by employees and employers and does not have the same base level at which the employees 'drop out'.

I will use approximations of these tax rates and base levels in order to illustrate the operation of the payroll taxes in an enterprise. Assume the social security tax is 6% and the Medicare tax is 2%. Assume an employee earns $50,000 in a year. The employee's and employer's shares of the payroll taxes would be determined as follows:

Employer:

Salary Amount	Type of Tax	Tax Rate	Amount of Tax
$60,000	FICA	6%	$3,600
$60,000	Medicare	2%	$1,200

Employee:

Salary Amount	Type of Tax	Tax Rate	Amount of Tax
$60,000	FICA	6%	$3,600
$60,000	Medicare	2%	$1,200

Consider the employer's summary journal entry for a whole year related to this employee and payroll tax consequences:

Salary Expense	$60,000	
Payroll Tax Expense	$4,800	
Cash		$55,200
Payroll Tax Liability		$9,600

The Payroll Tax Liability is the sum of the employer's half and the employee's half of the FICA tax. If this illustration had been for a salary amount in excess of the annual statutory base amount, the employee's portion of the FICA tax would have been capped at 6% of the statutory base and the employer's portion would *not* have been capped.

Employees' income taxes are usually withheld by employers and paid periodically to the appropriate governmental units. The employees' income tax is not an expense to the employers. To the employers, the employees' income tax merely 'flows through' the employer's accounting system and the net effect is 'no effect'.

Compensated Absences
Employers occasionally compensate employees who are *absent* from work. Paid vacations would be a recognizable example among numerous others. The important accounting issue is when to recognize the expense from compensating an employee who is not present. Should the expense be recognized when the employee is not present and is paid or should the expense be recognized when the employee earned the right to be absent and be paid despite the absence? Consistent with the accrual basis under which the FS are prepared, the expense should be recognized when the benefit is earned if these four requirements are met.

a. Have the services been rendered by the employee?
b. Is the employee's right to be paid vested?
c. Is the benefit probably to be paid in the future?
d. Is the amount of the benefit estimable?

If a future compensated absence meets all four of these tests it should be expensed when earned and a corresponding liability recorded in the FS. If a future compensated absence does not meet these four requirements, it should be expensed when the payment is actually made.

When employees have earned material amounts of vacation time that can be carried over to future accounting periods, the resulting aggregate expense and liability to the employers can be material. FS users can take comfort in that GAAP rules place the expense in the period when the benefit was *earned*, not when the benefit was taken.

Bonuses
Employers sometimes create bonus plans as part of the total compensation package in the attempt to provide adequate incentives for employees. Bonus calculations can be based on a wide range of variables. Thus, Bonus Expense is estimated at the end of one accounting period and also recognized as a liability in the B/S. This is consistent with

accrual accounting concepts. Bonus Expense is usually shown as part of Salaries Expense.

Calculating a bonus is a relatively simple calculation. For an example, assume the bonus rate is a percentage of the firm's income above an indicated base level and that the bonus will be based on income after the bonus. In algebraic terms,

Bonus = [Bonus rate] [Total income – base level income – Bonus]

Since this is one equation with one unknown, the bonus can be obtained by solving the equation for the unknown.

Consider this numerical example. Top management of the Anderson Company hired a top-performing manager away from another firm offering a bonus based on income earned by the firm above a $15,000,000 base amount after bonus. [The bonus is 4% of the income above $15,000,000 and after bonus.] During the first full year of the bonus plan's operation, the Anderson Company's income before tax and before bonus was $20,000,000. The firm's tax rate is 30%. What was the manager's bonus based on this information?

The bonus is $192,308 and the calculations are shown below.

Bonus = (4%) [$20,000,000 - $15,000,000 - Bonus]
Bonus = (4%) [$5,000,000 – Bonus]
Bonus = $200,000 - .04Bonus
1.04 Bonus = $200,000
Bonus = $192,308

Consider another example. Top management of Wayne Company hired a top-performing manager away from a competitor and offered the new manager a bonus based on income earned by the firm above a $15,000,000 base amount after bonus and after taxes. [The bonus is 4% of the income above $15,000,000 after tax and after bonus.] During the first full year of the bonus plan's operation, the firm's income before tax and before bonus was $20,000,000. The firm's tax rate is 20%. What was the manager's bonus based on this information?

Since the bonus is tax deductible, we have two equations and two unknowns. Tax influences the bonus and the bonus influences the tax.

Taxes = (30%) [$20,000,000 – Bonus]
Bonus = (4%) [$20,000,000 - $15,000,000 – Tax – Bonus]

If we substitute the expression for Tax into the bonus equation, we have one equation with one unknown and we can solve in the normal way. What was the manager's bonus based on this information?

89

The bonus is $38,760.

Bonus = (4%) [$20,000,000 - $15,000,000 – Bonus – (20%) ($20,000,000 – Bonus)]
Bonus = (4%) [$5,000,000 – Bonus -$4,000,000 + .2Bonus]
Bonus = (4%) [$1,000,000 -.8Bonus]
Bonus = $40,000 -.032Bonus
1.032Bonus= $40,000
Bonus=$38,760

Stock Options

Some firms create stock option plans to create incentives for executives to enhance share values. The stock options permit executives to acquire shares at a stated price [exercise price] until the options expire. If the price of the firm's shares rises above the exercise price when the options can be exercised, the executive can be richly rewarded for his/her services. Economic benefits to executives as a result of stock option plans can vastly outweigh their salaries. Typically, executives must remain with the firm through the end of a stated 'service period' or lose the option plan. This creates what are sometimes called 'golden handcuffs' since there could be a significant loss of opportunity if the executive leaves 'early'.

Stock option plans have been the source of much controversy within the accounting community for several years. The current state of accounting rules in this area recognizes two acceptable [GAAP] methods for determining whether there is any Compensation Expense as well as the amount of that Compensation Expense. The impact on the FS can be considerable. Managements of firms, as well as users of FS, should be aware of the methods and their implications.

The **intrinsic value method** is the 'older' of the two methods and is widely used. The Compensation Expense to be recognized over the service period equals the product of the number of shares in the option plan times the *excess* of the shares' fair market value *over* the exercise price. If the fair market value of the shares is higher than the exercise price, that difference times the number of shares under option will represent the total Compensation Expense recognized over the required service period. Usually this total expense is amortized using the straight-line method over that period. Note that if the fair market value of the shares is *less* than the exercise price when the option plan is created there will be no Compensation Expense whatsoever in the income statement as a result of the option plan *even if* the fair value later rises materially above the exercise price. The potential to structure the option plan and avoid recognizing any Compensation Expense is a significant reason for the popularity of this method. There is a required footnote disclosure indicating what the Compensation Expense *would have been* if the firm had selected the fair value method.

The **fair value method** is the 'newer' of the two methods and is the less widely used despite being recommended by FASB. The total Compensation Expense to be recognized over the required service period equals the *fair market value* of the options when granted. Usually this total expense is amortized using the straight-line method over the service period. Virtually all stock options have fair market values when granted to the executive and, thus, this method would result in some Compensation Expense being recognized regardless of the relationship of the exercise price and the fair market value. If the stock options are not publicly traded, the fair market value of the options can be approximated using the Black-Scholes options pricing model.

There is another type of stock option plan that does not involve any attempt to compensate employees for their services. These are called non-compensatory stock option plans and are characterized by a wide range of employees eligible for participation. Virtually all employees are eligible to buy shares at a small discount to the current fair market value without the employer recognizing Compensation Expense.

Pensions

A pension plan is an attempt to reward employees for services previously rendered by permitting them to enjoy a level of income after their careers have ended. Pensions plans come in two broad categories called defined-benefit pension plans and defined-contribution pension plans.

The accounting problem stemming from **defined benefit pension plans** is considerable as a result of having made promises to retirees regarding their pension benefits and the need to match the estimated present values of those future benefits against revenues on an annual basis. Actuaries estimate the present values of these future benefits. The Pension Expense is basically the net of three elements: (a) The present value of future retirement benefits earned in the current year but not expected to be paid until the employees have retired. This is the incremental present value of future benefits associated with the current year of service. (b) Interest earned on the estimated present value of the future benefits as a result of the passage of one more year. The present value of a liability to pay value in the future grows larger as the payment date draws nearer. We should think of this as interest and it is driven by the passage of time. (c) Pension plan returns *reduce* the current Pension Expense because income generated by the pension plan assets represents value that will *not* have to be paid by the employer. If pension plan managers can generate larger pension plan returns, the same levels of benefits in the future can be funded with *smaller* amounts of contributions.

Defined contribution pension plans pose no special accounting problem because the employer has made a 'promise' to contribute funds to the employee's pension plan and when that amount is funded on a current basis the employer's obligation is satisfied. There are no actuarial assumptions required here. '401k' pension plans are examples of these and they have been popular for some time.

Income Taxes in the Income Statement
Unlike the manner in which income statement tax consequences have been reflected to this point, Income Tax Expense in the I/S is usually comprised of two components: **Current Tax Expense** and **Deferred Tax Expense**. The Current Tax Expense reflects the taxes that are due on income that is reporting as taxable income in the tax return(s) of the entity. The Deferred Tax Expense only reflects the results of *temporary* differences between financial and tax accounting.

Accounting for Income Taxes
Financial accounting (FA) rules and tax accounting (TA) rules differ widely reflecting their different objectives. FA rules require standardized information in published FS reflecting some economic developments measured and reported according to GAAP. FA often uses estimates to derive values in the FS. Tax accounting rules have been adopted as a means by which governments generate adequate resources to pay for the goods and services that citizens have agreed government should provide. The goals of FA and TA differ widely. Differences between FA and TA rules can gathered into permanent and temporary differences reflecting whether these differences will not or will reverse in the future.

Permanent differences between TA and FA do not reverse and create no future tax consequences. Thus, permanent differences create no Deferred Tax Assets or Deferred Tax Liabilities in the balance sheet. We will explore the effects of permanent differences later in this topic.

Temporary differences between TA and FA will reverse and FS must reflect the expected *future* tax consequences of that reversal. These future tax consequences are Deferred Tax Liabilities or Deferred Tax Assets depending upon whether TA income or FA income will be larger in the reversal period(s). If the reversal of the temporary difference will cause TA income to be larger, *a* **Deferred Tax Liability** *(DTL) must be set up in the accounting records <u>at the time this temporary difference</u> <u>originates</u>*. Intuitively, the DTL will equal the expected future *incremental* tax to be paid when the temporary difference reverses [making TA income larger than FA income in that future year]. The DTL will be recognized as an amount equal to the future incremental difference between FA and TA income multiplied by the tax rate expected for the future reversal year(s). In the *originating* year, when initially recognizing a DTL, let a journal entry show you an important relationship:

       ??? $XXX
                DTL $XXX

When we are booking the DTL at an amount equal to the future differences in incomes times the future tax rate, we debit **Deferred Tax Expense**. [This is the missing account title in the above journal entry.]

Carefully consider the impact of this journal entry on this equation, our 'old friend'.

$$\text{Assets} = \text{Liabilities} + \text{OE}$$

[Liabilities would increase and OE would decrease. ☺]

If the reversal of a temporary difference in a future year would result in TA income being less than FA income, a **Deferred Tax Asset** [DTA] would be needed. The amount of the DTA would equal the amount of *future* difference between TA and FA incomes multiplied by the expected future tax rate. In the *originating* year, when initially recognizing a DTA, let a journal entry show you the important relationship:

```
DTA                              $XXX
       ???                              $XXX
```

When we are booking the DTA at an amount equal to the future differences in incomes ((FA and TA) times the future tax rate, what would we credit? The answer is that we would credit **Deferred Tax Expense** [DTE]. A credit entry to an expense is not intuitive. The correct name given to this account when it has a credit balance is Deferred Tax Benefit. However titled, the important result is that the credit to the expense account has the same effect on income as a revenue would have. I prefer to call it a DTE even though it has a credit balance instead of having to remember there is another name for the account when its balance is a credit.

What would be the impact of the journal entry above on the familiar equation below?

$$\text{Assets} = \text{Liabilities} + \text{OE}$$

[Assets would increase and OE would increase. ☺]

Deferred Taxes in Later Years
The introduction above explains what happens in the *originating* years when there are temporary differences. In later years, the important issue is to think 'cumulatively' and then to adjust the balance in the DTL (or DTA) to equal the ***future*** tax consequences resulting from the reversal of the cumulative temporary differences to date. This will be illustrated in the comprehensive example that follows shortly.

An Important Relationship
The effects in the *reversal* years are opposite to the differences in the *originating* years. Carefully follow these developments. In the originating year of a temporary difference, if FA income were larger than TA income, then we would expect the *reverse* to be true when the temporary difference reverses in some future year(s). [In the reversal year, TA income would exceed FA income and there would be an 'extra' amount of tax due on the difference.] Thus, it may be intuitive that in the *originating* year we would want to show an expense equaling the liability for the expected tax to be paid in the *future* when the

temporary difference reverses. The names we give this expense and liability, respectively, are DTE and DTL.

In all of the examples I will show you, I make two important simplifying assumptions. One, I assume that each year's tax rate is the same tax rate we expect to be in effect when the temporary difference reverses. The real world is not that simple and the differences between the current tax rates and the expected future tax rates would cause the concepts to become blurred in the calculations. The tax rates in the examples I will show you do change from year to year reflecting real world characteristics. Two, I assume that all DTA will result in future tax savings and, thus, avoid cluttering the presentation with Valuation Allowances for the DTA accounts that often are required in conjunction with DTA. These Valuation Allowances are contra asset accounts.

Current Tax Expense
Current Tax Expense [CTE] is determined by multiplying taxable income by the tax rate for the current year. Taxable income is the difference between taxable revenues and taxable expenses for a period. If taxable income is positive, then the entity will owe taxes for that year. For simplicity, ignore all of the means of paying taxes prior to filing a tax return. The journal entry to record the taxes payable in the accounting records of the entity involves debiting CTE and crediting Taxes Payable. [If the taxable income would be negative and ignoring the rules for carrybacks of net operating losses for tax purposes, imagine the journal entry would involve a debit to Tax Refund and a credit to CTE.]

Consider this example in which all of the differences between TA and FA are temporary.

Accounting for Current and Deferred Taxes:
The Jones Company was founded at the beginning of Year 1. The tax rates vary for Year 1 to Year 5, inclusive. The rates are shown along with the relevant data for each year.

The following information regarding FA and TA are shown below for each of the relevant years.

	Year 1	Year 2	Year 3	Year 4	Year 5
FA					
Revenues	$900	$660	$800	$500	$750
Expenses	540	440	500	600	610
TA					
Revenues	660	710	600	650	800
Expenses	420	410	320	810	540
Tax Rates	15%	20%	25%	15%	20%

At the end of each year, that year's tax rate is projected for all of the future years. That is, at the end of Year 1, the firm believes the tax rate for all future years will be 15%.

Compute taxes payable for each year. Use an amount equal to tax payable as the CTE for each condensed income statement for Year 1 to Year 5, inclusive. Calculate the amount that needs to be shown as the DTE in each year's I/S. Importantly, the DTL account needs to be updated at the end of each year to reflect the estimated future taxes that will need to be paid based upon future reversing differences. When the tax rates change there is no attempt to change the accounting that had been done in previous years.

Let us determine the values for these items:

Year 1 CTE (credit): $36 [This $36 is a debit since it is not presented parenthetically.]
[Taxable income] x [Current tax rate] = CTE
[$660 - $420] x [15%]

Year 1 DTE (credit): $18
In the current year FA income exceeds TA income by $120. In the future this temporary difference will reverse causing TA income to be larger. The tax rate expected in the future is 15% (same as the current tax rates and as explained above to simplify these examples). The $120 'extra' taxable income in the future times the future tax rate produces the need for a DTL balance of $18. The journal entry to record this is:

                DTE $18
                    DTL $18

Year 1 Net Income (Net Loss)
FA revenue less FA expense yields FA income before taxes: $360 [$900 - $540]
Then, subtracting CTE and DTE we can determine net income:
FA income before tax $360
Less: CTE $36
Less: DTE   18   -$54
Net Income $306

The ending balance in the DTL account at the end of Year 1 is $18.

Year 2 CTE (credit): $60
[Taxable revenues less taxable expenses] x [Current tax rate] = CTE
[$710 - $410] x [20%] = $60

Year 2 DTE (credit): ($8)
In the first two years *cumulatively*, FA income exceeds TA income by $40. [FA income exceeded TA by $120 in the first year and in the second year TA income exceeded FA by $80. Thus, cumulatively, FA exceeded TA accounting by $40 for the first two years combined.] In the future this temporary difference will reverse causing TA income to be larger than FA income by $40. The tax rate expected in the future is now 20% (same as the Year 2 current tax rate and as explained above to simplify these examples). The $40 'extra' taxable income in the future times the future tax rate produces the need for a DTL balance of $8. The journal entry to record this is:

```
    DTL             $10
        DTE                 $10
```

Year 2 Net Income (Net Loss)
FA revenue less FA expense yields FA income before taxes: $220 [$660 - $440]
Then, subtracting CTE and DTE we can determine net income:

FA income before tax		$220
Less: CTE	$60	
Less: DTE	(10)	-$50
Net Income		$170

The ending balance in the DTL account at the end of Year 2 is $8.

Year 3 CTE (credit): $70
[Taxable revenues less taxable expenses] x [Current tax rate] = CTE
[$600 - $320] x [25%] = $70

Year 3 DTE (credit): $7
In the first three years *cumulatively*, FA income exceeds TA income by $60. [FA income exceeded TA by $120 in the first year, in the second year TA income exceeded FA by $80, and in the third year FA income exceeds TA income by $20. Thus, cumulatively, FA exceeded TA accounting by $60 for the first three years combined.] In the future this temporary difference will reverse causing TA income to be larger than FA income by $60. The tax rate expected in the future is now 25% (same as the Year 3 current tax rate and as explained above to simplify these examples). The $60 'extra' taxable income in the future times the future tax rate produces the need for a DTL balance of $15. The journal entry to record this is:

```
    DTE             $7
        DTL                 $7
```

Year 3 Net Income (Net Loss)

FA revenue less FA expense yields FA income before taxes: $300 [$800 - $500]
Then, subtracting CTE and DTE we can determine net income:

FA income before tax		$300
Less: CTE	$70	
Less: DTE	7	-$77
Net Income		$223

Year 4 CTE (credit): ($24)

[Taxable revenues less taxable expenses] x [Current tax rate] = CTE
$650 - $810 = ($160) This is a tax loss. We will assume this loss will produce a refund using the current year's tax rate.
($160) x 15% = $24 refund. The journal entry would be debit Tax Refund and credit CTE both for $24.

Year 4 DTE (credit): $3

In the first four years *cumulatively,* FA income exceeds TA income by $120. [FA income exceeded TA by $120 in the first year, in the second year TA income exceeded FA by $80, in the third year FA income exceeded TA income by $20, and in the fourth year FA exceeded TA income by $60. Thus, cumulatively, FA exceeded TA accounting by $120 for the first four years taken as a whole.] In the future this temporary difference will reverse causing TA income to be larger than FA income by $120. The tax rate expected in the future is now 15% (same as the Year 4 current tax rate and as explained above to simplify these examples). The $120 'extra' taxable income in the future times the future tax rate produces the need for a DTL balance of $18. The journal entry to record this is:

DTE		$3	
	DTL		$3

Year 4 Net Income (Net Loss)
FA revenue less FA expense yields FA income before taxes: ($100) [$500 - $600]
Then, considering CTE and DTE we can determine net loss:

FA income before tax		($100)
Less: CTE	($24)	
Plus: DTE	3	(21)
Net Loss		($79)

Year 5 CTE (credit): $52
[Taxable revenues less taxable expenses] x [Current tax rate] = CTE
[$800 - $540] x [20%] = $52

Year 5 DTE (credit): ($18)
In the first five years *cumulatively,* FA income and TA income are equal. [FA income exceeded TA by $120 in the first year, in the second year TA income exceeded FA by $80, in the third year FA income exceeded TA income by $20, in the fourth year FA exceeded TA income by $60 and in the fifth year TA income exceeds FA income by $120. Thus, cumulatively, FA and TA accounting are equal for the first five years together.] This means that all temporary differences arising through the end of Year 5 have now reversed. There is no longer any need to have a DTL. The journal entry to record this is:

DTL		$18	
	DTE		$18

Year 5 Net Income (Net Loss)
FA revenue less FA expense yields FA income before taxes: $140 [$750 - $610]
Then, considering CTE and DTE we can determine net loss:

FA income before tax		$140
Less: CTE	$52	
Less: DTE	(18)	-34
Net Loss		$106

The DTL account plays a very important role because annually we have to change the balance in that account to equal the *future* tax consequences of *temporary* differences when they reverse. The journal entries made to change the balance in the DTL account annually provide the basis for determining DTE. These annual journal entries are very important to our understanding of the relationship between DTE and DTL.

Permanent Differences
Permanent differences do not cause any deferred tax consequences. Permanent differences do influence CTE because they either are or are not included in taxable

income. Recall, that CTE is derived from taxable income and the current year's tax rate. If a permanent difference is not a part of taxable income, then it cannot be part of CTE. If a permanent difference is part of taxable income, then it must be part of CTE.

Common Temporary Differences Between FA and TA
Depreciation differences are temporary. Depreciation for FA is commonly done using methods selected to provide the best matching of revenues and expenses in the income statement. Depreciation methods for use in the tax return are usually much more accelerated than those used in the income statement. Thus, in the early years of an asset's life, tax depreciation expense exceeds financial depreciation on the same asset. Later, in the asset's life these early differences reverse because the aggregate depreciation on an asset over its lifetime is generally the same for both financial and for tax purposes.

Bad Debts Expense [BDE] for FA is done using the allowance methods as explained earlier in this course. BDE for TA is done using the direct write-off method (unacceptable for FA). The differences between these methods for TA and FA are temporary.

Warranty Expense for FA is determined using management's estimates of the future warranty costs resulting from sales revenues in the current period. Warranty Expense for the tax return is based on amounts actually incurred based upon honoring warranty commitments for previous and current sales. It is as though the IRS is unwilling to allow a deduction based on estimated future warranty costs. These warranty expenses for FA and TA are temporary differences.

Rent Revenue for FA is recognized when it has been earned. Rent Revenue for TA purposes is considered taxable when it has been received. The resulting differences between TA and FA are temporary.

Interest Revenue on municipal bonds is not generally taxable income to the recipient. This interest revenue does appear in the income statement. The differences between the TA and FA treatments of municipal bond interest revenue are permanent.

Life insurance premiums made on life insurance policies where the firm is the beneficiary and the policyholder are not tax deductible. These premiums do appear as expenses in the (FA) income statement but are not allowed as deductions in the tax return. These policies are commonly referred to a 'key-person' policies. These differences between TA and FA treatments are permanent.

Life insurance proceeds from the death of a key person belong to the firm. The life insurance proceeds are not taxable to the firm. These proceeds do appear as revenues in the (FA) I/S but are not taxable in the tax return. These differences between TA and FA treatments are permanent.

Repairs and Maintenance
When operating assets have been owned for a period of time and resources are expended on them, it is important that the amounts spent be correctly treated in the FS as expenses or capitalized as additions to the asset.

If the expenditures are spent to make the asset like it was or more like it was when the asset was acquired, the expenditures should be expensed. Conceptually, the asset was 'wearing down' imperceptibly over time but no expense had been recorded for the decline.

If the expenditures have been incurred to make the asset more valuable in an economic sense, the expenditures should be capitalized (added to the cost of the asset). Capitalization of the expenditure will increase the carrying value of the asset and lead to more Depreciation Expense in the future periods of service. This treatment is consistent with accrual accounting and the matching principle.

In some cases, expenditures will be treated partly as an expense and partly as an addition to the asset. If the expenditure partly served to restore the asset to its original condition and partly served as an increase in the economic value of the asset, then management must exercise judgment regarding the amount to expense and the amount to capitalize.

Research and Development Activities
Under GAAP, expenditures classified as research and development activities must be expensed immediately rather than relying on management's judgment in assessing future benefits from such projects. Successful research and development outlays [R&D] are expensed under GAAP rules producing FS that may be unduly conservatively biased. Unsuccessful R&D outlays would have been expensed anyway assuming management was able to evaluate the success or failure of R&D project without bias. This accounting treatment might produce operating results that are excessively conservative. This is the price paid for taking away from management the ability to classify R&D projects are successful or unsuccessful. The concern inherent in the accounting standard adopted in the 1970's by FASB results from a wish to prevent manipulation of operating results by management through their ability to otherwise classify projects as successful or not in order to achieve a desired 'bottom line' for a period.

Users of FS should be aware that when R&D projects have been successful, the FS do not present the appropriate economic results.

R&D expenditures are activities undertaken that are sufficiently removed from the entity's current recurring commercial operations. Projects that are sufficiently related to the entity's recurring commercial activities are not classified as R&D and may be expensed or capitalized depending upon management's assessment about the future economic benefits that might result from the project.

This is an area requiring considerable judgment in establishing what is and what is not R&D. For those activities not classified as R&D, there is further judgment required to assess the future economic benefits resulting from the project, if any

Contingencies

Contingencies are situations where the outcome depends upon a future event. The outcome of an unsettled lawsuit is a contingency regardless of whether the firm is the plaintiff or the defendant.

Contingent gains are rarely disclosed in the footnotes and even more rarely accrued in the FS. The conservatism in GAAP, creates an environment where FS are biased against presenting operating results which might be overstated. If disclosing a contingent gains, care must be taken to avoid overstating the likelihood the contingent gain will materialize.

Conservatism makes it more likely that contingent losses will be disclosed or accrued depending upon circumstances. There are three relatively simple rules governing whether to disclose or accrue contingent losses. But, first, some terminology is appropriate to make the three rules easy to understand.

First, contingent losses must be classified according to whether or not the amount of the loss can be reliably estimated. Second, the likelihood of the loss actually materializing must be classified as 'probable', 'reasonably possible' or 'remote'.

The three simple rules for reporting contingent liabilities in the FS can be understood easily in the context of the matrix above.

1. All contingent losses that are at least 'reasonably possible' must be disclosed in the footnotes of the FS. [The top two horizontal rows must be disclosed in the footnotes to the FS.]

2. Contingent losses that are 'estimable' and 'probable' must be accrued and disclosed. [In the upper left cell, write the word 'Accrue' in addition to noting that it must be disclosed.]

3. Contingent losses that are 'remote' may be ignored or disclosed at the option of the firm's management. [The lowest horizontal row can be disclosed or ignored at the option of management.]

FS users should be on notice that the footnotes may contain 'juicy' information in relation to many issues including contingent liabilities. The more important it is that the user understand the entity's financial situation, the more important it will be that the user read the footnotes with special care. Users should remember that contingent gains will rarely be disclosed in the footnotes.

Operating Assets

Topic 9
This topic ties to Chapter 11 in the SSD text.

Operating assets are used in the operating activities conducted by the entity and have lives involving multiple accounting periods. Operating assets involve material amounts of the entity's invested resources and play a material role in the FS. Any manager of an entity or serious user of FS must appreciate the role of accounting methods and other practices involving operating assets.

We will examine operating assets from acquisition to disposition. During this period, we will see how expenditures on operating assets might be expensed or capitalized depending upon the facts. These assets must be reviewed periodically for impairments.

Operating assets are often referred to as Property, Plant and Equipment [PPE]. PPE covers buildings, equipment and land. PPE does not include intangible assets.

PPE is normally recorded as the sum of all of costs incurred to make the assets ready for their intended uses. This explanation is virtually identical to the one we used for inventory in topic 7.

Costs to be capitalized include invoice costs, delivery costs paid by the buyer (if any), installation costs, training costs, costs paid to others who assisted in the acquisition (fees paid by the buyer to real estate agents or to attorneys who helped in negotiating the transaction) and any other costs necessary to make the asset ready for its intended use. If a firm is given an opportunity to pay more for assets acquired in exchange for paying later, the difference is properly accounted for as Interest Expense. When included in the cost basis of PPE, costs are subject to depreciation in the future years accomplishing the matching principle's goal of comparing revenues and expenses properly in measuring of income properly according to GAAP.

Basket Purchases
Sometimes, several assets are acquired together requiring that price to be allocated to separate assets permitting subsequent depreciation expense to reflect the appropriate costs of using each asset. For example, if a firm bought a building and the building site (land), we would need to allocate some of the cost to the building and some to the land. The building cost has to be depreciated over the building's estimated useful life. Land cost is not depreciated under GAAP. Acquisition of several assets for one price is usually called a 'basket purchase'. The price paid for the assets is allocated to the components using their relative fair market values or appraisal values. The basket purchase method as described here is appropriate when the purchase price is _less_ than the sum of the fair values of the component assets. [If the single purchase price were _more_ than the sum of

the fair values of the component assets, the excess would probably be accounted for as Goodwill and is covered later in this topic.]

Consider an example:

The Leonte Company acquired three assets together for $300,000. These were the individual appraisal values for the components:

Component:	Appraisal Values
Asset A	$80,000
Asset B	180,000
Asset C	80,000
	$340,000

Determine the appropriate values at which the Leonte Company should record each of the four assets in its accounting records as a result of this acquisition.

Asset A $_____
Asset B $_____
Asset C $_____

Asset A: $70,588 = $80,000/ $340,000 x $300,000.

Asset B: $158,824 = $180,000/ $340,000 x $300,000.

Asset C: $70,588 = $80,000/ $340,000 x $300,000.

What are the totals of the four allocated costs to the four assets? _____

$300,000, the total price paid to purchase the set of assets.

Self-Constructed Assets

When firms construct assets for their own use or hire a construction company to build the asset for the firm, there are concerns about what the cost of the *completed* asset should be. Should it be the fair value that *would have been paid* if the asset had been purchased? Or should the asset be recorded as the necessary costs of construction?

GAAP rejects recording the asset at its fair market value in favor of the necessary costs to make the asset ready for its intended use. Necessary costs include amounts spent on materials and labor while building the asset. Overhead is considered a necessary cost even though it is indirect.

Interest Costs in the Construction Period

Interest costs incurred during the construction period, are treated like the overhead costs and capitalized. Interest costs during the construction period are treated as a necessary cost of making the asset ready for use and capitalized as part of PPE.

The construction period starts with planning the project and concludes when the project is ready for use. Except during the construction period, interest costs must be expensed directly.

Interest costs on money spent from construction loans obtained specifically for the current project can be capitalized during the construction period. Note carefully, you do not capitalize all of the interest from these construction loans, rather just the interest on the money spent out of the construction loan funds. [The construction loan amount could be larger than the amounts spent out of the loan or the construction loan might be for a period longer than the construction period.]

When funds from other sources are spent on a project, GAAP requires the opportunity costs of these funds be used to calculate interest that may be capitalized in the project. For example, assume some part of the funds used on the self-constructed asset came from internally generated operating cash flows. If not spent on the project, these internally generated operating cash flows could have been used to pay off loans *unrelated* to the construction loan (if any). This is one of the few times in financial accounting where GAAP requires that we consider the economic 'opportunity costs' of funds.

An important limit on interest to be capitalized is the interest costs *actually incurred* by the firm. At first glance the limit seems ridiculous, however, observe that if the total of loans *unrelated* to the project were small *and* the weighted-average interest rate derived from them was applied to large amounts of internally generated funds, the resulting value for interest to be capitalized might easily _exceed_ the firm's actual interest costs on the *unrelated* loans. In this situation, if the limit were not in place, the firm's income would be *increased* as a result of the project. This result would be way too 'liberal' for GAAP to tolerate and, thus, is forbidden. ☺

Consider a comprehensive example involving Capitalization of Interest During Construction Periods:

The Jess Construction Company decided to build a new headquarters office building at an estimated total cost of $5,000,000. To finance this project, the firm obtained a $3,000,000 construction loan at an interest rate of 8%. The remainder of the construction costs will be financed by the firm's considerable after-tax operating cash flow. The firm has loans *other than the construction loan* totaling $100,000 at a weighted-average interest rate of 6%.

The construction period began April 1, Year 1, and ended June 30, Year 3.

Spending on the project by year and source is shown below:

April 1, Year 1	$200,000	Construction loan
June 30, Year 1	500,000	Internal funds
September 30, Year 1	400,000	Construction loan
Monthly throughout Year 2	200,000	Construction loan
January 1, Year 3	1,500,000	Internal funds

How much interest can the Jess Construction Company capitalize in Year 1 from the **construction loan**?

Answer: $20,000 = [$200,000 x 8% x 9/12] + [$400,000 x 8% x 3/12]
Alternatively, the weighted average amount expended for the entire nine-month period is $333,333*. [*$200,000 x 9/9] + [$400,000 x 3/9]. Then, multiplying $333,333 by the construction loan's interest rate for the nine months of the construction period in Year 1, we obtain the same $20,000*. [*$333,333 x 8% x 9/12]

How much interest can the Jess Construction Company capitalize in Year 1 from **internally generated funds**?

$15,000* = [$500,000 x 6% x 6/12]
[*The amount capitalized from internally generated funds cannot exceed the *actual* interest on the loans unrelated to the project for the portion of Year 1 in the construction period [9/12]. $100,000 x 6% x 9/12 = $4,500.] Thus, the answer is $4,500.

How much interest can the Jess Construction Company capitalize in Year 2 from the **construction loan**?

$144,000 = $1,800,000* x 8% x 12/12
*$1,800,000 represents the weighted average amount from the construction loan invested in the project during Year 2. At the start of Year 2, the invested cost was $600,000 carried over from Year 1. During Year 2, another $2,400,000 was spent on the project evenly at the rate of $200,000 per month. [$600,000 for the whole year and half of the $2,400,000 sum to yield the $1,800,000. ☺]

How much interest can the Jess Construction Company capitalize in Year 2 from **internally generated funds**?

$30,000* = $500,000 x 6% x 12/12
[*The amount capitalized from internally generated funds cannot exceed the *actual* interest on the loans unrelated to the project for the portion of Year 1 in the construction period [12/12]. $100,000 x 6% x 12/12 = $6,000.] Thus, the answer is $6,000.

How much interest can the Jess Construction Company capitalize in Year 3 from the **construction loan**?

$120,000 = $3,000,000 x 8% x 6/12

How much interest can the Jess Construction Company capitalize in Year 3 from **internally generated funds**?

$60,000* = $2,000,000 x 6% x 6/12
[*The amount capitalized from internally generated funds cannot exceed the *actual* interest on the loans unrelated to the project for the portion of Year 1 in the construction period [6/12]. $100,000 x 6% x 6/12 = $3,000.] Thus, the answer is $3,000.

Intangible Assets
These assets are part of a firm's productive assets, but lacking physical substance. Examples of intangible assets include copyrights, patents, trademarks, leasehold improvements and goodwill. Intangible assets can have an economic value much larger than the recorded value.

Unless intangibles are purchased from other firms, they will be originally valued in the B/S at the costs expended to develop the intangible asset. See also the comments about R&D in this topic.

The initial B/S presentation of intangible assets can be best understood in the context of a two-by-two matrix and an understanding of a few basic terms related to intangible assets. [These initial amounts can be reduced later through amortization.]

Create in the margin here a '2 by 2' matrix according to these instructions. You should title the vertical columns with the terms 'Identifiable' and 'Unidentifiable'. The entire universe of intangible assets can be broken down into two sets. Conveniently, there is only one *unidentifiable* intangible asset: Goodwill [GW]. All the other intangible assets are identifiable.

The accounting for each of these four cells is different under GAAP. The accounting is not difficult but the differences are *material*.

Identifiable intangibles that have been acquired are recorded initially at the purchase price increased by any incidental amounts paid to complete the acquisition. Assume an attorney specializing in intellectual property was hired to help with the transaction. Any amounts paid to the attorney to facilitate the deal's successful completion would be capitalized as part of the intellectual property. In short, capitalize the purchase price plus all incidental costs.

When GW has been acquired, it will be capitalized in accordance with GAAP. GW is the *excess* of the purchase price over the sum of the identifiable net assets acquired measured at their fair market values. [Recall, if we pay less than the fair market values of the assets, we apply the 'basket purchase' approach as above.] I will provide an example calculating GW later.

If an entity *develops* an *identifiable* intangible asset, the intangible is recorded at the incidental costs to develop the intangible. If a firm developed a copyright on software at incidental costs of $5,000, the initial recorded value for the software in the firm's B/S would be the $5,000. The fair market value might be in the millions, but the B/S would only reflect the cost basis of the intangible.

If an entity expends resources to *internally* develop goodwill, the expenditures must be expensed immediately and no GW ever appears on the B/S. The expenditures might result in material amounts of economic goodwill but the FS will not report the GW as an asset because it had not been purchased. Users of FS should be aware that developed goodwill does not appear in the financial statements as GW. Moreover, economic goodwill is not reflected in the FS *at all* primarily due to significant problems associated with its measurement.

Goodwill Example
On May 1, Year 1, the Chris Company purchased a company with three recorded assets for a lump sum payment of $6,000,000. The three assets had separate recorded values as shown here: Land $2,000,000, Equipment $2,000,000 and Goodwill for $200,000. The fair market values of the Land and Equipment were $2,500,000 and $3,300,000, respectively. Chris Company amortizes all identifiable intangibles over a 10-year life.

How much GW, if any, should Chris recognize as a result of this purchase? $_____

[Answer: $200,000: Paid $6,000,000 and the sum of the fair market values of the identifiable net assets acquired is $5,800,000. Thus, the GW purchased in the transaction is $200,000. The GW in the books of the *acquired* company is ignored because it is not identifiable.]

Depreciation and Amortization

The costs of PPE (other than for Land) are subject to depreciation in the F/S. The depreciation process systematically and rationally recognizes that the costs of most assets decline over time despite interim periods of appreciation due to market conditions. This process allocates the original costs to expense in a systematic and rational manner. Depreciation Expense is not intended to represent the annual decrease in fair market value nor is the book value of PPE intended to approximate the fair market value of the asset at any point in time. Depreciation results from cost allocation and does not represent valuation changes or levels.

Depreciation in FA varies widely from depreciation as permitted in TA. Depreciation provides is one of the most significant differences between TA and FA. The deferred taxes resulting from temporary differences can be material to the firm. Generally, TA permits quicker depreciation of the assets' through Depreciation Expense than does FA. When a depreciable asset is relatively new, current year's TA income is lower than current year's FA income as a result of current TA Depreciation Expense exceeding current year FA Depreciation Expense. When these temporary differences reverse in the future, TA income will exceed FA income. Recall, this would require that Deferred Tax Liabilities be recognized in the current year at an amount equaling the extra amount of taxes we expect to pay in the future as a result of the temporary differences.

Accumulated Depreciation

When Depreciation Expense is debited, the corresponding credit is to Accumulated Depreciation, a contra-asset. What is the effect of this journal entry on this familiar equation?

$$\text{Assets} = \text{Liabilities} + \text{OE}$$

[Answer: Assets and OE both decrease.]

Book Value

A commonly used term in relation to PPE is 'book value'. In the context of PPE, book value means the cost of the asset *less* the Accumulated Depreciation account. Carrying value is frequently a synonym for book value.

Depreciation for Financial Accounting

You will only be responsible for two FA depreciation methods: straight-line and double-declining-balance methods. The double-declining-balance [DDB] method is an accelerated method characterized by having more Depreciation Expense in the early years of the asset's life than with the straight-line method. DDB Depreciation Expense generally declines from year to year as we will see shortly. The straight-line method generally puts the same amount of depreciation into each year's income statement over the life of the asset.

Straight-Line Method:

Depreciation Expense = ($Cost − $Salvage)/ Life

Depreciation Expense appears in the income statement.

$Cost represents all of the costs necessary to prepare the asset for its intended use.

$Salvage is the estimated value that can be obtained for the asset when it is retired from service.

Life is the estimated number of years during which the asset will be used for its intended purpose.

The book value of the asset at the end of its useful life equals salvage value.

Double-Declining Balance Method for Financial Accounting

Depreciation Expense = ($Cost − $Accumulated Depreciation) (2/ Life)

$Cost is the sum of all of the costs necessary to make the asset ready for its intended use.

$Accumulated Depreciation is the accumulation of all previous years' depreciation.

Life is the estimated number of years during which the asset will be used for its initial purpose.

When using DDB method in FA, depreciation must cease when the book value of the asset drops to salvage value. The method might result in the asset being fully depreciated *prior* to the end of its estimated useful life.

It may become necessary to change over to the straight-line method at some point in the life of the asset in order to depreciate the asset to the salvage value by the end of the asset's useful life. Failure to perform the 'switch-over' would leave the asset with a book value exceeding the salvage value at the end of the asset's useful life. While fairly confusing at first, the essentials of the 'switch-over' calculations are these:
1. At the start of any or every year, compare (1) the DDB depreciation for that year determined according to the procedures explained above to (2) Depreciation Expense determined under a modified 'straight-line' method calculation as presented in the next point.
2. The modified 'straight-line' method calculation is:
    ($Cost − Acc.Depr.at start of year - $Salv.)/ Remaining Life
3. The remaining life is the original life reduced by the years previously depreciated.
4. If the modified 'straight-line' Depreciation Expense is larger, then use it for the current and succeeding years. [Check the calculations for the previous year to see if the 'switchover' to modified 'straight-line' should have taken place in that year.] Alternatively, if the DDB Depreciation Expense is larger, we will use it for

the current year and repeat the comparison between the methods in the following year.
5. If the modified 'straight-line' Depreciation Expense for the current year is the *same* as for the DDB method, then it does not matter which method you use in the current year. Note that in later years the modified 'straight-line' method will always result in the larger Depreciation Expense than continued use of DDB.
6. Treating the Salvage Value as a negative in the numerator of the modified 'straight-line' depreciation method creates a bias *against* finding that the modified 'straight-line' Depreciation Expense will be larger in the current year.

Depreciation for Tax Accounting

You will only be responsible for one TA depreciation method: DDB (more commonly known in TA as Modified Accelerated Cost Recovery System ['MACRS']. This method is more accelerated than the FA version because tax laws permit the use of a cost recovery period that is shorter than the asset's estimated useful economic life. The result of the shorter life in the rate's denominator is that the MACRS depreciation *rate* is larger that would be the case in FA. Another subtle difference in this method is that tax laws permit the asset to be depreciated to *zero* rather than stopping the depreciation process when the book value reaches the salvage value. DDB Depreciation Expense in TA usually exceeds DDB Depreciation Expense for FA in the early years of an asset's life.

Double-Declining Balance Method for Tax Accounting

MACRS Depreciation Expense = ($Cost − $Acc. Depr.) (2/Cost Recovery Period)

All of the terms are as previously explained. The cost recovery period is determinable from a table presented on page 505 of the text. You are not responsible for knowing the details of that table. The cost recovery period is usually shorter than the estimated useful life. Depreciation recorded in the first year becomes Accumulated Depreciation in the formula for the second year. Thus, depreciation calculations are, in part, a function of prior years' Depreciation Expense.

As with DDB for FA, it may be necessary to change over to a modified 'straight-line' method in the life of the asset to depreciate the asset to *zero* by the end of the asset's cost recovery period. Failure to perform the 'switch-over' would leave the asset with a carrying value exceeding zero at the of the asset's cost recovery period. While fairly confusing at first, the essentials of the 'switch-over' calculations are these:
1. At the start of any or every year, compare the MACRS depreciation for that year determined according to the procedures explained above to Depreciation Expense determined under a modified 'straight-line' method calculation as presented in the next point.
2. The modified 'straight-line' method calculation is:
    ($Cost − Acc.Depr.at start of year)/ Remaining Cost Recovery Period
3. The remaining cost recovery period is the original cost recovery period reduced by the number of years the asset has been previously depreciated.

4. If the modified 'straight-line' Depreciation Expense is larger, then use it for that and succeeding years. Check the calculations for the previous year to see if the 'switchover' to modified 'straight-line' should have taken place in that year.
5. If the modified 'straight-line' Depreciation Expense for the current year is the same as for the DDB method, then it does not matter which method you use in the current year. Note, however, that in succeeding years the modified 'straight-line' method will always result in a larger Depreciation Expense.
6. Unlike the 'switch-over' calculation for DDB in FA, the 'switch-over' for MACRS *ignores salvage value in the numerator*. This makes it more likely that the 'switch-over' condition will be met when using MACRS in TA that when using DDB for FA.

Fractional Periods

In FA there are two common approaches for dealing with midyear acquisitions and disposals of assets. One approach involves counting the months of use of the asset in the acquisition or disposal year and pro rating the full-year depreciation determined through either the straight-line or DDB methods accordingly. The other approach is to adopt the half-year convention and depreciate assets for a half a year in both acquisition and disposal years without counting months.

There are other GAAP possibilities if followed consistently year after year.

In FA, you responsible for knowing you should count the months unless the firm has adopted the half-year convention. All of my examples will assume assets were acquired on the first or last day of a particular month. You will never have to count days for any of my examples.

In TA, we will assume the half-year convention is always used. We will overlook some TA rules governing acquisitions in the last quarter of a year and merely apply the half-year convention in all cases.

Disposals of Property, Plant & Equipment

When assets are sold at any point, the entity computes a gain or loss equals to the difference between the proceeds and the book value (or carrying value) of the assets when sold. The asset must be depreciated correctly up to the date of sale to have the proper book value in the gain/loss calculation. If the proceeds from the sale exceed the book value on the date of sale, the entity will report a *gain* on the disposal. If the proceeds from the sale are less than the book value on the date of sale, the entity will report a *loss* on the disposal.

A comprehensive example of TA and FA:

The Stephen Company purchased a new printing press on March 1, Year 1. The printing press was delivered on April 1, Year 1 and was installed on May 1. The firm had accepted the extended payment terms offered by the manufacturer and Stephen was obligated to pay $6,600,000 on April 30, Year 2. Stephen could have elected to pay $6,200,000 for the printing press on March 1, Year 1. Installation costs for the printing press were $120,000 for special wiring required for the printing press and $160,000 for the training of the firm's employees to use the new equipment. The firm began to use the new printing press on June 1, Year 1. The estimated life and estimated salvage value of the printing press were 6 years and $700,000, respectively. The cost recovery period for TA is five years. With TA, use the 'half-year' convention. *[The proper cost basis of this printing press is $6,480,000. The $6,200,000 could have been paid and thus should be used instead of the $6,600,000. The $400,000 difference should be called if interest if the Stephen Company decides to pay more and to pay later. The special wiring and training costs should be added to the $6,200,000 to get the proper cost basis of $6,480,000.]*

Required: Determine the proper values for the following:

Financial Accounting Straight-Line Method

Year 1: [($Cost – Salvage)/ Life] x [Fractional Period] = Depreciation Expense
[($6,480,000 - $700,000) / 6] x [7/12] = $561,944

Years 2-7, inclusive:
[($Cost – Salvage)/ Life] = Depreciation Expense
[($6,480,000 - $700,000) / 6] = $963,333

Year 8: [($Cost– Salvage)/ Life] x [Fractional Period] = Depreciation Expense
[($6,480,000 - $700,000) / 6] x [5/12] = $401,399

Financial Accounting Double-Declining Balance Method

Year 1: [($Cost –Acc. Depr.) (2/Life)] x [Fractional Period] = Depreciation Expense
[($6,480,000 – 0) (2/6)] x [7/12] = $1,260,000

Year 2: [($Cost –Acc. Depr.) (2/Life)]= Depr. Expense
[($6,480,000 - $1,260,000) (2/6)] = $1,740,000

Year 2: Calculations to Illustrate the 'Switch-over' to Straight Line Method'
[$Cost - $Acc. Depr. - $Salvage] / Remaining Life
([$6,480,000 - $1,260,000 - $700,000] / [6 – 7/12]) = $834,462
Do not use this as the Depreciation Expense for Year 2 because it is smaller than with DDB.

Year 3: [($6,480,000 - $3,000,000) (2/6)] = $1,160,000

Year 4: [($6,480,000 - $4,160,000) (2/6)] = $773,333

Year 5: [($6,480,000 - $4,933,333) (2/6)] = $515,556

Year 5: Calculations to Illustrate the 'Switch-over' to Straight Line Method'
[$Cost - $Acc. Depr. - $Salvage] / Remaining Life
([$6,480,000 - $4,933,333 - $700,000] / [6.0 – 3.58333]) = $247,805
Do not use this as the Depreciation Expense for Year 5 because it is smaller than with DDB.

Year 6: [($6,480,000 - $5,448,889) (2/6)] = $343,704*

*Would cause book value to be less than salvage value ($700,000). Thus, we must force a depreciation number that would leave the carrying value equal to salvage value and discontinue depreciation of this asset in future years even though the asset's useful life has not yet ended. The forced Depreciation Expense for Year 6 is $331,111.

No 'switch-over' to modified straight-line was necessary at any point throughout this FA DDB example.

Tax Accounting Double-Declining Balance Method [MACRS]:
The Cost Recovery Period [CRP] is 5 years. Use the 'half-year' convention with tax.

Year 1: [($Cost –Acc. Depr.) (2/CRP*)] x ['Half-Year'] = Depr. Expense
[($6,480,000 – 0) (2/5)] x [1/2] = $1,296,000

Year 2: [($Cost –Acc. Depr.) (2/CRP)]= Depr. Expense
[($6,480,000 - $1,296,000) (2/5)] = $2,073,600

Year 2: Calculations to Illustrate the 'Switch-over' to Straight Line Method' in MACRS
[$Cost - $Acc. Depr] / Remaining CRP
([$6,480,000 - $1,296,000] / [5 – 1/2]) = $1,152,000
Do not use this as the Depreciation Expense for Year 2 because it is smaller than with MACRS.

Year 3: [($6,480,000 - $3,369,600) (2/5)] = $1,244,160

Year 4: [($6,480,000 - $4,613,760) (2/5)] = $746,496

Year 4: Calculations to Illustrate the 'Switch-over' to Straight Line Method' in MACRS
[$Cost - $Acc. Depr.] / Remaining CRP
([$6,480,000 - $4,613,760] / [5.0 – 2.5]) = $746,496
When there is a tie as in this case, you may use either method to obtain Depreciation Expense for the current year. However, in subsequent years, the calculations using the modified straight-line method must be used.

Year 5: [($6,480,000 - $5,360,256)] / (5.0 – 3.5)] = $746,496

Year 6: [($6,480,000 - $6,106,752)] / (5.0 – 4.5)] = $373,248*
*Reduces the carrying value to zero. This is all of the depreciation that is allowed as a tax deduction in Year 6.

Amortization
Amortization is to identifiable intangible assets what depreciation is to PPE. As the cost basis of identifiable intangibles is allocated to expense in a systematic and rational manner it becomes amortization. I have only seen amortization done through use of the straight-line method although other methods could be used. Salvage value is ignored for intangibles. GW is the only unidentifiable intangible asset.

In amortizing identifiable intangible assets, the only interesting issue involves determining the proper life for the asset. Identifiable intangibles have three lives: remaining legal life, FASB's imposed maximum life for amortization purposes [40 years], and remaining useful economic life.

Some intangibles, like patents and copyrights, have finite legal lives. This provides one of the three 'lifetimes' considered by accountants for amortizing the value of the intangible asset over time. Trademarks do not have finite legal lifetimes.

FASB has imposed a maximum amortization period for identifiable intangibles of 40 years. This period was chosen as being arbitrarily long and, conservatively, no identifiable intangibles should be amortized over a period exceeding 40 years even in the case of Trademarks that do not have legal finite life. For example, if someone were to buy a company and properly allocate $500,000,000 to the value of the Trademark at the time of acquisition, that value would have to be amortized over a period not to exceed 40 years under GAAP.

The remaining useful economic life is the third 'lifetime' of identifiable intangibles. Management and accountants must examine the intangible asset to evaluate the period over which the identifiable intangible can be expected to provide measurable economic benefits from ownership. Often, the remaining useful economic life is shorter than the remaining legal life for intangibles with finite legal lives.

Impairments
When applied to PPE, impairments refer to some diminishment in utility or value as a result of owning (controlling) some asset. GAAP currently requires meeting two tests before impairment losses can be recognized.

The first test involves comparing the carrying value of the asset owned (controlled) against the cash flows to be received (or outlays avoided) as a result of use of and/or eventual sale of the asset. For example, the carrying value of an asset could be easily determined by subtracting the Accumulated Depreciation from the cost basis of the asset as explained previously in this topic. Estimating the cash flows from the use of an asset and/or sale is an easy but subjective task. If the carrying value exceeds the sum of future cash flows from the use of and/or sale of an asset, there is deemed to be an impairment loss. [It is important to note that the estimated future cash flows from use and/or sale of the asset are not considered at their 'present values' in this calculation. Thus, the impairment test contains an inherent bias *against* determining that there is an impairment loss. The 'present values' would be smaller than the undiscounted future cash flows and, *if used in the first test*, would cause more impairments than when using the undiscounted future cash flows.]

The second test involves comparing the carrying value of the asset against the fair market value of the asset deemed to be impaired in the first test. If the fair market value of the asset is lower than the carrying value at the time of the test, then the difference is deemed to be the impairment loss and the asset's carrying value is written down to the fair market value.

Choosing Depreciation Methods for Tax and Financial Accounting
For FA purposes, the choice of depreciation methods should be based upon whatever method does the best job of matching revenues and expenses (specifically Depreciation Expense). Management must consider the pattern of benefits to be enjoyed through control of the asset. If the benefits are clearly greater in the early years of the asset's life, an accelerated depreciation method should be selected. The method illustrated in this lecture is the DDB method. [The sum-of-the-years' digits is another accelerated method sometimes used in financial accounting. I did not cover sum-of-the-years' digits method in this semester and it was not mentioned in the text.]

TA permits use of a different depreciation method than that used in FA. This enables management to select a depreciation method that will postpone the payment of taxes if that is in the firm's best interest. For example, selection of DDB Depreciation method will result in larger Depreciation Expenses in the early years of the assets' lives and less Depreciation Expense later. The temporary differences between depreciation methods in FA and TA create the largest single source of deferred taxes.

In the long run, the total expense associated with use of an asset is the same for TA as for FA. The timing of the Depreciation Expenses varies widely as a result of which methods are employed for which purposes. A common mistake is to think that an accelerated method is preferable for the FS because that will result in lower taxes to be paid in the early years. Tax returns and FS are usually very different with respect to PPE.

Accounting for Investments

Topic 10
This topic ties to Chapter 12 in the SSD text.

Firms may have several important goals when buying and holding investments. One possible short-term goal might be a desire to hold assets providing 'instant' liquidity in the event of unplanned economic opportunities or threats. Another short-term goal might be to earn a (positive) rate of return on temporary cash balances. Management must weigh its desire for safety when making these investments against the desire to earn (higher) positive rates of return. The risk/return tradeoff drives many of these decisions regarding where to 'park' excess funds temporarily.

Sometimes firms have long-term goals. These include investing funds for known needs many years in the future. Life insurance companies invest money that will not be needed until many years later. Another long-term objective might be to acquire some *influence* over the operating policies of another firm in order to promote some mutual business interests or to prevent a competitor from gaining a foothold with the **investee**. Still another long-term objective might involve obtaining *actual control* of another firm in order to better develop the business interests of the investor.

When selecting investments from the investment spectrum, **debt securities** and **equity securities** have long been considered based upon their risk and return characteristics.

What Are the Implications for Management and Other Financial Statement Users?
Managers of firms and FS users must have some knowledge about accounting rules for investments. Managers of firms must appreciate how those investments will be reported in the firm's FS and influence apparent financial performance. No one would ever attempt to manage a football team without a full appreciation of game strategy including knowledge of how to keep score in football. Similarly, in business, managing involves many skills including having an accurate sense of how business decisions will impact a very public 'report card': the firm's FS. Investors must have enough skill to interpret correctly what the FS reveal about investment positions taken by an investor firm. GAAP presumes that FS users have enough information to understand information contained in FS.

Some investments are made in equity securities of another firm. Common shares would be an example of equity investments representing an ownership interest in the investee. Sometimes the investor would prefer to have an investment that would be a liability to the investee. The investor will call these debt investments. Debt investments have *due dates* and usually involve *interest rates*. Equity securities do not have due dates and do not involve interest rates. Equity securities are ordinarily regarded as more risky although generalizations may not be appropriate.

What Are the Accounting Treatment Possibilities Along the Investment 'Continuum'?

Let's begin by creating a continuum of relative sizes of investments that one firm can make in the ownership of another firm. The 'smallest' investment in the equity of another firm is zero percent. The other end of the relative equity investment continuum is 100%. In the lower part of the continuum, the investor does not exercise any **significant influence** over the investee because the percentage ownership is too small or there are other factors preventing significant influence. The **cost method** is the name of the accounting method appropriate for use when the investor does not have significant influence. Moving to the right on the continuum and for investments in equity securities, at some point the investor may have significant influence over the investee but will not have **control**. Investors with significant influence over the investee should use the **equity method** when accounting for the investment. Investors with control over the investee should still use the equity method but should prepare **consolidated financial statements** that include the investee's assets and liabilities. Control is defined as an equity ownership interest exceeding 50%. Recall from early in the course that assets do not have to be owned, but merely controlled.

Investments in debt securities do not convey any elements of influence or control and, thus, would be accounted for using the *cost method* regardless of the percentage of the firm's debt securities might be owned. Investments in preferred shares [Topic 12] do not provide any elements of influence or control and should be accounted for using the cost method.

A few years ago some special rules for 'marketable' debt and equity investments were adopted for use with the cost method. 'Marketable' means a reliable market price is available. When the investor in marketable securities has no significant influence, the investor will use as many as three portfolios depending on the circumstances: **trading securities portfolio, available for sale securities portfolio,** and **debt securities held to maturity.** The financial statement reporting of these investments is done at the *portfolio* level. The investor would keep detailed internal records of each individual investment, but group investments into portfolios for financial reporting.

What Are the Important Implication of Trading Securities Portfolios?

This portfolio is comprised of marketable debt and equity securities that do not provide any significant influence or control over the investee. The trading securities portfolio [Tr/S] is comprised of securities that are *intended* for active trading by the investor. Because of the required intent for active trading, Tr/S are always classified as current assets.

The Tr/S portfolio is considered 'close enough' to the firm's 'operating' activities to reflect Tr/S transactions as operating activities in the SofSF. Otherwise, these transactions would have been shown as investing activities.

How Are Trading Securities Reported in the Balance Sheet?

Tr/S must be reported at their fair market value. Since these investments are carried at cost in the Tr/S account, we need a **Valuation Allowance** to adjust the Tr/S up or down to fair market value at each B/S date. These adjustments up or down are accomplished by journal entries to make them easier to understand correctly. Valuation Allowances can have debit balances when the fair market value is higher than cost or credit balances when the fair market value is lower than cost. Observe these simple relationships and then consider an elementary, but important, example.

Tr/S Relationships		
Tr/S Portfolio at Cost	$600	$600
Valuation Allowance [debit/(credit)]	180	(210)
Tr/S Portfolio at FMV	$780	$390

Tr/S Example:
The Stephen Company acquired some Tr/S early in Year 1 paying $800 cash. At the end of Year 1, the fair market value of these securities was $600. How large a balance would we need in the Valuation Allowance and would it be a debit or a credit? [Answers: $200 credit.]

Consider the *journal entry* needed to obtain the proper ending Valuation Allowance balance at the end of Year 1. We would need to credit the Valuation Allowance for $200. What account would we debit for the $200 balancing the journal entry? The debit would be to *Unrealized Loss* on Tr/S for $200. If you had purchased these securities for $800 and they were now worth $600, you would have experienced an *economic* loss.

The 'economic loss' is reflected in the debit to Unrealized Loss and the balance needed in the Valuation Allowance comes from the credit to the Valuation Allowance in the journal entry.

What Are the Accounting Implications for the Income Statement From Tr/S?

Unrealized Gains and Unrealized Losses are recognized when the Valuation Allowance must be adjusted. *Unrealized Gains and Unrealized Losses* are reported in the I/S even though the related securities have *not* been sold. Unrealized Gains and Losses are directly related to the adjustment needed to create the proper ending balance in the

Valuation Allowance. The proper ending balance in the Valuation Allowance reflects whatever must be added to or subtracted from the Tr/S cost basis in order to obtain the fair market value of the portfolio in the B/S at year-end. In the example above, the Valuation Allowance had to have an end of year credit balance in order that Tr/S would be reported at fair market value of $600. The desired year-end B/S would appear like this:

Tr/S at cost	$800	
Less: Valuation Allowance	(200)	
Tr/S at Market Value, 12/31/Yr. 1		$600

The $600 would be included with the other current assets.

The I/S would appear like this:

Unrealized Loss on Tr/S   ($200)

The more important test of your understanding occurs at the end of the *second* year. Let's assume for simplicity that the Stephen Company did not buy or sell any Tr/S during Year 2. Further, let's assume the fair market value of the same securities that had been purchased in Year 1 has increased to $950 at the end of Year 2.

What is the proper ending balance needed in the Valuation Allowance at the end of Year 2 for presentation with Tr/S in the B/S?

The desired year-end balance sheet would appear like this:

Tr/S at cost	$800	
Plus: Valuation Allowance	+150	
Tr/S Portfolio at Market Value, December 31, Yr. 2		$950

Importantly, think about the *journal entry* to make this result appear in the Stephen Company's B/S. What accounts would debited and credited and for what amounts?

Intuitively, from this example the rise in the fair market value of the Tr/S portfolio feels like an economic gain and the I/S reflects that by containing a line item for Unrealized Gain on Tr/S for $350. The B/S will report the fair market value of the portfolio and the I/S will reflect economic increases and decreases in fair market values for the *unsold* securities classified in the Tr/S portfolio.

What Are Realized Gains and Losses?
When securities are sold, we measure *Realized* **Gains and Losses** as the difference between their original cost and their sale price. Realized Gains and Losses are reported in the I/S the same as if they had resulted from the sale of land. These Realized Gains and Losses in the I/S are the same as would be reported in the firm's *tax return*. [*Unrealized* Gains and Losses reflect changes in the fair market values of unsold securities.]

Are there Important Implications from Holding an Available for Sale Securities Portfolio?
This 'Available for Sale' [AFS] portfolio is comprised of marketable debt and equity securities that do not provide the investor with any significant influence or control over any investee. Moreover, the AFS portfolio is comprised of securities that *cannot* be properly placed in either of the other two marketable securities portfolios by the investor. Recall, the other two marketable securities portfolios are the Tr/S portfolio previously discussed and 'debt securities to be held until maturity' portfolio that we will briefly mention later. Because the AFS portfolio operates as a 'catch all' for marketable securities that are not properly placed in one of the other two portfolios, the AFS portfolio could contain current asset and non-current asset securities. However, I will disregard the likelihood of 'splitting' the portfolio into these two components.

How Is an AFS Portfolio Reported in the Balance Sheet?
The AFS portfolio has two important consequences in the B/S. One, the AFS portfolio must be reported at fair market value among the assets in the B/S Two, in the OE section of the B/S there will be an account containing the Unrealized Gains [Losses] on the AFS portfolio. Since these investments are carried at cost in the AFS account, we need a Valuation Allowance to adjust the AFS up or down to fair market value over time. These adjustments up or down are accomplished through use of journal entries to make them easier to understand correctly. Valuation Allowances can have debit balances when the fair market value is higher than cost or credit balances when the fair market value is lower than cost. Observe these simple relationships and then consider a simple, but important, example.

AFS Securities Relationships
AFS Securities Portfolio at Cost	$700	$700
Valuation Allowance [debit/(credit)]	280	(210)
AFS Securities Portfolio at FMV	$980	$490

AFS Securities Example:
The Kyle Company acquired some AFS early in Year 1 paying $800 cash. At the end of Year 1, the fair market value of these securities was $600. How large a balance would we need in the Valuation Allowance and would it be a debit or a credit?

With the AFS portfolio, we use the same mechanics to adjust the Valuation Allowance at the end of every period for proper reporting in the B/S. The Valuation Allowance is adjusted to get the carrying value of the portfolio up or down to its fair market value. The Valuation Allowance carries over from year to year and must be adjusted using a journal entry as we have previously seen. Consider this basic example illustrating the adjustment process. Assume at the end of the *previous* year, the AFS portfolio properly appeared like this in the B/S.

AFS Portfolio at Cost	$800
Less: Valuation Allowance	(200)
AFS Portfolio at Market Value, December 31, Yr. 1	$600

For simplicity, assume no purchases or sales of any securities in the AFS portfolio. At the end of the *current* year, assume the AFS portfolio had a fair market value of $980. What balances would be needed for the AFS portfolio in the balance sheet? What is the necessary journal entry to adjust the Valuation Allowance from its carried over credit balance of $200 to the desired debit balance of $180?

With the AFS portfolio, *Unrealized* Gains and Losses do not appear in the I/S. Instead, they are treated as special components in the OE section of the B/S. As special OE accounts, the Unrealized Gains and Losses on the AFS portfolio carry over from year to year instead of being 'closed out' as with the Tr/S portfolio. The lack of I/S involvement for the *Unrealized* Gains and Losses on the AFS portfolio reflects that this portfolio is not closely identified with the firm's operating activities as is the Tr/S portfolio.

In connection with the AFS portfolio, an interesting relationship occurs involving the *Valuation Allowance* and the special OE account, *Unrealized Gains and Losses on AFS Securities*. In each B/S, these accounts will have *equal* dollar amount balances, but if one is a debit the other must be a credit. Consider the fortunate economic implications of having a *debit* balance in the Valuation Allowance. The debit balance in the Valuation Allowance means that since acquisition, the AFS securities have gone *up* in value and that is a good thing ☺. The corresponding account in the OE section, Unrealized Gain on AFS Securities, reflects this fortunate economic result ☺.

If there was an Unrealized Loss on AFS Securities in the OE section for $500, what proper balance would we find in the Valuation Allowance for the AFS portfolio? Name the amount and whether it would be a debit or a credit.

What Happens in the Income Statement as a Result of Owning an AFS Portfolio?
The income statement implications for the AFS portfolio are straightforward. There would be *no* Unrealized Gains and Losses on AFS securities found there. Just as for the Tr/S portfolio, *realized* gains and losses, interest income and dividend income would be found in the I/S as appropriate.

Financial statement users and managers of firms should realize that the AFS portfolio will have a lower level of impact on the income statement during periods of market price volatility. However, *economic* gains and losses will still occur, but will be reported in the OE section.

What Are the Implications of Having a Portfolio of Debt Securities Held Until Maturity?
This discussion is for your information only and you will not be held accountable for this material on exams or quizzes.] This portfolio can *only* contain debt securities unlike the other two marketable securities portfolios. The investor must demonstrate it has the ***ability*** and ***intent*** to hold these debt securities until they mature. Some debt securities may mature in a relatively short time, while others may mature in a relatively long time. This portfolio can have current asset and non-current asset components. Any marketable debt securities where the investor does not have intent and ability to hold until maturity would have to be classified in the Tr/S or the AFS portfolios.

Because the investor must have the intent and ability to hold these debt securities until maturity, the portfolio is presented in the B/S at original cost as adjusted for amortization of premiums and discounts on the securities, if any. The fair market value of this portfolio is required to be disclosed in the footnotes to the F/S. We will not pursue the implications of amortizing premiums/discounts at this point since they are presented in detail in Topic 11.

Realized gains/losses and interest revenue are recognized in the I/S.

A Comprehensive Example of Accounting for Marketable Securities:

The Trojan Company has these portfolios with information available for your use as needed. All securities were acquired in Year 1, the firm's first year.

	Cost Basis	FMV at Dec. 31, Yr 1	Sale Proceeds	FMV at Dec. 31, Yr 2
Tr/S Portfolio:				
Lavach Corp	$40,000	$37,000	$18,000(1)	*$18,000
Fenolio Corp.	35,000	31,000		32,000
Unruh Corp	32,000	22,000	$28,000(2)	N/A
Totals	$107,000	$90,000		$50,000
AFS Portfolio:				
Leonte Corp.	$45,000	$49,000	N/A	$46,000
Tuckey Corp.	38,000	41,000	$22,000(3)	*23,000
Totals	$83,000	$90,000		$69,000

*The fair market value of the unsold securities.

(1) 40% of the Lavach Corp. securities were sold for $18,000.

(2) All of the Unruh Corp. securities were sold for $28,000.

(3) Half of the Tuckey Corp. securities were sold for $22,000.

Based on the information given and for these portfolios, what items would appear in the I/S of the USC Company for the year ended December 31, Year 2? [Indicate whether the gains/losses would be realized and/or unrealized.]

Tr/S $_____
[Realized Gain of $2,000 from Lavach securities, Realized Loss of $4,000 on Unruh securities, and Unrealized Gain of $1,000 from adjusting the Valuation Allowance from $17,000 (credit) to $18,000 (credit).]

AFS $_____
[Realized Gain of $3,000 from Tuckey securities.]

Based on the information given and for these portfolios, what items would appear in the B/S of the Wayne Company for the year ended December 31, Year 2?

Tr/S $_____

[Tr/S @ cost $59,000
 -Val. Allow   -18,000
 Tr/S @ FMV $41,000]

AFS $_____

[AFS @ cost $64,000
 +Val. Allow.   +5,000
 AFS @ FMV $69,000

In Owners' Equity: Unrealized Gain of $5,000

Here are the journal entries related to the above results.
There would be a Realized Gain of $2,000 from the sale of Lavach securities.
    Cash $18,000
        Realized Gain $2,000
        Tr/S   16,000

There would be a Realized Loss of $4,000 from the sale of Unruh securities.
    Cash $28,000
    Realized Loss   4,000
        Tr/S $32,000

There would be an Unrealized Gain on Tr/S of $1,000.
    Unrealized Gain on Tr/S $1,000
        Valuation Allowance $1,000

This will bring the Valuation Allowance from the credit $17,000 balance that carried over from the previous year to the $18,000 credit balance that is needed at the end of Year 2.

There would be a Realized Gain of $3,000 from the sale of Tuckey securities [AFS].
    Cash $22,000
        Realized Gain $3,000
        Tr/S   19,000

No Unrealized Gain or Loss would appear in the I/S because this is the AFS portfolio.

What Should Managers of Firms and Users of FS Know About Tr/S and AFS Portfolios?

Managers of firms that choose to hold Tr/S and/or AFS portfolios as well as users of their FS should understand that volatility in market price will appear in the asset section of the B/S. Whether price volatility flows into the I/S as Unrealized Gains/Losses or whether those Unrealized Gains/Losses will flow directly into OE depends upon which portfolio produced it.

Cost Method Financial Statement Implications When Securities Are Not Marketable:
The previous discussion of marketable securities was a subset of the cost method when the securities were marketable. When there is no available market price, and the equity securities do not provide significant influence or control, the cost method is used in accounting for the investments. Similarly, we would properly account for the investment using the cost method if they were non-marketable debt securities or non-marketable preferred shares.

The cost method is relatively easy to understand. The investment is recorded at cost when acquired. Subsequently, if the investee declares dividends the investor would recognize Dividends Receivable and Dividends Revenue for its share of the dividends. [If the investments are debt securities, the investor would have Interest Receivable and Interest Revenue.] Investors use the accrual basis and declaration of the dividends would trigger Dividends Revenue. Receipt of dividend payments would not trigger Dividend Revenue, rather Dividends Receivable would be credited.

Non-marketable cost method investments are subject to impairment rules as explained in topic 9 previously. If written down, the value to which the investment is lowered becomes the new cost basis and any subsequent recoveries in value cannot be recognized. The 'fair market value' for use in the impairment tests has to be estimated.

Sales of securities from portfolios using the (non-marketable) cost method produce Realized Gains and Losses. Other than through the impairment tests, changes in value do not become part of the investor's I/S.

Goodwill is not separately recognized as being a component of the Investment account when the investor uses the cost method.

A Comprehensive Example of the Cost Method for Non-Marketable Securities.

The Hopkins Company purchased 20,000 shares of Lavach Company for $50 per share on January 1, Year 1. Hopkins owns 4% of the outstanding shares of Lavach. This investment does not give Hopkins any significant influence over the Lavach Company and Lavach Company shares do not have an established market price.

During Year 1, Lavach Company earned $600,000 and declared a $200,000 dividend payable in January Year 2.

During Year 2, Lavach Company earned $1,200,000 and declared a $300,000 dividend. This dividend was partially paid in Year 2 ($100,000) and the remainder was to be paid in January Year 3.

During Year 3, Lavach Company earned $1,500,000 and declared a $50,000 dividend payable in January Year 4.

On January 1, Year 4, Lavach Company suffered a serious loss due to a change in governmental regulations and Hopkins Company felt it should write down the value of its remaining investment to $600,000. This is an impairment loss and was determined properly according to the terms of the two impairment tests.

Prepare journal entries to record this information in the financial records of the Hopkins Company.

Yr. 1   Investment $1,000,000
            Cash $1,000,000
Recognizes having paid $50 per share for 20,000 shares of Lavach.

Yr. 1   Dividend Receivable   8,000
            Dividend Revenue   8,000
Recognizes Hopkins' 4% of Lavach's declared dividend of $200,000 in Year 1.

Yr. 2   Cash   12,000
        Dividend Receivable   8,000
            Dividend Receivable   8,000
            Dividend Revenue   12,000
To recognize receipt of $8,000 from the Year 1 dividend *and* $4,000 of the dividend declared and paid in Year 2. Two-thirds of the $300,000 Year 2 dividend will not be paid until January Year 3. Hopkins' share is 4% or $8,000 and this becomes a Dividend Receivable. The credit to Dividends Receivable is for the $8,000 received from the Year 1 dividend. Dividend Revenue is on the accrual basis and recognizes 4% of the dividend declared in Year 2 [$300,000 x 4%].

Yr. 3   Cash   8,000
            Dividend Receivable   8,000
Records the receipt of $8,000 dividends declared in Year 2 payable in Year 3.

Yr. 3   Dividend Receivable   2,000
            Dividend Revenue   2,000
Records Hopkins' share of Lavach's dividend declared in Year 3, but payable in Year 4.

Yr. 4   Impairment Loss   400,000
            Investment   400,000

Records Hopkins' impairment loss in Year 4 related to the investment in Lavach. The investment is being written down to $600,000.

Yr. 4   Cash   2,000
            Dividend Receivable   2,000

Records Hopkins' share of Lavach's dividends declared in Year 3, but paid to Hopkins in Year 4.

What Are the FS Implications of the Equity Method?

If equity investments provide significant influence, the investor must use the equity method without regard to the investments marketability. The investor's apparent desire to exert significant influence over the investee and the implied long-term business implications resulting from the investment seem more important than recording changes in market values even if available.

When making an investment that provides significant influence, record the investment at its cost. Implicitly reflected in the investment transaction might be some amount related to differences in the book values and fair market values of assets and liabilities in the investee's balance sheet. The price paid by the investor would have reflected the market's assessment of the investee's net assets at *fair market value*. Also, there might be some **Goodwill** implied in the investor's purchase transaction if the investor paid more than the investor's share of the investee's net assets measured at fair market value. Any measured difference between book value and fair market value for the investee's assets must be amortized over the remaining life of the assets giving rise to this difference. Any **Goodwill** must remain in the Investment account and will not be subsequently amortized in a systematic way.

How Do Investors Treat Their Share of the Investee's Income in the Equity Method?

One important feature of the equity method is that the investor records *its share* of the investee's net income as a debit to the Investment account and a credit to 'Equity in Earnings of (investee)'. The 'Equity in Earnings of (investee)' functions as if it were a revenue in the I/S of the investor. For the investor, what is the effect on the basic accounting equation resulting from debiting Investment and crediting 'Equity in Earnings of (investee)'?

$$\text{Assets} = \text{Liabilities} + \text{OE}$$

[Answer: Assets increase and OE *both* increase by the same amounts representing the investor's share of the investee's net income.]

The investee's income might be different than the income the investor *would have* calculated because of the possibility of differences between the fair values and the carrying values of assets in the books of the investee. If those 'book value-fair market value' differences are linked to depreciable assets or inventory in the investee's books, an adjustment must be made by the investor to reflect that the investor's 'cost basis' for those assets differs from the cost basis considered by the investee when calculating the investee's own income.

For example, if the 'book value-fair market value' difference is attributable to a single piece of depreciable equipment in the investee's books and the fair value exceeds the book value by $200,000. Assume further the equity method investor owns 30% of the investee and the depreciable asset has a remaining depreciable life of six years. The investee would have calculated the equipment's depreciation on the lower book value, while the investor would have calculated the equipment's depreciation based on the equipment's fair market value. Thus, the investee's annual income would be *overstated* by $33,333 when viewed from the *investor's* perspective. [$200,000/6 = $33,333. I will always assume both parties use straight-line depreciation method and no salvage in these illustrations.] One final and important calculation: since the investor did not pay for *all* of the $200,000 difference between book value and fair market value, we must multiply the $33,333 by the investor's ownership percentage (30%).

The implication of this example in the context of the journal entry recorded earlier when the investor recognized *its share* of the investee's income requires that we *reduce* the debit to the Investment account and the credit to the Equity in Earnings of (investee) each by $10,000. [$33,333 x 30%]

In the equity method, all dividends are treated as 'liquidating' dividends and reduce the value in the Investment account. This is very different that in the cost method, where dividends trigger Dividend Revenue.

If Goodwill was indicated by the price paid by the investor, that Goodwill must be tested annually to determine if any impairment has occurred. If there has been no impairment, Goodwill is not adjusted. If there has been any impairment of Goodwill, the investor must adjust downward its Investment account and reduce the Equity in Earnings of (investee) in the same kind of journal entry as illustrated in the previous paragraph. I will not illustrate or hold you accountable for Goodwill impairments in the context of investments.

A Comprehensive Example of the Equity Method:

The Lakers Company purchased a 40% interest in the Magic Company on January 1, Year 1 paying $7,000,000 in cash. This investment gives Lakers significant influence over Magic.

When Lakers made the investment, the book value of Magic's net assets was $3,000,000. The fair market value of Magic's net assets was $10,000,000 on that same date. The difference between the book values and fair market values are attributable entirely to assets having remaining depreciable lives of 10 years.

In Year 1, Magic reported net income of $1,000,000. There were no inter-company transactions in Year 1. Magic declared and paid a $100,000 dividend in Year 1.

<u>Required</u>: Prepare journal entries recording this information in the books of the Lakers Company for Year 1:

Investment $7,000,000
    Cash $7,000,000
Recording the investment in Magic by the Lakers Company.

Investment $400,000
    Equity in Earnings of Magic $400,000
Recording Lakers' share of Magic's income for Year 1

Equity in Earnings of Magic $280,000
    Investment $280,000
Reducing Lakers' share of Magic's income for the depreciation on the book value-fair market value difference. [($10,000,000 - $3,000,000) x (40%) /10 years = $280,000]

Cash $40,000
    Investment $40,000
Recording Lakers' share of Magic's dividends as a *liquidating* dividend

Goodwill in the Investment account is $3,000,000. [The excess of $7,000,000 over (40%)($10,000,000) is $3,000,000.]

In Year 2, Magic reported earnings of $2,000,000. Magic declared and paid dividends of $200,000 in Year 2.

Lakers did not change its ownership interest over Magic during Year 2.

Required: Prepare proper journal entries recording this information in the books of Lakers for Year 2.

Investment $800,000
    Equity in Earnings of Magic $800,000
Recording Lakers' share of Magic's income for Year 2

Equity in Earnings of Magic	$280,000	
Investment		$280,000

Reducing Lakers' share of Magic's income for the depreciation on the book value-fair market value difference. [($10,000,000 - $3,000,000) x (40%) / 10 years = $280,000]

Cash	$80,000	
Investment		$80,000

Recording the dividend received by Lakers as a *liquidating* dividend.

Consolidated Financial Statements for Companies With Subsidiaries

When an investor has subsidiaries, the economic substance is that they are one economic unit. Frequently, the motive for having subsidiaries reflects legal requirements in those foreign or domestic jurisdictions where the subsidiaries operate. Whatever the reason for having subsidiaries where ownership exceeds 50%, the substance is that the entities together represent one economic unit. Legally, the entities are separate, but FA is based on the economic substance. The important result of preparing and distributing consolidated FS is that users can see the sum of the consolidated entity's activities and holdings in one convenient place. Consolidated FS have eliminated inter-company investments, receivables/payables and inter-company transactions to avoid 'double counting' these.

What are the Basic Principles of Consolidated Financial Statements?

The basic principles chiefly reflect the desire to present the FS as if it were one legal entity after elimination of inter-company transactions to avoid 'double counting' assets/liabilities and revenues/expenses.

A simple example will illustrate the need to eliminate some inter-company transactions and assets/liabilities. Suppose a husband earns $90,000 per year from his employer and he pays his wife $30,000 to manage his personal financial affairs. Would it be appropriate for the *couple* to report their combined incomes at $120,000? Of course not, since her $30,000 of income is *also* an expense for the husband. On a consolidated basis we understand the *couple* has consolidated income of $90,000 after eliminating the inter-couple transactions.

Similarly, suppose the husband owed his wife $9,000 for financial services rendered. Would it be appropriate for the *couple* to report the $9,000 as part of their total receivables in a loan application the *couple* might be preparing? The answer is obvious ☺.

Consider another related motive for elimination of inter-company transactions. Suppose a man owns a painting that he just bought for $10,000. Assume the true fair market value is $10,000. The man's sister promises to pay him $90,000 for the painting and offers a note payable [NP] for that amount. The man agrees to these terms. Two weeks later the man offers his sister $1,000,000 for the *same* painting and offers to sign a NP for

$910,000 and to cancel her NP to him. On a *separate basis* the man and his sister have experienced gains of $80,000 and $910,000, respectively. However, on a *consolidated basis*, what is the *substance* of their inter-family transactions? It is easy to see the fallacy in thinking that they have had gains aggregating nearly $1,000,000 from these two transactions.

How do we account when the investor owns more than 50% and is using the equity method?
To simplify your understanding of accounting for inter-company investments with control, we assume no 'book value-fair market value' differences for assets owned by the subsidiary. Additionally, we assume no Goodwill in any of the acquisitions. As a result, the investor's Investment account will contain an amount equal to its percentage ownership times the subsidiary's OE.

What eliminations are required when consolidating subsidiaries into the investor's financial statements?
(1) Inter-company receivables and payables are eliminated avoiding 'double-counting'.
(2) The Investment account itself must be eliminated since it is better to show the underlying assets and liabilities instead of showing an Investment account in the consolidated FS. The other half of this elimination makes the OE accounts of the subsidiary 'disappear'.
(3) If the subsidiary is *not* 100% owned, **Minority Interest** must be created in the consolidated B/S reflecting the part of the subsidiary's OE the investor does *not* own. The Minority Interest account is a 'hybrid' between the liability and OE classifications in the consolidated B/S. From the economic perspective of the consolidated entity, the Minority Interest seems like part of equity. However, from the perspective of the investor, the Minority Interest account seems more like a 'liability' since *all* of the subsidiary's assets and liabilities are shown in the consolidated B/S *without* the investor actually owning *100%* of those assets and liabilities.

A Basic Consolidation Example Where the Subsidiary is 100% Owned

The Li Company has a 100% ownership interest in Chan Company. The separate FS of the Li Company and Chan are shown below.

	Li	Chan	Consolidated
Cash	$250	$450	$ 700
Accounts Receivable	250	250	$ 420
Investment in Chan	900	---	$
PPE (net)	800	700	$ 1500
Total Assets	$2,200	$1,400	$ 2620
Accounts Payable	$350	$350	$ 620
Mortgage Payable	450	150	$ 600
Contributed Capital	800	400	$ 800
Retained Earnings	600	500	$ 600
Total Liab. & Owners' Equity	$2,200	$1,400	$ 2620

Chan owes $80 to Li.

The book values of Chan's assets and liabilities equal their fair market values.

Prepare a consolidated B/S for the Li Company.

The Investment account and the subsidiary's OE accounts 'disappear'. Thus, the consolidated B/S will not have an Investment account and the Contributed Capital and RE accounts will have balances, respectively, of $800 and $600.

Eliminating the inter-company receivable and payable will result in consolidated AR of $420. [$250 + $250 - $80 = $420] Consolidated AP will be $620. [$350 + $350 - $80 = $620]

All of the other accounts can be added horizontally to obtain the consolidated values that will appear in the FS. The consolidated B/S will balance at $2,620.

A Basic Consolidation Example With a Subsidiary That is Less Than 100% Owned
The Tony Company has 70% ownership interest in Crystal Company. The separate FS of the Tony Company and Crystal Company are shown below.

	Tony	Crystal	Consolidated
Cash	$300	$500	$ 800
Accounts Receivable	500	1,400	1700
Investment in Crystal	1,400	---	
PPE (net)	900	700	1600
Total Assets	$3,100	$2,600	$ 4100
Accounts Payable	$400	$400	600
Mortgage Payable	700	200	900
Minority Interest	---	---	600
Contributed Capital	1,200	1,300 .30%	1200
Retained Earnings	800	700	800
Total Liab. & Owners' Equity	$3,100	$2,600	$ 4100

Crystal owes $200 to Tony. The book values of Crystal's assets and liabilities equal their fair market values.

Prepare a consolidated B/S for the Tony Company.

The Investment account and the subsidiary's OE accounts 'disappear'. Thus, the consolidated B/S will not have an Investment account and the Contributed Capital and Retained Earnings accounts will have balances, respectively, of $1,200 and $800. A Minority Interest account will 'appear' in the amount of $600. This amount represents the part of Crystal's OE that is *not* owned by Tony [($1,300 + $700) (30%) = $600].

Eliminating the inter-company receivable and payable will result in consolidated A/R of $1,700. [$500 + $1,400 - $200 = $1,700]   Consolidated A/P will be $600. [$400 + $400 - $200 = $600]

All of the other accounts can be added horizontally to obtain the consolidated values that will appear in the FS. The consolidated B/S will balance at $4,100. How did you do?

Accounting for Liabilities Incurred Through Financing Activities

Topic 11
This topic ties to Chapter 13 in the SSD text

One of the first relationships in the early part of the semester was the basic accounting equation: Assets = Liabilities + OE. In this topic we will explore some of the details about *both* sources of capital that managers of businesses and FS users must understand to communicate in the accounting medium.

Previously, liabilities chiefly involved current operating liabilities. Typical examples from previous coverage included A/P, Salaries Payable, Rent Payable and Interest Payable. Borrowing transactions created N/P. In the early part of this topic, we will discuss the interactions between the use of debt and equity capital and the resulting impacts on returns to owners. Later, we will cover long-term borrowing arrangements including N/P and Bonds Payable [BP].

Most long-term liabilities are accounted for on the basis of the *present values* of their future cash payments. The interest rate at the time the loan was created will usually serve as the interest rate throughout the term of the loan. These loans are known as fixed rate loans and they are the basis for most borrowing transactions. We will also discuss variable rate loans so you will understand the accounting and financial implications.

Basic Building Blocks
Simple and compound interest concepts as well as present value calculations underlie most of the FS relationships related to long-term borrowing transactions.

Simple Interest
Simple interest is based on the *original* principal only. That's why we call it 'simple'. ☺

A Simple Interest Example:
The Hopkins Company was formed on March 1, Year 1. On August 31, Year 1, the firm borrowed $500,000 on its line of credit at an interest rate of 9%. The principal and all of the interest are due on the note's maturity date, May 1, Year 2. [Hint: interest rates are *always* annual, unless *otherwise* stated.]

Interest Expense for Year 1:
The basic formula for interest calculations is: Principal x Rate x Time.
In the example above, Interest Expense for Year 1 becomes:
$500,000 x 9% x 4/12 = $15,000

At the end of Year 1, the adjusting journal entry to record this is:
    Interest Expense $15,000
        Interest Payable $15,000

Interest Expense for Year 2:
Principal x Rate x Time: $500,000 x 9% x 4/12 = $15,000
[The principal remained at $500,000 and did not include the previously accrued $15,000 because there was no *compounding* date on December 31, Year 1 when we accrued interest for the four months ended then.]

More Complex 'Simple' Interest Examples:

You should understand the math and then how accounting is done for simple interest.

1. On January 1, Year 1, a firm lent $5,000 at 8% *simple* interest for three years. How much Interest Revenue would the firm recognize in each of the three years?
Year 1: $5,000 x 8% x 1 = $_____ [$400 ☺]
Year 2: $5,000 x 8% x 1 = $_____ [$400 ☺]
Year 3: $5,000 x 8% x 1 = $_____ [$400 ☺]

[Interest for all three years is based on the *original* principal since there are no compounding dates as we move through the three years.]

2. On September 1, Year 1, a firm agreed to pay $2,000,000 on September 1, Year 3. *Simple* interest on this obligation was 7%.

How large a liability must the firm record on September 1, Year 1? $_____
[$1,652,893 = $2,000,000/[1 + (7%)(3). This liability is the 'present value' of the $2,000,000 determined using *simple interest* concepts.]

How much Interest Expense will the firm recognize in Year 2? $_____
[$115,702 = $1.652,893 x 7%]   Interest Expense is based on the original liability.

Compound Interest
Compound interest gets its name from the *compounding* dates on which accrued interest to that point in time becomes *part of the principal for <u>subsequent</u> interest calculations.* <u>Almost all long-term liabilities in finance and accounting use compound interest.</u>

Compound Interest Examples:
We need to understand compound interest and how they appear in the FS. First, the math, then, the accounting implications. You will probably want to refer to present value tables as you work these examples. Remember, unless stated to the contrary, interest rates are *annual* and involve (annual) *compounding*.

1. On December 31, Year 1, a firm invested $10,000 at 9% compound interest for four years.

Interest Revenue for each of the four years is calculated from the 'carrying value' or 'book value' of the investment at the *start* of the 'compounding' year. The carrying value of the investment at the time of the investment is $10,000, the amount invested.

How much Interest Revenue would the firm recognize in *each* of the four years?

Interest Revenue for Year 2: $_____ [$900= $10,000 x 9% x 1]

Interest Revenue for Year 3: $_____ [$981= $10,900 x 9% x 1]

Interest Revenue for Year 4: $_____ [$1,069= $11,881 x 9% x 1]

Interest Revenue for Year 5: $_____ [$1,166= $12,950 x 9% x 1]

What amount would be received at maturity? $_____ [☺ $14,116 = $10,000 + $900 + $981 + $1,069 +$1,166]

We could have arrived at this same answer using present value tables. In a table of present value factors for a single payment, find the factor when there are four compounding periods and the interest rate is 9%: .70843. The present value of the future amount is $10,000 and we can use this equation:
Present Value = Factor x Future Amount

Divide the factor into $10,000 to obtain $14,116. ☺

2. On December 31, Year 1, a firm agreed to pay $5,000,000 as a lump sum in exactly three years. The interest rate on this obligation was 6%.

The liability recorded on December 31, Year 1, must be the *present value* of the future payment. We will have to compute the *present value* of the future cash payment *before* recording the liability on December 31, Year 1. The present value of the future cash payment can be determined as follows:
$5,000,000 / (1.06)(1.06)(1.06) = $4,198,096

How large a liability must the firm record on December 31, Year 1? $_____
[$4,198,096]

How could we have done the math with present value tables?
Present Value = Factor x Future Amount
In the table for factors showing the present value of a single payment, find the factor for three periods (n=3) and the interest rate is 6%. The factor is .83962.
Present Value = (.83962)($5,000,000)
Present Value = $4,198,100
The $4 difference is due to the rounding in the tables.

Interest Expense for any period is based upon the carrying value of the liability at the *start* of that period. The carrying value of the liability is the present value of the cash flows at that moment in time. Interest Payable is part of the carrying value of the liability for purposes of compound interest.

How much Interest Expense will the firm recognize in Year 3? $_____ This question is really asking how much Interest Expense would we recognize during the Year 3 based on the carrying value of the liability at the start of the Year 3. [$266,999 = [$4198,100 + ($4,198,100)(6%)] (6%)]

Another way to obtain this answer is to establish the carrying value of the liability at the start of Year 3 by working backward from the future value. Using the present value table for lump sums, find the factor where n=2 and I=6%. The factor is .89000. The present value after one year (the end of Year 2 or the start of Year 3) is $5,000,000 x .89000 = $4,500,000. Then multiply that present value by 6% for Year 3 to obtain $270,000. None of us will worry about the $1 difference that comes from the rounding.

Helpful Concept: the carrying value is always equal to the present value of the future cash flows at that moment in time ☺.

Annuities and Lump Sums
Lump sums are 'one time' payments to be made or received in connection with the financial arrangements. Annuities are equal, regular payments over time with a constant interest rate. Lump sum and annuity applications are routine in accounting and finance. When we combine these concepts with present and future value concepts and compound interest applications, we begin to appreciate how important it is for business people to understand the basic concepts.

Borrowing with Long-Term N/P
Suppose an amount is borrowed at the present time (present value) and the liability will be fully repaid over time with a series of periodic equal payments. The following expression captures the essence of what's needed to solve for the size of the equal periodic payments:

Present Value = (Factor) (Payment Size)

The factor comes from the tables of present value of annuity factors. The 'N' represents the number of payments and the 'I' represents the interest rate per compounding period. Even though the payments will occur in the future, we know the present value of the annuity equals the borrowed amount.

Consider this example of borrowing with a N/P
The Marshall Company has borrowed $4,000,000 from its neighborhood bank for business expansion. The bank charges 10% interest requiring semi-annual payments of

equal size for four-years to amortize the loan. The first payment will be made six months after taking out the loan.

1. Determine the size of each of the equal payments made to amortize the loan.
Present Value = (Factor) (Payment Size)
The present value is the $4,000,000.
The factor, 6.46321, is from the table for present value of an ordinary annuity when N=8 and I=5%. The repayment period is four years long and the payments are semi-annual. Thus, there will be eight payments. The interest rate is 5% because we need to use the interest _per compounding period_. The 10% interest rate given is an annual rate and with semi-annual compounding, we need to 'cut that rate in half' to get the appropriate rate for use in the tables. Substituting the known values into the equation and solving for the payment size we obtain $618,887 as the semi-annual payment size.

2. Show the proper journal entry that would be made when the _first_ semi-annual payment on the loan is made.

Interest Expense ($4,000,000 x 5%)	$200,000	
Note Payable (plugs as the difference ☺)	418,887	
Cash (as calculated above)		618,887

    We will need the 'new' carrying value caused by this payment:
    $4,000,000 - $418,887 = $3,581,113

3. Show the journal entry that would be needed to pay the _second_ semi-annual payment.

Interest Expense ($3,581,113 x 5%)	$179,056	
Note Payable (plugs as the difference ☺)	439,831	
Cash (as calculated above)		618,887

    We will need the 'new' carrying value caused by this payment:
    $3,581,113 - $439,831 = $3,141,282

4. Immediately after making the fourth payment, what would be the carrying value of the N/P? *The carrying value is equal to present value of the remaining payments.* Conceptually, there are two ways to derive the answer. The 'low tech' way would be to do two more journal entries and determine the carrying value after the fourth semi-annual payment. The 'high tech' way to derive the answer is to establish that there are four more payments remaining after the fourth payment had been made and, then, to calculate the present value of those four *remaining* payments. I will illustrate both approaches below.

    The journal entry needed when making the _third_ semi-annual payment:

Interest Expense ($3,141,282 x 5%)	$157,064

Note Payable (plugs as the difference ☺) 461,823
    Cash (as calculated above)   618,887

We will need the 'new' carrying value caused by this payment:
$3,141,282 - $461,823 = $2,679,459

The journal entry needed when making the *fourth* semi-annual payment:

Interest Expense ($2,679,459 x 5%) $133,973
Note Payable (plugs as the difference ☺)   484,914
    Cash (as calculated above)   618,887

The 'new' carrying value caused by this payment:
$2,679,459 - $484,914 = $2.194,545

To determine the carrying value by calculating the present value of the remaining *four* payments, apply the familiar equation from above.

Present Value = (Factor) ($Payment Size)

Here, the present value will be equal to the carrying value of the remaining two payments. Each payment will be $618,887. From the table of present value of an ordinary annuity, when N=4 and I=5%, we have the factor 3.54595. Substituting the *known* values into the expression above we determine the present value (carrying value) is $2,194,543. The dollars of difference are due to rounding in the tables and we will not worry about that.

Borrowing by Issuing Bonds Payable [B/P]

B/P differ from N/P in a few important ways. Bonds make semi-annual interest payments of equal size through the maturity date of the bonds. When bonds mature, the face amount of the bonds is due as a lump sum payment *in addition to* the final interest payment due on the same date. In contrast, recall, that when the last periodic payment was made on a note, the carrying value would have been *fully amortized.*

Importantly, observe that the cash payments associated with bonds come in two distinct types: (1) a one-time lump sum payment on the maturity date and, (2) semi-annual interest payments starting six months after the issuance of the bond and concluding on the maturity date.

Calculating the issue price of the bond essentially involves determining the present values of *both* the periodic interest payments *and* the one-time lump-sum payment. The sum of these present values is the issue price of the bond.

It will be useful to discuss some terms before getting into the mechanics of B/P. Bonds have *two* interest rates associated with them: the **coupon rate** is used to determine the *size of the periodic interest payments*, the **market rate** is used to *'present value'* all of the cash outflows associated with the bond. The stated rate is a synonym for the coupon rate. Effective rate and 'yield' are synonymous with market rate. Most of the time I use coupon rate and market rate.

The **'face' value** of the B/P is the lump sum payment due on the maturity date and is also known as the *maturity value*. All of the examples I have ever created have face values per bond of $1,000.

The interest payments on B/P refer to the periodic payments that are required by the bonds' terms. The interest payments are determined my multiplying the face value of the bonds times the coupon rate of interest and then multiplying for 'time' [Face x CR% x T]. Like other interest rates, given coupon rates are annual and must be adjusted downward to fit the semi-annual interest payment and compounding periods that dominate the world of accounting and finance.

Interest expense on B/P is determined by multiplying the carrying value of the B/P at the start of the interest payment period times the market rate of interest and then adjusting for time [P x R x T]. This is virtually the same approach as to calculate interest expense on N/P as explained earlier.

IMPORTANT MATERIAL:
B/P can be issued for more than face value or for less than face value. Stated alternatively, the present values of all of the cash outflows related to the B/P can be *greater* than the face value of the bonds, or the present values of all of the cash outflows related to the B/P can be *less* than the face value of the B/P. Whichever of these situations occurs in any example depends upon the **relation** between **coupon rate** and **market rate**. Recall, the *coupon rate* drives the *size of the interest payments*. The *market rate* drives the size of the *Interest Expense*. If the coupon rate is higher than the market rate of return demanded by investors considering buying these bonds, the B/P's prices will be bid up to exceed the face value of the B/P. This excess above the face value will be effectively returned to the investors through higher than normal cash payments every six months. Alternatively, if the coupon rate is lower than the market rate of return demanded by investors considering buying these B/P, the bonds' prices will be bid down below the face value of the B/P. Because the cash payments are not as large as the investors required at the time the B/P were issued, the investors will be rewarded at the end of the B/P term when receiving the face value of the B/P, an amount *larger* than the investors had paid when purchasing the B/P.

When BP are issued for *more* than face value, the excess is recorded in a special account called the **Premium on Bonds Payable**, an 'adjunct' account because it carries a credit balance as does the B/P account. When bonds are issued for *less* than face value, the difference is accounted in the Discount on Bonds Payable. The **Discount on Bonds Payable** is a 'contra' account because it carries a debit balance in contrast to the B/P account.

The carrying value of B/P issued at a premium is the B/P account at face value *plus* the Premium on B/P. The carrying value of B/P issued at a premium has to be greater than the face value (maturity value). Alternatively, the carrying value of B/P issued at a discount has to be *less* than the face value (maturity value). The carrying value of B/P issued at a discount is the BP account at face value *less* the Discount on BP. Consider these important relationships:

As we will soon see, Premiums and Discounts are both amortized to zero over the lifetime of the BP. For now, consider the effects of amortizing a Premium. What would amortizing a Premium do to the carrying value of bonds issued at a premium? *[The carrying value would decrease over time.]*

What would amortizing the Discount on Bonds Payable do to the carrying value of bonds issued at a discount? *[The carrying value would increase over time.]*

Consider this graphic representation of the results of amortizing premiums or discounts.

B/P issued at a premium will have carrying values *decreasing* over their lifetimes. B/P issued at a discount will have *increasing* carrying values over their lifetimes.

Let's calculate the issue price for the B/P in this example.

Bonds Payable: Issuance and Subsequent Accounting:
The Merle Company issued one bond with a maturity amount (face amount) of $1,000. This bond was issued on October 1, Year 1 and matures on October 1, Year 5. The effective rate being earned by the investors is 10% while the coupon rate (stated rate) of interest is 12%. The bond pays interest on October 1 and April 1. For simplicity, you may ignore the need for adjusting journal entries in this exercise.

Calculating the issue price of the bond from the data above:

Issue price = [$Int. Payment][PV Ann. Factor N=8 and I=5%] + [$Face][PV of a Single Payment N=8 and I=5%]
$Interest Payment = **$60.00**= Face Value x Coupon Rate x time= $1,000 x 12% x ½
[PV Annuity Factor N=8 and I=5%] =   **6.46321**
$Face =   **$1,000**
[PV of a Single Payment N=8 and I=5%] =   **.67684**

Issue Price = **$1,064.63**

Now, let's create the journal entries made throughout the life of the bond.

October 1, Year 1
    Cash $1,064.63
        Bonds Payable   1,000.00
        Premium on B/P   64.63
Carrying Value = $1,064.63

April 1, Year 2
    Interest expense   53.23
    Premium on B/P   6.77
        Cash   60.00
Interest Expense: $1,064.63 x 5% x 6/12 = $53.23
New Carrying Value = $1,057.86

October 1, Year 2
    Interest expense   52.89
    Premium on B/P   7.11
        Cash   60.00
Interest Expense: $1,057.86 x 5% x 6/12 = $52.89
New Carrying Value = $1,050.75

April 1, Year 3
    Interest expense   52.53
    Premium on B/P   7.46
        Cash   60.00
Interest Expense: $1,050.75 x 5% x 6/12 = $52.53
New Carrying Value = $1,043.29

October 1, Year 3
    Interest expense   52.16
    Premium on B/P   7.84
        Cash   60.00
Interest Expense: $1,043.29 x 5% x 6/12 = $52.16
New Carrying Value = $1,035.45

April 1, Year 4
  Interest expense   51.77
    Premium on B/P   8.23
      Cash   60.00
Interest Expense: $1,035.45 × 5% × 6/12 = $51.77
New Carrying Value = $1,027.22

October 1, Year 4
  Interest expense   51.36
    Premium on B/P   8.64
      Cash   60.00
Interest Expense: $1,027.22 × 5% × 6/12 = $51.36
New Carrying Value = $1,018.58

April 1, Year 5
  Interest expense   53.93
    Premium on BP   9.07
      Cash   60.00
Interest Expense: $1,018.58 × 5% × 6/12 = $50.93
New Carrying Value = $1,009.51

October 1, Year 5
  Interest expense   *50.49
    Premium on B/P   *9.51
      Cash   60.00
Interest Expense: $1,009.51 × 5% × 6/12 = $50.49*
New Carrying Value = $1,000.00
*Adjusted to cause the Premium account to have a zero balance after the October 1, Year interest payment has been made and recorded.

October 1, Year 5
  Bonds Payable   1,000.00
    Cash   1,000.00
This shows the payment of the 'lump sum payment' on the bond's maturity date. The two journal entries on October 1, Year 5, could be done together.

Let's examine another example but where the bond is issued at a *discount*.
The Hopkins Company issued one bond on August 1, Year 1 that matures at $1,000.00 on August 1, Year 4. This bond pays interest semiannually on August 1 and February 1. The stated rate (coupon rate) of interest is 9% while the effective rate of interest for the investors is 12%.

Let's first calculate the issue price:

Issue price = [$Int. Payment][PV Ann. Factor N=6 and I=6%] + [$Face][PV of a Single Payment N=6 and I=6%]
$Interest Payment = **$45.00**= Face Value x Coupon Rate x time= $1,000 x 9% x ½
[PV Annuity Factor N=6 and I=6%] = **4.91732**
$Face = **$1,000**
[PV of a Single Payment N=6 and I=6%] = **.70496**

Issue Price = **$926.24**

August 1, Year 1
    Cash $926.24
    Discount on B/P   73.76
        Bonds Payable   1,000.00
Carrying Value = $926.24 = $1,000.00 - $73.76

February 1, Year 2
    Interest expense   55.57
        Discount on B/P   10.57
        Cash   45.00
Interest Expense: $926.24 x 6% x 6/12 = $55.57
New Carrying Value = $936.81 = $926.24 + $10.57

August 1, Year 2
    Interest expense   56.21
        Discount on B/P   11.21
        Cash   45.00
Interest Expense: $936.81 x 6% x 6/12 = $56.21
New Carrying Value = $948.02 = $936.81 + $11.21

February 1, Year 3
    Interest expense   56.88
        Discount on B/P   11.88
        Cash   45.00
Interest Expense: $948.02 x 6% x 6/12 = $56.88
New Carrying Value = $959.90 = $948.02 + $11.88

August 1, Year 3
    Interest expense   57.59
        Discount on B/P   12.59
        Cash   45.00
Interest Expense: $959.90 x 6% x 6/12 = $57.59
New Carrying Value = $972.49 = $959.90 + $12.59

February 1, Year 4
    Interest expense   58.35
        Discount on B/P   13.35
        Cash   45.00

Interest Expense: $972.49 \times 6\% \times 6/12 = \$58.35$
New Carrying Value = $985.84 = \$972.49 + \$13.35$

August 1, Year 4
    Interest expense   *59.16
        Discount on B/P   *14.16
        Cash   45.00

Interest Expense: $985.84 \times 6\% \times 6/12 = \$59.15$
New Carrying Value = $\$1,000.00 = \$985.84 + \$14.16*$

August 1, Year 4
    Bonds Payable   1,000.00
        Cash   1,000.00

To pay off the 'face' amount on August 1, Year 4. The two journal entries on August 1, Year 4 could have been done as one entry.

Variable Rates and Borrowing Transactions

Liabilities with variable rates are also known as 'adjustable' rate loans. Lenders are usually willing to lend at lower rates when the rates can be adjusted later to reflect then current market rates. Alternatively, if lending at a fixed rate for a long-term, the interest rates are usually higher to allow for future inflation and other financial risks not known at the present time. Borrowers find lower interest rates attractive and may be willing to face the risks of future adjustments in rates [up or down] in exchange for the lower interest rate in the present. These same borrowers are hoping that interest rates will not rise over time and dreaming that those rates might even fall. Usually 'yield curves' are upward sloping indicating that borrowing/lending money at the shorter end of the spectrum involves lower interest rates.

Conceptually, when the interest rate is adjusted, the *carrying value* of the liability at that time becomes the *present value* in the equation below. The *new* interest rate and the *remaining* number of payments to maturity provide the 'I' and the 'N' when finding the factor from the table of present values of an annuity. We can then determine the new payment size for use until the interest rate is adjusted again according to the terms of the note.

Present Value = (PV of Annuity Factor) ($Payment Size)

Consider this example of an adjustable rate N/P.

A firm has negotiated an adjustable rate N/P in exchange for receiving $600,000 cash on April 1, Year 1. The initial interest rate is 8% and equal quarterly payments are required on July 1, October 1, and January 1 and April 1. This note was to be amortized over five years. The interest rate is adjusted each year on April 1 using a widely-known interest rate index.

Required: Calculate the *new* payment size if, after making four payments to the lender, the interest rate is adjusted to 12% on April 1, Year 2.

First, we must determine the amount of each payment to be made *prior* to the first adjustment of the rate on April 1, Year 2.

Present Value = (PV of Annuity Factor) ($Payment Size)
$600,000 = (27.35548, N=40, I=2%) ($Payment Size)
$Payment Size = $21,933.45

Now, let's determine the *carrying value* of the loan after the first four payments. This carrying value will be the present value of the remaining 36 payments at the original interest rate. Recall, that the carrying value equals the present value in this equation still using the original interest rate. [The 'high-tech' approach explained earlier. ☺]

Present Value = (PV of Annuity Factor) ($Payment Size)
Present Value = (25.48884, N=36, I=2%) ($21,933.45)
Present Value = $559,058.25

We could have obtained this same carrying value tediously by recording the first four journal entries at the times of the first four loan payments. [The low-tech approach. ☹]

Now, treating the carrying value of the note on April 1, Year 2, as the present value in the familiar equation below we have:

Present Value = (PV of Annuity Factor) ($Payment Size)
$559,058.25 = (21.83225, N=36, I=3%) ($Payment Size)
$Payment Size = $25,606.99 for the payments starting on July 1, Year 2

Now, assume the interest rate will be adjusted upward to 16% on April 1, Year 3. First, we must obtain the carrying value of the note after making four payments of $25,606.99.

Carrying Value = (PV of Annuity Factor) ($Payment Size)
Carrying Value = (20.38877, N=32, I=3%) ($25,606.99)
Carrying Value = $522,094.92

Then, solving for the size of payments starting on July 1, Year 3, in the familiar way:

Present Value = (PV of Annuity Factor) ($Payment Size)
$522,094.92 = (17.87355, N=32, I=4%) ($Payment Size)
$Payment Size = $29,210.48 for the payments starting on July 1, Year 3

Identifying Annuity Cases Requiring Use of Present Value Tables and Cases Requiring Use of Future Value Tables

Suppose you are buying a speedboat at a cost of $60,000 and you wish to finance $45,000 of the purchase price. You plan to pay off the portion financed by making 36 monthly payments at an interest rate of 12%. The payments and the compounding will be monthly starting one month after your purchase of the car. How large will each of the payments be?

Is this a present value or a future value of an annuity problem? [This is a *present value* problem. The amount financed equals the *present value* of the 36 monthly payments that will amortize the loan.]

How large will *each* payment be?
[Answer: $1,494.64 determined as follows:
Present Value = (PV of Annuity Factor, N=36, I=1%) ($Payment Size)
$45,000 = (30.10751)($Payment Size)
$Payment Size = $1,494.64]

Some business situations make it desirable to accumulate a sum of money for a future purpose. Suppose you seek to accumulate $500,000 over the next four years. You have identified a bank that will pay 12% per year compounded bi-monthly. How much do you have put into the account starting in two months and every two months thereafter to accumulate $500,000 in exactly four years from today's date?

Is this a present value or a future value of an annuity problem? [This is a *future value* problem since the payments will be accumulating at interest over the four years to $500,000.]

How large must each of the 24 payments be to accomplish the goal? [$16,435.55 determined as follows:
Future Value = (FV of Annuity Factor, N=24, I=2%) ($Payment Size)
$500,000 = (30.42186)($Payment Size)
$Payment Size = $16,435.55

Handy Way to Differentiate 'Future Value' and 'Present Value' Situations

If the *interest and* the *payments* both *increase* the 'balance' in the account, it is a future value situation.

If the *interest increases* the balance in the account and the payments *decrease* the balance in the account, it is a present value situation.

In the first of the preceding examples, interest increased the amount owed to the bank and the payments decreased the amount owed to the bank (present value situation). In the second of the preceding examples, interest increased the balance in the bank and the payments also increased the balance in the bank (future value situation).

Comprehensive Example of Fixed Rate Notes Payable and Bonds Payable

The Piketty Company decided to borrow $22,718 on December 31, Year 1. The firm was considering two options: issuing twenty B/P and signing a N/P. Under both options, the firm would receive $22,718 as a result of the borrowing transaction. The face value of each bond is $1,000. Thus, the face value of all twenty bonds is $20,000.

The N/P would bear interest at a rate of 10% and require six equal annual payments starting on December 31, Year 2. The note would be entirely amortized by making the six payments.

The bonds would pay interest semiannually on June 30 and December 31. The bonds would have a coupon rate of 10% and the effective [market] rate of interest on the bonds would be 8%. The bonds have a maturity date of December 31, Year 11. The first interest payment would be due on June 30, Year 2.

1. What would be the carrying value of the N/P on December 31, Year 2 after the payment on that day had been properly recorded? $_____?

[Answer: $19,744. One way to establish the carrying value would be to record the journal entry on December 31, Year 2 and to determine the carrying value after the journal entry had been recorded.

$5,216 is the annual payment required by the terms of the note. [$22,718= (4.35526, N=6, I=10%) (Payment Size)] On December 31, Year 2:

Interest Expense	$2,272	
Note Payable	2,944	
Cash		5,216

The carrying value at December 31, Year 2, after recording the payment on that date would be: $19,774 = $22,718 - $2,944

Another way to obtain the same answer would be to determine the present value (carrying value) on December 31, Year 2 of the remaining five payments. This is the 'high-tech' approach. ☺

(Present Value) = (3.79079, N=5, I=10%) ($5,216)
Present Value = $19,773 (differences due to rounding)

2. How much Interest Expense would Piketty Company recognize during Year 3 as a result of issuing the NP? $_____?

Answer: $1,977
Interest expense in Year 3= (carrying value at the start of Year 3)(interest rate)(time)
$1,977 = ($19,773)(10%)(1)

3. How much interest expense would Piketty Company recognize during Year 2 if it chooses to issue the twenty B/P? $_____?

[Answer: $1,814
Total Interest Expense for Year 2 on the bonds would be $1,814. [$909 + $905]

First, let's establish the issue price of the bonds was $22,718.
Issue Price = ($Int. Payment)(F, N=20, I=4%) + ($Face amount)(F, N=20,I=4%)
$Interest Payment = $Face amount x 5% = $20,000 x 5% = $1,000
$Face amount = $10,000
$22,718= ($1,000)(13.59033, N=20, I=4%) + ($20,000)(.45639, N=20,I=4%)

Second, Interest Expense for the first six months of Year 2 would be determined from the carrying value of the bonds on December 31, Year 1.

Interest Expense ($22,718 x 4% x 1)	$909	
Premium on Bonds Payable	91	
Cash		1,000

New Carrying Value on June 30, Year 2: $22,627 = $22,718 - $91

Third, Interest Expense for the last six months of Year 2 would be determined from the carrying value of the bonds on June 30, Year 2.

Interest Expense ($22,627 x 4% x 1)	$905	
Premium on Bonds Payable	95	
Cash		1,000

New Carrying Value on December 31, Year 2: $22,532 = $22,627 - $95

4. What would be the carrying value of the twenty B/P in the books of the Piketty Company on December 31, Year 4 after the interest payment for that day had been properly recorded? $_____?

[Answer: $22,113*. The answer can be most easily determined by calculating the carrying value of the bonds on December 31, Year 4, after the interest payment for that day had been properly recorded.
$Carrying Value = ($Int. Payment)(F, N=14, I=4%) + ($Face)(F, N=14, I=4%)
$Carrying Value = ($1,000)(10.56312) + ($20,000)(.57748)
$Carrying Value = $10,563 + $11,550= $22,113*]

Owners' Equity Topics Including Common and Preferred Shares, Dividends, Treasury Stock and Earnings Per Share Considerations

Topic 12
This topic ties to chapter 14 in the SSD text.

Assets = Liabilities + OE
This familiar equation gives us the basic structure of the B/S and creates the role played by OE (also known as 'net assets'). OE as measured in the B/S would likely differ widely from OE measured at fair market values because of the significant limitations in both the historical accounting model and GAAP with respect to many important economic developments.

What Are the Important Differences Between Liabilities and Equity?
Liabilities are characterized by maturity dates and often involve Interest Expense if the debt resulted from a borrowing transaction. Equity positions do not have due dates and do not have any Interest Expense. The cost associated with using equity capital (cost of capital) is not explicitly or implicitly recognized in the FS.

Which Is the Riskier Source of Capital?
Most people instinctively respond by saying that debt is the riskier of the two. In business, if a firm is primarily concerned with the risk of bankruptcy, then I might agree in that context that debt is the riskier. But for entities where bankruptcy is a theoretical possibility relative to the firm's attempts to create value for the shareholders, equity is the riskier source of capital. If you don't meet your contractual obligations with debt holders, then bankruptcy is the extreme result [the less serious result might be having lackluster credit ratings]. If you do not meet the expectations of your owners, then share prices decline and access to further equity capital infusions becomes far more difficult [or the terms of such infusions make them undesirable].

Understanding the risks of debt and equity to the firm is easy if you consider which investment vehicle is the more risky to the *investor*. No doubt you already knew that equity investments were more risky that debt investments when considered from the *investor's* perspective.

What is Return on Equity About?
Return on equity [ROE] is a ratio expressing the relationship between income available to equity holders (numerator) and OE in the B/S (denominator). Both numerator and denominator are expressed in values measured according to GAAP. I use this discussion to build a bridge between the roles of debt and equity in an entity and to show how financial leverage can be favorable sometimes and unfavorable at others.

Let's Look at Some Examples In Which We Compute Return on Equity Measures

Calculating ROE

The Alliance Company was formed on January 1, Year 1 when its three owners each invested $40,000 into the firm. One of them *lent* the firm an additional $100,000 at an interest rate of 10%.

The firm is considering several options and has asked you to compute the firm's ROE under each of the alternatives.

Required: Compute the return on equity (ROE) for each of the following *independent* alternatives.

Alternative #1: If the firm could earn 20% return on assets, the firm's ROE would be ____%. [28.333% = [($220,000)(20%) –($100,000)(10%)] / $120,000]

Alternative #2: If the firm could earn 30% return on assets, the firm's ROE would be ____%. [46.667% = [($220,000)(30%) –($100,000)(10%)] / $120,000]

Alternative #3: The firm is considering borrowing *an additional* $100,000 at an interest rate of 15%. The extra cash would then be invested in assets with none of the cash being used to repay the original loan from one of the owners. If the firm could earn a rate of return on assets of 20% **and** the firm did borrow the additional $100,000, the firm's ROE would be ____%. [32.5% = [($320,000)(20%) –($100,000)(10%) – ($100,000)(15%)] / $120,000]

Alternative 4: Instead of borrowing the additional $100,000 as described in #3 above, the firm is considering allowing another equity investor into the firm. The proposed new investor would invest $100,000 equity in the firm. If the firm would invest all of the incremental $100,000 in assets and the return on assets would be 20%, the firm's ROE would be ____%. [24.545% = [($320,000)(20%) –($100,000)(10%)] / $220,000]

One final question on ROE issues: If the firm has no debt, what is the relationship between return on assets and ROE? [ROA and ROE are identical when the firm has no debt.]

Variability in ROE measures comes from variability in the ROA and also reflects the firm's degree of financial leverage.

Does It Matter Whether the Enterprise Organizes as a Partnership or as a Corporation?
The discussion in the textbook regarding the *form* of organization is interesting and informative. Today, there are hybrid forms of organization available from which to choose. The important points for business founders involve the issue of investors' levels of liability for *business* debts and the issue of whether the business profits should be taxed at the corporate level or at the individual level. The corporate form of enterprise dominates the business landscape and generally provides investors with liability that is limited to the amount of their *investment* (**limited liability**). The corporate form of

enterprise requires that corporate income tax be assessed on *corporate* profits and then income tax is applied again at the investor level on any dividends received from the corporation (***double taxation***). In this topic, we will assume the *corporate form* of organization because the frequency of its selection indicates it is the preferred organizational form.

What Are the Basic Forms of Equity Investments Within a Firm?
The basic equity investments within a firm are preferred and common shares. Preferred shares appear to be the more important from the description that follows but appearances are deceiving. Preferred equity investments are *insignificant* sources of equity capital for almost all corporations. If preferred shares exist at all, it is usually in response to some special desire by some investors. The vast majority of equity investment is in common shares. I will mention the basic preferences extended contractually to some investors in 'preferred' shares and will cover those characteristics in detail or in examples.

The basic preferences extended to preferred shareholders may include (a) the right to be 'paid off' first in the event of corporate liquidation, (b) the right to be paid dividends in full and first when dividends are declared by the board of directors, (c) the right to be paid later if for any previous year(s) the full amount of dividends were not paid to the preferred shareholders, and (d) the right to participate in 'mega' dividends that might be declared by the board on an irregular basis.

What Are the Important Distinctions Between Contributed Capital and Retained Capital?
Generally, owners invested the CC and RE was earned and kept within the firm. We will complicate this fundamental relationship as we move through this lecture. GAAP is based on users of FS being reasonably well informed about accounting rules and, thus, able to understand information in the FS as well as its limitations.

The textbook correctly describes the relationship between 'par' values, 'additional paid-in capital' and RE. The more valuable distinction for our purposes is between CC and retained capital. The legal necessity to account for 'par' values has been substantially and recently reduced.

When investors in the corporation make investments in the firm, the firm will increase the contributed capital component in the OE section. When the firm earns income, the RE account will increase (retained capital). Dividends in any form will decrease RE.

What journal entry is made when issuing shares?
Debit Cash for the amount received and credit CC for the same amount.

    Cash $XXX
            Contributed Capital   XXX

What Are Treasury Shares [T/S] and How Do They Differ From Other Investments?
T/S (Treasury Stock) result when the firm repurchases shares from its own shareholders. It appears that the firm owns part of itself, but the correct perspective is that the

remaining shareholders actually own a larger portion of the firm than they had previously owned. The *remaining* shareholders each own a *relatively larger portion* of the corporation that they owned prior to the purchase of the T/S.

If I own 500 shares of a corporation (5% ownership interest) and the firm 'buys out' the entire interest of another investor who had owned 1,000 shares of the firm, what percentage of the firm do I own *after* the purchase of T/S by the corporation? [5.55% = 500 shares / [10,000 – 1,000 shares]

How Are Treasury Shares Accounted for in the Balance Sheet of the Corporation?
Treasury shares are contra OE accounts reducing OE. Treasury Shares are not 'investments' and are not treated as assets in the corporation's B/S. In terms of debits and credits, Treasury Shares is a debit balance account that is presented in the OE section as a *reduction* in total OE. The typical OE accounts are normal credits and T/S, as a debit balance account, makes total OE *smaller*.

A small example to illustrate the basic principles will help.

The Chris Crafty Corporation has assets of $15,000 and liabilities of $4,200. The firm spends $300 cash to buy shares back from some of its shareholders. What dollar amount of OE is there *after* the purchase of these T/S is completed? [$10,500 = $10,800 - $300]

Normally, the corporation cannot spend more on T/S than the balance in the RE account. Distributing assets to any shareholders reduces the assets available to satisfy claims of the corporation's creditors. Corporate law normally prohibits companies from intentionally causing the total OE to be less than CC. The firm's creditors generally consider CC to be available to satisfy their claims in the event of a corporate liquidation. [Note: there is no legal prohibition to having less total equity than CC if this results from corporate losses.]

Why Would a Corporation Want to Buy Back Some of Its Own Shares?
There are many different motives for buying back some of a firm's own shares. One frequently cited reason is to have shares available for issuance to employees when they might exercise their options to purchase shares as part of a stock option plan *while avoiding* dilution of the earnings per share [EPS]. [See also the EPS coverage later in this lecture.)

Another motive is to take advantage of temporary decreases in the price of the firm's shares. Shares repurchase plans are announced in advance and cannot be based on inside information. For example, if the firm might have knowledge that a subsequent earnings announcement or some other good news would be released it would be illegal for the firm to buy shares based on non-public information the same as for any individual to trade on non-public information. When firms announce **stock repurchase plans**, usually there is a commitment to spend up to a specified dollar amount over an extended period of time.

Then within the scope of the announced plans, firms will buy shares on a day-to-day basis being careful not to inappropriately manipulate share prices in the process.

In pursuing a stock repurchase plan, the normal impact on the price is positive because the firm is indicating that it thinks the firm's share prices make the shares attractive *even for the firm* to buy. There is another more basic reason why the share price might move upward, the firm yet is another buyer of the shares. The normal increase in share price is definitely not automatic. If the market participants sense the firm has nothing better to do with the money than to buy back shares, the marketplace may react in a negative way to the firm's future prospects of generating cash for the long run.

The firm may plan to use the shares in some future acquisition and want to avoid using unissued shares to consummate the acquisition. Occasionally, when announcing an acquisition for cash, stock or a combination of the two, the acquirer's stock price will fall. Commonly cited reasons for the stock price decline include the prospective earnings dilution from the acquisition or the fear the acquirer has paid too much in the deal. If an intended future acquisition was to be consummated using recently purchased treasury shares, the dilution concern would be reduced.

What If Some or All of the Treasury Shares Are Sold Later?
When *buying* T/S, the firm will debit T/S for the cost of the shares and credit cash for the same amount. Visually, the journal entry looks like this:

Treasury Shares	$XXX	
Cash		XXX

Later, if *selling* some or all of the shares for *more* than had been paid on a per share basis to buy them the firm will make the following entry:

Cash	$XXXX	
Contributed Capital from T/S		X
Treasury Shares		XXX

I can make these relationships intuitive. The shares were sold for *more* than had been paid to buy them. We recognize this as an economic profit. However, dealing in your own shares cannot produce any increase in the firm's net income so we could not correctly credit Gain on Sale of T/S. Similarly, this economic gain is not taxable either. At a more basic level, the debit to Cash has to be larger than the credit to T/S because, after all, the shares were sold for *more* than had been paid to buy them…..☺.

If some of the T/S were to be sold for *less* than what had been paid to buy them, we would need a debit to balance the entry showing the difference between the amount paid to buy them earlier and the amount received for them now. The first place we look is to determine if there is a Contributed Capital from T/S transactions with a credit balance sufficient to absorb the necessary debit. [This account would exist if earlier T/S sales transactions had been for prices *higher* than had been paid to buy those shares.] If the account exists and has a sufficient credit balance to absorb the debit we need to balance the present entry, then we are done. However, if the Contributed Capital from T/S account does not exist *or* if it does not have a big enough credit balance to 'handle' the debit needed to balance the present entry, then we must put the rest of the necessary debit into RE. [We cannot cause the Contributed Capital from T/S transactions account to have a *debit* balance. There is not a problem if it does not exist or if it has a credit balance.] The journal entry to record a sale of T/S for less than had been paid to buy them earlier might look like this:

Cash	$XXX	
Contributed Capital from T/S (possibly)	X	
Retained Earnings (possibly)	X	
Treasury Shares		XXXX

The method explained above is the cost method of accounting for treasury shares. There is another method that is acceptable [GAAP] but I will not hold you accountable for it. It is the par value method.

Let's try a little example to see how well this is working for you.

Accounting for T/S:

The Kyle Company has 30,000 shares of its common shares outstanding. In its first ever, T/S transaction, the firm bought 2,000 of these shares when the fair market value of the stock was $35 per share. Several weeks later the firm sold 600 of these shares for $60 per share. Several months later the firm sold 400 of the remaining T/S for $32 per share.

1. What is the journal entry to record the purchase of 2,000 shares of T/S? [Debit T/S and credit Cash, both for $70,000.]

2. What is the journal entry to record the sale of 600 of the treasury shares at $60 per share? [Debit Cash for $36,000. Credits to T/S for $21,000 and to Contributed Capital from T/S Transactions for $15,000.]

3. What is the journal entry to record the sale of 300 of the treasury shares at $32 per share? [Debit Cash for $9,600. Debit to Contributed Capital from T/S Transactions for $900. Credit T/S for $10,500.]

4. What is the balance in to Contributed Capital from T/S Transactions after transaction '3' above? [$14,100]

5. On a related note, what is the balance in T/S after all three of the above transactions had been properly recorded? [$38,500 = $35/share x 1,100 shares]

Cash Dividends: What Steps Are Involved Here?
The board of directors has the exclusive authority to declare dividends when the declaration and payment of these dividends will not cause liquidity problems for the firm. I will assume the dividend meets all of the legal requirements. We will assume throughout that the declaration of dividends would not cause a legal problem or a liquidity problem. In real world situations these potential problems cannot be so easily assumed away.

When the board declares a dividend, RE is debited and Dividends Payable is credited for the cash to be distributed on the payment date. The board also selects a date of record on which the parties to receive the dividend on the payment date are determined. No journal entry is needed on the date of record. On the date of payment, the journal entry to record the payment involves a debit to Dividends Payable and credit to Cash.

The shareholders are unsecured creditors of the corporation between declaring the dividend are declared and the payment date.

How are Stock Dividends Different Than Cash Dividends?
Stock dividends involve distributing additional shares to the current shareholders *in proportion* to their current holdings. No cash is involved. If a 10% stock dividend is declared, then each shareholder will receive *additional shares* equal to 10% of their current holdings.

Accounting principles for stock dividends hinge on whether the stock dividend is considered large or small. A small stock dividend is 20% or smaller. A large stock dividend is 25% or larger. While stock dividends between 20%-25% are possible, we will not cover them in any examples here. GAAP indicates that stock dividends between 20-25% must be treated with professional judgment.

How Do We Account for Small Stock Dividends?
Small stock dividends are accounted for at their *fair market value* on the date of declaration. The shares will not be distributed until the date of distribution (payment). The journal entry involves debiting RE for the fair market value of the shares to be distributed later and crediting CC. Consider what this journal entry does to total OE. [Total OE is unchanged when declaring a small stock dividend. RE decreases and CC increases.

How Do We Account for Large Stock Dividends?

Large stock dividends are accounted for at their board-designated value and not at their fair market values on the declaration date. When declared, large stock dividends involve a debit to RE and a credit to CC for the board-designated value of the shares to be distributed on the distribution date. Consider what this journal entry does to total OE. [Total OE is unaffected by declaring a large stock dividend. RE decreases and CC increases.]

Is a Stock Split Different Than a Stock Dividend?
Yes, stock splits are different than stock dividends. In a stock split only the board-designated value and the number of shares outstanding change. In a 2-for-1 stock split, the number of shares doubles and the board-designated value is cut in half. The total effect on CC is nil. This analogy seems appropriate: If you have ten $20 bills and changed them at the bank for forty $5 bills you would have the same amount of money as you started with. This example would be analogous to a 4-for-1 stock split. No journal entry is required with stock splits. The real reason I mention stock splits at all is for you to avoid any confusion between stock dividends and stock splits.

Let's work through an example involving large and small stock dividends.

Various Topics Related to Common and Preferred Shares:

1. Issuance of Shares: The Hopkins Company issued 50,000 common shares for $640,000 cash early in Year 1. The land is worth one-fourth what the building is worth.

Show the journal entry to record the issuance of these shares. [Debit Buildings for $480,000 and Land for $160,000. (This is the equivalent of the 'basket purchase' methodology explained with PPE.) Credit CC for $640,000.]

2. In Year 1, The Hopkins Company had Net Income of $400,000. Early in Year 2, the firm decided to issue a 40% common stock dividend when the shares had a fair market value of $110 per share. The board of directors determined that these shares warrant a CC valuation of $300,000. No cash dividends were paid in Year 2. During Year 2, the firm had Net Income of $500,000.

Determine the firm's ending RE balance at December 31, Year 2, as a result of this information. [$400,000 -$300,000 + $500,000 = **$600,000**]

3. Early in Year 3, the firm decided to distribute a 20% common stock dividend when the fair market value of the common shares was $20 each. Net Income in Year 3 was $500,000. The firm declared and distributed a cash dividend in November Year 3 in the amount of $200,000.

Determine the firm's ending RE balance at December 31, Year 3 as a result of this information. [$600,000 as determined above -$280,000* + $500,000 - $200,000 = **$620,000**]

*(50,000 shares + 20,000 shares) x 20% = 14,000 shares
14,000 shares @ $20 per share = $280,000

4. Early in Year 4, the firm declared and distributed a '3 for 1' stock split when the fair market value of each common share was $40. Cash dividends declared and distributed late in Year 4 amounted to $160,000. Net Income for Year 4 was $200,000.

Determine the firm's Ending RE balance at December 31, Year 4 as a result of this information. [$620,000 as determined above - $160,000 + $200,000 = $660,000]

How Can We Interpret the Cumulative Balance in the RE Account?
Earlier in the semester we could answer this question easier than at this time. That's the problem with increasing your knowledge. More knowledge makes things *more* complicated ☹. Earlier, all we had to consider was income increasing RE and dividends decreasing RE. Now, large and small stock dividends both *reduce* RE while *increasing* Contributed Capital.

Why Would Firms Issue Stock Dividends?
The most likely answers would be either to 'cheer up' the shareholders by giving them 'something' or to reduce the fair market values of the shares in the marketplace. As the stock dividend percentage gets bigger, the latter reason probably becomes the dominant motivation.

What Is Comprehensive Income and How Does It Differ From Net Income?
Comprehensive income includes everything that is part of net income plus/minus each item that increases or decreases OE other than transactions with the owners. One example of an item that would so adjust net income comes from the investments lecture where saw that the Valuation Allowance for the AFS portfolio and a special OE account (Unrealized Gains/Losses on AFS) would go up or down in response to changes in the fair market value of the securities in the AFS portfolio.

In the OE section of the B/S, there is a caption titled Accumulated Other Comprehensive Income. This caption contains cumulatively all of the differences between net income and comprehensive income for current and previous periods. The best way to see how all this ties together is in the following graphic:

How Are Earnings Per Share Computed?

The goal of earnings per share [EPS] disclosures is to express the firm's income available to common shareholders *on a per share basis* to help users of the FS have a better 'feel' for how much income 'belongs' to one share. EPS is inherently a *per common share* concept. Probably it could be better titled 'earnings per (common) share' in order to isolate out any part of net income that flows to the benefit of preferred shareholders and not to common shareholders.

Let's assume there are no preferred shares, or almost the equivalent, that the portion of Net Income 'belonging' to the preferred shareholders is immaterial. This will allow us to see the important concepts in a less cluttered manner. Net Income is placed in the numerator of a fraction and the weighted average of the common shares outstanding for the period is placed in the denominator. The fraction equals EPS.

Do not be 'spooked' by the phrase 'weighted average of the common shares outstanding'. This average is computed to acknowledge that some shares may not have been outstanding for the entire period. For example, if the firm issued 8,000 shares on May 31, Year 3, those shares would enter into the EPS calculations for all of Year 3 as 4,667 shares [8,000 shares x 7/12]. Shares issued in stock dividends or splits are treated as having been issued at the *start* of their issuance year simplifying our work since that means they were outstanding for the *entire* year ☺.

Why Do Some Firms Have *Two* EPS Numbers Presented in Their Income Statements?

To this point, accountants describe these calculations as the basic EPS disclosure since they do not consider any of the possible future dilutions that might occur as a result of the firm having issued convertible securities [convertible bonds and/or convertible preferred shares]. Moreover, the potential dilutions from stock option plans and similar arrangements have not been considered. The important point for you to take away from this discussion is this: when there are *two* EPS disclosures, the first is the basic EPS disclosure as described above and the second shows the level to which the basic EPS value could be lowered as a result of dilutive securities (etc.) outstanding at this time.

If a security is currently antidilutive it is ignored for the purposes of the current EPS calculations. In a later period, however, these securities might become dilutive and might be included at that time in the EPS calculations.

Cash Basis and Accrual Basis of Accounting: [1084a]
1. $2,300, $700 and $2,300, respectively.
2. $2,400, $500 and $3,300, respectively.
3. Net credit $500, net debit $300 and net credit $300, respectively.
4. Net prepayment of $400, net liability of $200 and net liability of $600, respectively.

Cash Basis and Accrual Basis of Accounting: [1085a]
5. $2,300, $700 and $2,300, respectively.
6. $2,400, $500 and $3,300, respectively.
7. Net credit $500, net debit $300 and net credit $300, respectively.
8. Net prepayment of $400, net liability of $200 and net liability of $600, respectively.

Financial Statement Relationships: [1086a]
Directions: Respond to each of the requirements below. The questions are independent unless otherwise noted.

1. $550
2. $3,500
3. $15,000
4. $9,600
5. $2,500
6. $900
7. $3,500
8. $2,000
9. Increase by $100,000
10. Decrease $50,000

Financial Statement Relationships: [1087a]

	Balance Sheet			Income Statement	
Assets	Liabilities	Owners' Equity	Revenues	Expenses	Income
1. +	+				
2. + -					
3.	no changes			no changes	
4. -		-		+	-
5. +		+			
6. + -					
7. -	+	-		+	-
8. -	-				
9. +		+	+		+

Exercise on Journal Entries: [1088a]
Answers:
1. Debits to Cash for $76,000 and Land for $10,000. Credits to Notes Payable for $20,000 and Owners' Equity for $66,000. Debit Interest Expense and credit Interest Payable both for $2,000.
2. Debits to Cash for $105,000 and Accounts Receivable for $71,000. Credits to Unearned Revenues for $90,000 and Revenues for $86,000.
3. Debits to Supplies Inventory for $8,000 and to Prepaid Supplies* for $1,000. Credit Cash for $9,000. [* an asset account]

Exercise on Journal Entries (continued): [1088a]
4. Debit Supplies Expense for $3,200 and credit Supplies Inventory for $3,200.
5. Debit Prepaid Rent for $6,000 and credit Cash for $6,000.
6. Debit Rent Expense for $500 and credit Prepaid Rent for $500.
7. Debit Salaries Expense for $30,000 and Prepaid Salaries for $6,000. Credits to Salaries Payable for $6,000 and Cash for $30,000.
8. Debits to Salaries Expense for $30,000. Credits to Prepaid Salaries for $6,000 and Cash for $24,000.
9. Debit Cash for $90,000 and credit Unearned Revenues for $90,000.
10. Debits to Cash for $25,000, Unearned Revenues for $90,000 and Accounts Receivable for $15,000. Credit Revenues for $130,000.

Exercise on Journal Entries: [1089a]
Answers:
1. Debit Cash for $35,000. Credits to Notes Payable for $10,000 and Owners' Equity for $25,000. At the end of the year, Debit Interest Expense and credit Interest Payable both for $1,100.
2. Debits to Cash for $40,000 and Accounts Receivable for $40,000. Credits to Revenues for $50,000 and Unearned Revenues for $30,000.
3. Debit Supplies Inventory for $5,000. Credits to Cash for $3,000 and Accounts Payable for $2,000.
4. Debit Supplies Expense for $4,000 and credit Supplies Inventory for $4,000.
5. Debit Prepaid Rent for $3,200 and credit Cash for $3,200.
6. Debit Rent Expense for $800 and credit Prepaid Rent for $800.
7. Debits to Salaries Expense for $10,000 and Prepaid Salaries for $5,000. Credit Cash for $15,000.
8. Debit Salaries Expense for $20,000. Credits to Prepaid Salaries for $5,000 and Cash for $15,000.
9. Debit Cash for $70,000. Credit Unearned Revenues for $70,000.
10. Debits to Unearned Revenues for $70,000 and Accounts Receivable for $50,000. Credit Revenues for $120,000.

Financial Statement Relationships: [1090a]

	Balance Sheet			Income Statement		
	Assets	Liabilities	Owners' Equity	Revenues	Expenses	Income
1.	+	-			No change	
2.		No change			No change	
3.	+	-			No change	
4.	-		-		+	-
5.	+		+			
6.	+	-				
7.	+	-		-	+	-
8.	+	+				
9.	++		+	+		+

Accounting for Advertising Costs: [1091a]
Year 1: -$0-
Year 2: $3,000,000
Year 3: -0-
 [The financial statements can be overly conservative due to accounting rules requiring advertising costs to be expensed because future economic benefits are difficult to estimate.]

Recording Transactions and Adjusting Journal Entries: [1092a]

Cash	$ 5,305	Consulting Revenues	$ 750
Prepaid Rent	40	Rent Revenue	-0-
Supplies Inventory	15	Rent Expense	200
Accounts Receivable	50	Supplies Expense	75
Prepaid Utilities	5	Utilities Expense	35
Prepaid Salaries	5	Salaries Expense	150
Accounts Payable	20		
Rent Payable	-0-		
Notes Payable	2,000		
Unearned Revenues	100		
Utilities Payable	-0-		
Salaries Payable	10		

Recording Transactions and Adjusting Journal Entries: [1093a]

Cash	$ 4,045	Consulting Revenues	$ 750
Prepaid Rent	20	Rent Revenue	-0-
Supplies Inventory	15	Rent Expense	100
Accounts Receivable	50	Supplies Expense	65
Prepaid Utilities	15	Utilities Expense	25
Prepaid Salaries	5	Salaries Expense	150
Accounts Payable	30		
Rent Payable	-0-		
Notes Payable	1,500		
Unearned Revenues	200		
Utilities Payable	-0-		
Salaries Payable	10		

Deriving Financial Statement Implications: [1094a]

1.
    __+90,000_ Total Assets   _____ Revenues
    __+20,000_ Total Liabilities   _____ Gains
    __+70,000_ Owners' Equity   _____ Expenses
    _____ Losses
    _____ Income

2.
    ___N/C___ Total Assets   _____ Revenues
    _____ Total Liabilities   _____ Gains
    _____ Owners' Equity   _____ Expenses
    _____ Losses
    _____ Income

3.
    ___+15,000 Total Assets   _____ Revenues
    _____ Total Liabilities   _+15,000_ Gains
    ___+15,000_ Owners' Equity   _____ Expenses
    _____ Losses
    __+15,000_ Income

4.
    ___+10,000_ Total Assets   _____ Revenues
    _____ Total Liabilities   ___+10,000_ Gains
    ___+10,000_ Owners' Equity   _____ Expenses
    _____ Losses
    ___+10,000_ Income

5.
    ___-1,000__ Total Assets   _____ Revenues
    ___+7,000__ Total Liabilities   _____ Gains
    ___-8,000__ Owners' Equity   __+8,000__ Expenses
    _____ Losses
    __-8,000___ Income

6.
    __+520,000_ Total Assets   _+500,000__ Revenues
    ___+20,000_ Total Liabilities   _____ Gains
    __+500,000_ Owners' Equity   _____ Expenses
    _____ Losses
    _+500,000__ Income

7.
    __-120,000_ Total Assets   _____ Revenues
    ___+30,000_ Total Liabilities   _____ Gains
    __-150,000_ Owners' Equity   _+150,000_Expenses
    _____ Losses
    __-150,000_ Income

8.
    ___N/C___ Total Assets   _____ Revenues
    _____ Total Liabilities   _____ Gains
    _____ Owners' Equity   _____ Expenses
    _____ Losses
    _____ Income

9.
    __-2,400___ Total Assets   _____ Revenues
    _____ Total Liabilities   _____ Gains
    __-2,400___ Owners' Equity   __+2,400__ Expenses
    _____ Losses
    __-2,400___ Income

Deriving Financial Statement Implications (continued): [1094a]

10.
- +700,000 Total Assets
- +250,000 Total Liabilities
- +450,000 Owners' Equity

- +450,000 Revenues
- _____ Gains
- _____ Expenses
- _____ Losses
- +450,000 Income

Deriving Financial Statement Implications: [1095a]

1.
- +75,000 Total Assets
- +15,000 Total Liabilities
- +60,000 Owners' Equity

- _____ Revenues
- _____ Gains
- _____ Expenses
- _____ Losses
- _____ Income

2.
- +630,000 Total Assets
- +30,000 Total Liabilities
- +600,000 Owners' Equity

- +600,000 Revenues
- _____ Gains
- _____ Expenses
- _____ Losses
- +600,000 Income

3.
- -160,000 Total Assets
- +40,000 Total Liabilities
- -200,000 Owners' Equity

- _____ Revenues
- _____ Gains
- +200,000 Expenses
- _____ Losses
- -200,000 Income

4.
- -2,000 Total Assets
- +8,000 Total Liabilities
- -10,000 Owners' Equity

- _____ Revenues
- _____ Gains
- +10,000 Expenses
- _____ Losses
- -10,000 Income

5.
- -1,200 Total Assets
- _____ Total Liabilities
- -1,200 Owners' Equity

- _____ Revenues
- _____ Gains
- +1,200 Expenses
- _____ Losses
- -1,200 Income

6.
- _____ Total Assets
- _____ Total Liabilities
- _____ Owners' Equity
- NO CHANGE AT ALL

- _____ Revenues
- _____ Gains
- _____ Expenses
- _____ Losses
- _____ Income

Deriving Financial Statement Implications (continued): [1095a]

7.
    ___N/C___ Total Assets   _____ Revenues
    _____ Total Liabilities   _____ Gains
    _____ Owners' Equity   _____ Expenses
                                                          _____ Losses
                                                          _____ Income

8.
    _+15,000_ Total Assets   _____ Revenues
    _____ Total Liabilities   _+15,000_ Gains
    _+15,000_ Owners' Equity   _____ Expenses
                                                            _____ Losses
                                                          _+15,000_ Income

9.
    _-10,000_ Total Assets   _____ Revenues
    _____ Total Liabilities   _____ Gains
    _-10,000_ Owners' Equity   _____ Expenses
                                                            +10,000___ Losses
                                                          _-10,000_ Income

10.
    _+650,000_ Total Assets   _+400,000_ Revenues
    _+250,000_ Total Liabilities   _____ Gains
    _+400,000_ Owners' Equity   _____ Expenses
                                                            _____ Losses
                                                          _+400,000_ Income

Assumptions, Principles and Conventions: [1096a]

1. __b__ .

2. _f_

3. __c__

4. __e__
5. _a or f_
6. _J_
7. _J_
8. __d__

Financial Statement Elements: [1097a]

1. Assets increase and owners' equity increases. [Gains increase and this causes the increase in owners' equity.]

2. Total Assets are unchanged. One asset goes up and another goes down.

3. Assets decrease and Liabilities decrease.

4. Assets increase and Owners' Equity increases. The increase in Owners' Equity is caused by Revenues being earned which causes income and the increase in Owners' Equity

Financial Statement Elements (continued): [1097a]
5. Assets increase and Liabilities increase.

6. Assets decrease and Liabilities decrease. The firm has some Expense for Interest that causes income to decrease. The decrease in income causes lower Owners' Equity.

7. Assets decrease and Owners' Equity decreases. The decrease in Owners' Equity is caused by an increase in expenses and a decrease in income.

8. Assets increase and Owners' Equity increases.

9. Assets decrease and Owners' Equity decreases. There is no expense when dividends are declared or paid.

10. Assets increase and Owners' Equity increases. The gain increases income and this causes the increase in Owners' Equity.

Financial Statement Elements: [1098a]
1. [A+, OE+]

2. [A+, L+]

3. [no change]

4. [A-, OE-, E+]

5. [A+, OE+, R+]

6. . [L+, OE-, E+]

7. . [A-, OE-, E+]

8. [A-, L-, OE-, E+]

9. [A+, L+]

10. [L+, OE-, E+]

11. [A-, L-]

12. . [A-, OE-, E+]

13. [A-, OE-, E+]

14. [no change]

15. [A-, L-]

16. . [A+, L+]

17. [A+, OE+, G+]

18. [A-, L-, OE-, E+]
19. [no change]
20. [A-, OE-, Loss+]

Accrual Accounting Terminology: [1099a]
1. [unearned or deferred]
2. [accrued]
3. [prepaid]
4. [accrued]
5. [prepaid]
6. [unearned or deferred]

Cash Basis and Accrual Basis of Accounting: [1171a]
1. $700, $600 and $600, respectively.
2. $1,500, ($500) and $400, respectively.
3. Unearned Revenue $500, AR $200 and AR $1,200, respectively.
4. December Year 1 liability of $300, December Year 2 prepayment of $100, and December Year 3 liability of $700.

Adjusting Journal Entries: [1172a]
1. Year 1: Debit Insurance Expense for $1,600 and credit prepaid Insurance for $1,600. Year 2: Debit Insurance Expense for $2,400 and credit Prepaid Insurance for $2,400].
2. Year 1: Debit Depreciation Expense for $5,000 and credit Accumulated Depreciation for $5,000. Year 2: Debit Depreciation Expense for $6,000 and credit Accumulated Depreciation for $6,000.
3. Debit Unearned Rent Revenue for $9,000, debit Rent Receivable for $8,400, credit Rent Revenue for $17,400
4. Debit Supplies Expense for $6,000 and credit Supplies Inventory for $6,000. The correct Supplies Expense for the year in the income statement is $12,000.

Accounting Cycle: [1174a]
After the adjustments and closing entries, assets total $2,445,000,[in 000's: Cash $1,925, Rent Deposit $15, Prepaid Rent $15, Supplies Inventory $20, Prepaid Insurance $70, Accounts Receivable $400] Liabilities total $32,000 [in 000's: Notes Payable $20, Salaries Payable $10, Interest Payable $2] and Capital is $2,413,000 [Contributed $40, Retained Earnings $2,373]. The firm's income for Year 1 was $2,373,000. The revenues were $3,000,000. The expenses totaled $627,000 [Insurance $50,000, Supplies $80,000, Interest $2,000, Rent $165,000 and Salaries $330,000].

[Debit to Revenues and credits to the Expenses. The number needed as a credit to balance the Closing Journal [CJE} would be $2,373,000 and that would be a credit to Retained Earnings.]

The firm's income for Year 2 is $1,353,000. Revenues are $2,075,000 [$75,000 for Interest Revenue and $2,000,000 for Consulting Revenue]. Total Expenses are $722,000. [Rent $180,000, Salaries, $360,000, Interest $2,000, Supplies $120,000 and Insurance $60,000]

The firm's Total Assets are $5,200,000 [Cash $2,225,000, Rent Deposit $15,000, Prepaid Rent $15,000, Supplies Inventory $60,000, Prepaid Insurance $10,000, Accounts Receivable $800,000, Certificate of Deposit $2,000,000, Interest Receivable $75,000]. The firm's total liabilities are $1,434,000 [Salaries Payable $10,000, Notes Payable $20,000, Interest Payable $4,000 and Unearned Revenues $1,400,000]. The firm's ending Capital is $3,766,000 [$40,000 invested by the owners and $3,726,000 earned by the firm and not paid out to the owners.]

Recording Transactions: [1175a]
1. Debits to Cash for $28 and Truck for $8. Credits to Capital for $26 and Notes Payable for $10.
2. Debit Truck for $15 and credits to Notes Payable for $10 and Cash for $5.
3. Debit Prepaid Rent for $12 and credit Cash for $12.
4. Debit Land for $5 and Credit Cash for $5.
5. Debit Supplies Inventory for $4 and credit Accounts Payable for $4.
6. Debit Computer for $12 and credits to Cash for $1 and Notes Payable for $11.
7. Debit Cash for $20 and credit Notes Payable for $20.
8. Debit Cash for $40 and credit Unearned Revenues for $40.

Recording Transactions (continued): [1175a]
Account balances after all of these transactions have been recorded: (credits)

Cash	$65,000
Trucks	23,000
Prepaid Rent	12,000
Land	5,000
Supplies Inventory	4,000
Computer	12,000
Unearned Consulting Revenue	(40,000)
Accounts Payable	(4,000)
Notes Payable (includes lease liability)	(51,000)
Capital	(26,000)

Recording Transactions: [1176a]
[all numbers in 000's]:
1. Debit Cash $200 and credit Capital $200.
2. Debit Supplies Inventory $10 and credit Cash $10.
3. Debit Salaries Expense for $18 and credit cash for $18.
4. Debit AR for $32 and Cash for $8. Credit Revenues for $40.
5. Debit Cash for $32 and credit AR for $32.
6. Debit Supplies Expense for $2 and credit Supplies Inventory for $2.
7. Debit Training Expense for $9 and credit AP for $9.
8. Debit AP for $9 and credit Cash $9.
9. Debit Cash for $60 and credit Unearned Revenues for $60.
10. Debit AR for $40 and Unearned Revenues for $60. Credit Revenues for $100.
11. Debit Salaries Expense for $126 and credit Cash for $126. [7x18=126]

At the end of September, the accounts have the following balances:

Cash	$137	
Supplies Inventory	8	
AR	40	
AP	0	
Unearned Revenues	0	
Revenues		(140)
Salaries Expense	144	
Supplies Expense	2	
Training Expense	9	
Capital		(200)

The firm's loss would be ($15).

The firm's ending capital would be $185.

Accounting Cycle: [1177a]
1. Debit Cash for $250,000. Credits to Notes Payable for $50,000 and Owners' Equity for $200,000.
2. On October 31, Year 1: Debit Office Rent Expense for $6,000 and Prepaid Office Rent for $18,000. Credit Cash for $24,000.
3. [Debit Prepaid Equipment Rental for $900 and credit Cash for $900. This entry will be recorded twice in Year 1.
4. Debit Supplies Inventory for $3,000 and credit Accounts Payable for the same amount.]
5. Debit Accounts Payable for $300 and credit Supplies Inventory for $300.
6. No journal is made when the employees are hired. All of the paydays for Year 1 are part of item 10 below.
7. Debit Investments for $3,600 and credit Cash for the same amount.
8. Debit Accounts Payable for $2,700 and credit Cash for $2,700.
9. Debit Cash for $120,000 and Accounts Receivable for $80,000. Credit Revenues for $200,000.

Accounting Cycle (continued): [1177a]
10. August payday: Debit Salaries Expense for $10,000 and credit Cash for the same amount. September through December inclusive: Debit Salaries Expense for $80,000 and credit Cash for the same amount.]
11. Debit Cash for $105,000 and credit Unearned Revenues for the same amount.
12. Debit Unearned Revenues for $42,000 and credit Revenues for the same amount.
13. Debit Loss for $1,600 and Cash for $2,000. Credit Investments for $3,600.

Net Income is $124,100. Total Assets at the end of Year 1 are $449,600. Total Liabilities are $125,500. Total Owners' Equity is $324,100.

The Wizard Company
Balance Sheet
December 31, Year 1

Assets:	
Cash	$354,900
Accounts Receivable	80,000
Prepaid Office Rent	14,000
Prepaid Equipment Rent	300
Supplies Inventory	400
Total Assets:	$449,600
Liabilities:	
Unearned Revenues	$63,000
Notes Payable	50,000
Salaries Payable	10,000
Interest Payable	2,500
Total Liabilities:	$125,500
Owners' Equity:	
Contributed Capital	$200,000
Retained Earnings	124,100
Total Owners' Equity:	$324,100
Total Liab. & Owners' Equity:	$449,600

The Wizard Company
Income Statement
For the Five Months Ended December 31, Year 1

Revenues	$242,000
Expenses and Loss:	
Salaries	$100,000
Office Rent	10,000
Supplies	2,300
Equipment Rent	1,500
Interest	2,500
Loss on Sale of Investments	1,600
Total Expenses and Loss:	$117,900
Net Income	$124,100

Closing Journal Entry: Debit Revenues for $242,000. Credits to all expense accounts, the loss account and to Retained Earnings [Credit Salaries Expense for $100,000, Office Rent Expense for $10,000, Supplies

Accounting Cycle (continued): [1177a]
Expense for $2,300, Equipment Rent expense for 1,500, Interest Expense for $2,500, Loss on Sales of Investments for $1,600 and to Retained Earnings for $124,100].

In Year 2, the following events occurred.
1. *[No journal entry is required based on this information until paydays occur (item 6 below)]*
2. The firm finished the remainder of the project described in items 11 and 12 from Year 1. *[Debit Unearned Revenues for $63,000 and credit Revenues for $63,000.]*
3. *[Debit Cash for $80,000 and credit Accounts Receivable for the same amount.]*
4. *[Debit Notes Payable $50,000, Interest Payable for $2,500 and Interest Expense for $500. Credit Cash for $53,000.]*
5. *[Debits to Cash for $184,000 and Accounts Receivable for $46,000. Credit Revenues for $230,000.]*
6. *[January payday: Debits to Salaries Expense for $10,000 and Salaries Payable for $10,000. Credit Cash for $20,000. February-December inclusive: Debit Salaries Expense for $374,000 and credit Cash for the same amount.]*
7. *[Debit Supplies Inventory for $5,000 and credit Accounts Payable for the same amount.]*
8. *[Debit Investments for $7,000 and credit Cash for the same amount.]*
9. On July 31, Year 2, the firm moved to larger office space signing a one-year lease for the year beginning on that day. The monthly rent on the new office space was $3,000. This rental agreement required the year's rent to be paid at the time the firm moved into the new offices. *[Let's expense the Prepaid Office Rent that had been carried over into Year 2: Debit Office Rent Expense for $14,000 and credit Prepaid Office Rent for the same amount. Then let's record the payment for the year's rent in advance on the new office: Debit Prepaid Office Rent for $36,000 and credit Cash for the same amount.]*
10. *[Debit Prepaid Equipment Rental for $3,600 and credit Cash for the same amount. This summarizes four journal entries made in Year 2.]*
11. *[Debit Cash $250 and credit Dividend Revenue for the same amount.]*
12. *[Debit Cash for $8,000. Credits to Investments for $7,000 and to Gain on Sales of Investments for $1,000.]*

Total Assets in the balance sheet are $201,950. Net Loss is $144,150. Total Liabilities in the balance sheet are $22,000. Owners' Equity is $179,950.

The Wizard Company
Balance Sheet
December 31, Year 2

Assets:
Cash	$133,550
Accounts Receivable	46,000
Prepaid Office Rent	21,000
Prepaid Equipment Rent	300
Supplies Inventory	1,100
Total Assets:	$201,950

Liabilities:
Salaries Payable	$17,000
Accounts Payable	5,000
Total Liabilities:	$22,000

Owners' Equity:
Contributed Capital	$200,000
Retained Earnings	(20,050)
Total Owners' Equity:	$179,950

Accounting Cycle (continued): [1177a]
Total Liab. & Owners' Equity: $201,950

The Wizard Company
Income Statement
For the Year Ended December 31, Year 2

Revenues	$293,000
Dividend Revenues	250
Gain on Sale of Investments	1,000
Total Revenues and Gain:	$294,250
Expenses:	
Salaries	$401,000
Office Rent	29,000
Supplies	4,300
Equipment Rent	3,600
Interest	500
Total Expenses:	$438,400
Net Loss	($144,150)

Accounting Cycle: [1178a]
14. Debit Cash $250,000. Credits to Notes Payable for $70,000 and to Contributed Capital for $180,000.
15. No journal entry is made on May 1, Year 1. On September 30, Year 1: Debit Office Rent Expense for $15,000 and Prepaid Office Rent for $21,000. Credit Cash for $36,000.
16. Debit Prepaid Equipment Rent for $4,500 and credit Cash for the same amount.
    Debit Supplies Inventory for $9,000. Credits to Cash for $6,000 and to Accounts Payable for $3,000.
17. Debit Accounts Payable for $1,800 and credit Supplies Inventory for $1,800.
18. Record no journal entry on the hiring date. All of the Salary payment journal entries for the year are to be made in item 10 below.
19. Debit Investments for $20,000 and credit Cash for the same amount.
20. Debit Accounts Payable for $1,200 and credit Cash for the same amount.
21. Debits to Cash for $76,000 and Accounts Receivable for $114,000. Credit Revenues for $190,000.
22. Debit Salaries Expense for $230,000. Credit Cash for the same amount.
23. Debit Cash for $300,000 and credit Unearned Revenues for $300,000.
24. Debit Unearned Revenues for $180,000 and credit Revenues for the same amount.
25. Debits to Cash for $14,000 and Loss on Sale of Investments for $6,000. Credit Investments for $20,000.

Net Income is $83,667. Total Assets at the end of Year 1 are $469,000. Total Liabilities are $205,333. Total Owners' Equity is $263,667.

The Wayne Company
Balance Sheet
December 31, Year 1

Assets:	
Cash	$342,300
Accounts Receivable	114,000
Prepaid Office Rent	12,000
Prepaid Equipment Rent	500
Supplies Inventory	200
Total Assets:	$469,000

Accounting Cycle (continued): [1178a]

Liabilities:
Unearned Revenues	$120,000
Salaries Payable	10,000
Interest Payable	5,333
Notes Payable	70,000
Total Liabilities:	$205,333

Owners' Equity:
Contributed Capital	$180,000
Retained Earnings	83,667
Total Owners' Equity:	$263,667
Total Liab. & Owners' Equity	$469,000

The Wayne Company
Income Statement
For the Eight Months Ended December 31, Year 1

Revenues	$370,000
Expenses:	
Salaries	$240,000
Office Rent	24,000
Supplies	7,000
Equipment Rent	4,000
Loss on Sale of Investments	6,000
Interest	5,333
Total Expenses:	$286,333
Net Income	$83,667

Closing Journal Entry: Debit Revenues for $370,000. Credits to each of the Expenses and to the Loss account to zero out each. [Salaries $240,000, Office Rent $24,000, Supplies $7,000, Equipment Rent $4,000, Interest $5,333 and Loss on Sale of Investments $6,000]

In Year 2, the following events occurred.
1. No journal is made when hiring the new employee. Journal entries for all paydays are requested in item 6 below.
2. Debit Unearned Revenue for $120,000 and credit Revenues for $120,000.
3. Debit Cash for $114,000 and credit Accounts Receivable for the same amount.
4. Debits to Notes Payable for $70,000, Interest Payable for $5,333 and Interest Expense for $667. Credit Cash for $76,000.
5. Debits to Cash for $245,000 and Accounts Receivable for $105,000. Credit Revenues for $350,000.
6. January: Debits to Salaries Payable for $10,000 and Salaries Expense for $20,000. Credit Cash for $30,000. February-December [paydays inclusive: Debit Salaries Expense for $451,000 and credit Cash for the same amount.
7. Debit Supplies Inventory for $11,000 and credit Accounts Payable for the same amount.
8. Debit Investments $25,000 and credit Cash for the same amount.
9. Debit Prepaid Equipment Rental for $5,500 and credit Cash for $5,500.
10. Debit Cash for $300 and credit Dividend Revenue for the same amount.
11. Debit Cash for $33,000. Credits to Gain on Sale of Investments for $8,000 and to Investments for $25,000.

Total Assets in the balance sheet are $229,200. Net Loss is $59,134. Total Liabilities in the balance sheet are $24,667. Owners' Equity is $204,533.

Accounting Cycle: (continued) [1178a]
The Wayne Company
Balance Sheet
December 31, Year 2

Assets:
Cash	$123,100
Accounts Receivable	105,000
Supplies Inventory	1,100
Total Assets:	$229,200

Liabilities:
Accounts Payable	$11,000
Salaries Payable	13,667
Total Liabilities:	$24,667

Owners' Equity:
Contributed Capital	$180,000
Retained Earnings	24,533
Total Owners' Equity:	$204,533
Total Liab. & Owners' Equity:	$229,200

The Wayne Company
Income Statement
For the Year Ended December 31, Year 2

Revenues	$470,000
Dividend Revenues	300
Gain on Sale of Investments	8,000
Total Revenues and Gain:	$478,300

Expenses:
Salaries	$484,667
Office Rent	36,000
Supplies	10,100
Equipment Rent	6,000
Interest	667
Total Expenses:	$537,434
Net Loss	($59,134)

Accounting Cycle: [1179a]
The Merlin Company
Balance Sheet
December 31, Year 1

Cash	**$348,800**
Prepaid Rent	**14,000**
Prepaid Equipment Rent	**5,700**
Supplies Inventory	**1,000**
Accounts Receivable	**260,000**
Total Assets	**$629,500**
Notes Payable	**$8,000**
Interest Payable	**375**
Total Liabilities	**$8,375**

Accounting Cycle (continued): [1179a]

Contributed Capital	**$90,000**
Retained Earnings	**531,125**
Total Owners' Equity	**$621,125**
Total Liab. & Owners' Equity	**$629,500**

The Merlin Company
Income Statement
For the Five Months Ended December 31, Year 1

Sales Revenue	**$600,000**
Expenses:	
Salaries	$54,000
Rent	10,000
Supplies	3,000
Equipment Rental	1,500
Interest Expense	375
Net Income	**$531,125**

Accounting Cycle: [1180a]
After the adjustments and closing entries at the end of Year 1, assets total $2,445,000, liabilities are $32,000 and Capital is $2,413,000. The firm's income for Year 1 was $2,373,000. The revenues were $3,000,000. The expenses totaled $627,000 [Insurance $50,000, Supplies $80,000, Interest $2,000, Rent $165,000 and Salaries $330,000].

The firm's income for Year 2 is $1,353,000. Revenues are $2,075,000. Total Expenses are $722,000. [Rent $180,000, Salaries, $360,000, Interest $2,000, Supplies $120,000 and Insurance $60,000]

At the end of Year 2, the firm's Total Assets are $5,200,000 [Cash $2,225,000, Rent Deposit $15,000, Prepaid Rent $15,000, Supplies Inventory $60,000, Prepaid Insurance $10,000, Accounts Receivable $800,000, Certificate of Deposit $2,000,000, Interest Receivable $75,000]. The firm's Total Liabilities are $1,434,000 [Salaries Payable $10,000, Notes Payable $20,000, Interest Payable $4,000 and Unearned Revenues $1,400,000]. The firm's ending Capital is $3,766,000 [$40,000 invested by the owners and $3,726,000 earned by the firm and not paid out to the owners.]

Adjusting Journal Entries: [1181a]
1. AJE December 31, Year 1: debit Insurance Expense and credit Prepaid Insurance both for $1,066.67 [8 x $4,800/36]
AJE December 31, Year 2: debit Insurance Expense and credit Prepaid Insurance both for $1,600.00 [12 x $4,800/36]

2. AJE December 31, Year 1: debit Depreciation Expense and credit Accumulated Depreciation both for $5,333.33 [($44,000 - $20,000)/3] x 8/12 = $5,333.33
AJE December 31, Year 2: debit Depreciation Expense and credit Accumulated Depreciation both for $8,000.00
[($44,000 - $20,000)/3] = $8,000.00

3. AJE December 31, Year 1: debit Unearned Rent Revenue for $10,800, debit Rent Receivable for $7,000, and credit Rent Revenue for $17,800.
[$14,400/12] x 9 = $10,800 and $1,000/month x 7 = $7,000]

4. AJE December 31: debit Supplies Expense and credit Supplies Inventory both for $8,000.

Financial Statement Preparation: [1182a]

The Trojan Company
Balance Sheets
December 31, Year 2 and Year 1

	Year 2	Year 1
Current Assets:		
Cash	$1,500	$1,000
Accounts Receivable	400	300
Supplies Inventory	200	300
Prepaid Salaries	200	100
Prepaid Rent	100	400
Total Current Assets	$2,400	$2,100
Non-Current Assets:		
Property, Plant & Equipment	$5,000	$4,000
(Accumulated Depreciation)	(1,500)	(1,000)
Investments	1,500	2,000
Total Non-Current Assets	$5,000	$5,000
Total Assets	$7,400	$7,100
Current Liabilities:		
Accounts Payable	$400	$600
Salaries Payable	200	500
Taxes Payable	200	300
Rent Payable	900	800
Total Current Liabilities	$1,700	$2,200
Non-Current Notes Payable	$2,000	$2,000
Total Liabilities	$3,700	$4,200
Owners' Equity:		
Contributed Capital	$1,200	$1,000
Retained Earnings	2,500	1,900
Total Owners' Equity	$3,700	$2,900
Total Liabilities & Owners' Equity	$7,400	$7,100

The Trojan Company
Income Statement
For the Year Ended December 31, Year 2

Sales Revenues	$7,000
Operating Expenses:	
Salaries	$1,800
Rent	2,000
Selling & Administrative	1,000
Travel	600
Depreciation	500
Supplies	500
Total Operating Expenses	$6,400
Operating Income	$600
Other (Revenues), Expenses and (Gain):	
Interest Revenue	($100)
Gain on Sale of Investment	(400)
Interest Expense	200
Other (revenues), Expenses and (Gain) net	($300)

Financial Statement Preparation (continued): [1182a]

Earnings Before Income Taxes	$900
Tax Expense	300
Net Income	$600

Closing Journal Entries: [1183a]

The CJE would include debits to Sales [$7,000], Interest Revenue [$100] and Gain [$400]. The CJE would also include these credits: Rent Expense [$2,000], Supplies Expense [$500], Depreciation Expense [$500], Selling & Administrative Expense [$1,000], Consultants Salary Expense [$1,800], Travel Expense [$600], Interest Expense [$200] and Tax Expense [$300]. Balancing the CJE requires a $600 credit to Retained Earnings. This is how Retained Earnings becomes $2,500 in the balance sheet for Year 2.

Adjusting journal entries have a very different purpose. AJEs exist to cause all of the accounts to have the correct balances before the financial statements are prepared. Thus, financial statements would contain accounts with correct balances *if* the AJEs had been correctly done.

Financial Statement Preparation: [1184a]

The Oreo Corporation
Balance Sheet
December 31, Year 1

Assets:

Cash	$31,000
Prepaid Salaries	10,000
Prepaid Rent	24,000
Supplies Inventory	11,000
Total Assets	$76,000

Liabilities:

Accounts Payable	$6,000
Salaries Payable	2,000
Unearned Revenues	20,000
Notes Payable	10,000
Utilities Payable	1,000
Total Liabilities	$39,000

Owners' Equity:

Contributed Capital	$3,000
Retained Earnings	34,000
Total Owners' Equity	$37,000
Total Liab. & Owners' Equity	$76,000

The Oreo Corporation
Income Statement
For the Nine Months Ended December 31, Year 1

Revenues		$170,000
Expenses:		
Salaries	$72,000	
Rent	36,000	
Supplies	21,000	
Utilities	7,000	136,000
Net Income		$34,000

Closing Journal Entry for December 31, Year 1:
Debit Revenues for $170,000 and credits to Salaries Expense for $72,000, Rent Expense for $36,000, Supplies Expense for $21,000, Utilities Expense for $7,000 and Retained Earnings for $34,000.

Financial Statement Preparation (continued); [1184a]
The Oreo Corporation
Balance Sheet
December 31, Year 2

Assets:
Cash	$174,000
Supplies Inventory	12,000
Prepaid Utilities	2,000
Total Assets	$188,000

Liabilities:
Accounts Payable	$9,000
Unearned Revenues	50,000
Notes Payable	10,000
Total Liabilities	$69,000

Owners' Equity:
Contributed Capital	$3,000
Retained Earnings	116,000
Total Owners' Equity	$119,000

Total Liab. & Owners' Equity $188,000

The Oreo Corporation
Income Statement
For the Year Ended December 31, Year 2

Revenues: $290,000

Expenses:
Salaries	$120,000	
Rent	48,000	
Supplies	29,000	
Utilities	11,000	208,000
Net Income		$82,000

Closing Journal Entry for December 31, Year 2:
Debit Revenues for $290,000. Credits to Salaries Expense for $120,000, Rent Expense for $48,000, Supplies Expense for $29,000, Utilities Expense for $11,000 and Retained Earnings for $82,000.

Adjusting Journal Entries: [1185a] Assume all fiscal years end on December 31.
1.
Year 1
Debit Depreciation Expense for $4,500 and credit Accumulated Depreciation for the same amount.
Year 2
Debit Depreciation Expense for $10,800 and credit Accumulated Depreciation for the same amount.

2.
Year 1
Debit Unearned Rent Revenue for $22,000 and credit Rent Revenue for the same amount.

Adjusting Journal Entries: [1186a]
1.
AJE December 31, Year 1: debit Depreciation Expense and credit Accumulated Depreciation both for $3,889
[($58,000 - $30,000)/3] x 5/12 = $3,889]
AJE December 31, Year 2: debit Depreciation Expense and credit Accumulated Depreciation both for $9,333
[($58,000 - $30,000)/3] = $9,333]

2.
AJE December 31, Year 1: debit Unearned Rent Revenue and credit Rent Revenue for $44,000.

Journal Entries: [1187a]
1. [Debit Cash for $70,000. Credits to Notes Payable and Owners' Equity for $35,000 each.]

2. [Debits to Cash for $75,000 and to Accounts Receivable for $120,000. Credits to Unearned Revenue for $25,000 and to Revenues for $170,000.]

3. [Debit Supplies Inventory for $14,000. Credits to Accounts Payable for $8,400 and to Cash for $5,600.]

4. [Debit Supplies Expense for $9,800 and credit Supplies Inventory for the same amount.]

5. [Debit Prepaid Rent for $8,800 and credit Cash for the same amount.]

6. [Debit Rent Expense for $2,200 and credit Prepaid Rent for the same amount.]

7. [Debit Salaries expense for $24,500 and credits to Cash and Salaries Payable for $21,000 and $3,500, respectively.]

8. [Debits to Salaries Payable for $3,500 and to Salaries expense for $49,000. Credit Cash for $52,500.]

9. [Debit Cash for $60,000 and credit Unearned Revenues for the same number.]

10. [Debits to Accounts Receivable and Unearned revenues for $130,000 and $60,000, respectively. Credit Consulting Revenues for $190,000.]

Journal Entries: [1188a]
1. Debit Cash $100,000. Credits Owners' Equity and Notes Payable each for $50,000.

2. Debits to Cash for $55,000 and to Accounts Receivable for $85,000. Credits Unearned Revenue for $20,000 and Revenues $130,000.

3. Debit Supplies Inventory $8,000. Credits Cash for $3,200 and Accounts Payable $4,800.

4. Debit to Supplies Expense $5,600 and credit to Supplies Inventory for the same amount.

5. Debit Prepaid Rent $5,200 and credit Cash for the same amount.

6. Debit Rent Expense $1,300 and credit Prepaid Rent for the same amount.

7. Debit Salaries Expense $20,000. Credits Salaries Payable $4,000 and Cash $16,000.

8. Debits to Salaries Expense for $40,000 and to Salaries Payable for $4,000. Credit Cash for $44,000.

9. Debit Cash $80,000. Credit Unearned Revenues $80,000.

Journal Entries: [1188a cont.]
10. Debits to Unearned Revenues for $80,000 and to Accounts Receivable for $110,000. Credit Revenues for $190,000.

Accounting Cycle: [1189a]

For Year 1:
Prepaid Equipment Rent	$ 400
Office Rent Payable	$ 5,600
Notes Payable (including Accounts Payable)	$ 8,000
Net Income <Net Loss>	$ 41,850
Cash	$ 25,100

For Year 2:
Salaries Expense	$ 20,875
Consulting Revenues	$ 36,000
Supplies Expense	$ 1,300

Accounting Cycle: [1190a]

For Year 1:
Prepaid Equipment Rent	$ 200
Office Rent Payable	$ 2,400
Notes Payable (including Accounts Payable)	$ 4,000
Net Income <Net Loss>	$ 36,635
Cash	$ 22,500

For Year 2:
Salaries Expense	$ 17,785
Consulting Revenues	$ 38,000
Supplies Expense	$ 700

Accounting Cycle: [1191a]

For Year 1:
Prepaid Equipment Rent	$ 200
Office Rent Payable	$ 4,000
Notes Payable (including Accounts Payable)	$ 5,000
Net Income <Net Loss>	$ 26,760
Cash	$ 31,160

For Year 2:
Salaries Expense	$ 14,875
Consulting Revenues	$ 36,000
Supplies Expense	$ 600

Accounting Cycle: [1192a]
For Year 1:
Prepaid Equipment Rent	$	250
Office Rent Payable	$	1,600
Notes Payable (including Accounts Payable)	$	2,000
Net Income <Net Loss>	$	21,290
Cash	$	20,760

For Year 2:
Salaries Expense	$	9,500
Consulting Revenues	$	30,000
Supplies Expense	$	500

Accounting for Revenues and Expenses: [1193a]

The Dorsey Company
Income Statement
For the Year Ended December 31, Year 1

Sales Revenue		$120,000	$ 95,000
Expenses:			
Salaries		32,000	23,000
Rent		26,000	26,900
Supplies		9,000	6,000
Utilities		7,000	7,500
Total Expenses		74,000	
Net Income		$46,000	31,600

Accounting for Revenues and Expenses: [1194a]

The Tynesha Company
Income Statement
For the Year Ended December 31, Year 1

Sales Revenue		$120,000	$ 100,000
Expenses:			
Salaries		32,000	25,000
Rent		26,000	27,100
Supplies		10,000	7,000
Utilities		7,000	7,600
Total Expenses		75,000	
Net Income		$45,000	33,300

Recording Transactions and Adjusting Journal Entries: [1195a]

Cash	$ 4,045	Consulting Revenues	$	750
Prepaid Rent	20	Rent Revenue		-0-
Supplies Inventory	15	Rent Expense		100
Accounts Receivable	50	Supplies Expense		65

Recording Transactions and Adjusting Journal Entries (continued): [1195a]

Prepaid Utilities	_____15	Utilities Expense	_____25
Prepaid Salaries	_____5	Salaries Expense	_____150
Accounts Payable	_____30		
Rent Payable	_____-0-		
Notes Payable	_____1,500		
Unearned Revenues	_____200		
Utilities Payable	_____-0-		
Salaries Payable	_____10		

Accounting Cycle: [1196a]
On December 31, Year 1, the accounts were properly adjusted and closed resulting in the following *adjusted trial balance.* Supplies on hand at the end of the year had been $1,200 by actual count. Income in Year 1 had been $112,450.

In Year 2, the following events occurred.
1. *No journal entry is to be made based on this information.*

2. *Debit Unearned Revenues and credit Revenues each for $70,000.*

3. *Debit Cash and credit Accounts Receivable each for $27,000.*

4. *Debits to Cash and Accounts receivable for $105,000 and $45,000, respectively.*

5. *January 15, Year 2; Debit Salaries Expense and salaries Payable, both for $5,000. Credit Cash for $10,000. February 15 through December 15 paydays, inclusively, Debit Salaries Expense and credit Cash for $191,400 (sum of all 11 paydays). The adjustment for the end of the year: Debit Salaries Expense for $8,700 and credit Salaries Payable for the same amount.*

6. *Debit Supplies Inventory and credit Accounts Payable for $8,000 each.*

7. *Debit Rent Expense for $4,000 (January and February), Rent Payable for $10,000 and prepaid Rent for $14,000. [There are alternative ways to record this.] Credit Cash for $24,000.*

8. *Debit Investments and credit Cash both for $10,000.*

9. *Debit Notes Payable for $20,000, Interest Expense for $1,050 and Interest Payable for $750. Credit Cash for $21,800.*

10. *Debit Rent Expense and credit Prepaid Rent both for $14,000. Debit Rent Expense for $15,000 and debit Prepaid Rent for $21,000. Credit Cash for $36,000. There are a variety of ways in which the journal entries could be made in Year 2. Please check to see if your results for the end of the year are correct. If so, do not sweat the details.*

11. *The simplest 'shortcut' is to debit Equipment Rent Expense and credit Cash both for $3,600. If you do this on August 1, there is no need to adjust these accounts at the end of the year.*

12. *Debit Cash and credit Dividends revenue, both for $250.*

Accounting Cycle (continued): [1196a]

13. Debits to Cash and loss on Sale of Investments for $8,000 and $2,000, respectively.

Carefully analyze the Supplies Inventory account. It started the year with a $1,200 balance and $8,000 more were purchased in the current year. If $700 were not used, then Supplies Expense needs to be $8,500 for Year 2 reflecting the value of supplies that were consumed. Debit Supplies Expense and credit Supplies Inventory, both for $8,500.

The Merlin Company
December 31, Year 2
Adjusted Trial Balance Before Closing Journal Entries:

Cash	$151,350	
Accounts Receivable	45,000	
Prepaid Eq. Rent	2,100	
Supplies Inventory	700	
Prepaid Office Rent	21,000	
Salaries Payable		$8,700
Accounts Payable		8,000
Contributed Capital		120,000
Retained Earnings		112,450
Revenues		220,000
Salaries Expense	205,100	
Office Rent Expense	29,000	
Interest Expense	1,050	
Eq. Rent Expense	3,600	
Supplies Expense	8,500	
Loss	2,000	
Dividends revenue		250
Totals	$469,400	$469,400

Accounting Cycle: [1197a]
Net Income for Year 1 is $2,527.
Total Assets at the end of Year 1 are $4,565. Total Liabilities are $1,138. Total Owners' Equity is $3,427.

Prepare a balance sheet at December 31, Year 1 and income statement for the four months ended December 31, Year 1. Prepare Closing Journal Entries at the end of Year 1.

Journal entries necessary to record items 1 through 13 in Year 1:
1. Debit Cash $1,400. Credits to Notes Payable for $500 and Owners' Equity for $900.
2. No journal entry is required. This is an executory contract when created.
3. Debit Prepaid Equipment Rental and credit Cash both for $180.
4. Debit Supplies Inventory and credit Accounts Payable both for $400.
5. Debit Accounts Payable and credit Supplies Inventory for $100 each.
6. No journal entry is required at this time. The arrangement is executory.
7. Debit Investments and credit Cash both for $350.
8. Debit Accounts Payable and credit Cash both for $300.
9. Debits to Cash for $800 and Accounts Receivable for $1,200. Credit Revenues for $2,000.
10. Debit Salaries Expense for $75 and credit Cash for $75. This is the payday journal entry on October 15. The journal entries at November 15 and December 15 will be identical to this.
11. Debit Cash and credit Unearned Revenue for $1,500 each.
12. Debit Unearned Revenue and credit Revenues both for $1,000.
13. Debit Cash for $500. Credits to Gain on Sale of Investments for $150 and Investments for $350.

Accounting Cycle (continued): [1197a]

Based upon the recording of journal as done above, there are five adjusting entries required.

14. Debit Salaries Expense and credit Salaries Payable for $38 each. This will recognize the expense for employee services *after* the December payday and it will recognize that the firm owes the employees for services rendered in the last half of December. [Round up to $38 for simplicity.]
15. Debit Interest Expense and credit Interest Payable both for $20. This is to recognize that part of the annual cost of the interest has been 'used up' and needs to be an expense in the accounting records. Also, the accounting records need to show that there is interest owed to the investor
16. Debit Supplies Expense and credit Supplies Inventory both for $200. The Supplies Inventory account needs to be adjusted from its $300 unadjusted balance down to $100 reflecting that $200 of the supplies had been used up since they were purchased.
17. Debit Office Rent Expense and credit Office Rent Payable for $80 each. The accounting records need to reflect that the firm has used up $80 worth of rent despite not having paid that amount to the landlord yet. The accounting records also need to show that this amount is owed to the landlord even though the payment is not due at this time.
18. Debit Equipment Rent Expense for $60 and credit Prepaid Equipment Rental for $60 each. The accounting records have to show that part of the prepayment has expired and needs to be reflected as an expense.

The Merlin Company
Balance Sheet
December 31, Year 1

Assets:
Cash	$3,145
Accounts Receivable	1,200
Prepaid Equipment Rent	120
Supplies Inventory	100
Total Assets	$4,565

Liabilities & Owners' Equity:
Office Rent Payable	$80
Salaries Payable	38
Interest Payable	20
Unearned Revenues	500
Notes Payable	500
Total Liabilities	$1,138

Owners' Equity:
Contributed Capital	$900
Retained Earnings	2,527
Total Owners' Equity	$3,427
Total Liabilities & OE	$4,565

The Merlin Company
Income Statement
For the Year Ended Dec. 31, Year 1

Revenues	$3,000
Gain on Sale of Investments	150
	$3,150

Accounting Cycle (continued): [1197a]

Expenses:
Salaries	$263
Interest	20
Supplies	200
Office Rent	80
Equipment Rent	60
	$623
Net Income	$2,527

Closing Journal Entry:
Revenues	$3,000	
Gain on Sale of Investment	150	
Salaries Expense		$263
Interest Expense		20
Supplies Expense		200
Office Rent Expense		80
Equipment Rent Expense		60
Retained Earnings		2,527

At the end of Year 2, identify the accounts that need to be adjusted in order that their ending balances are correct for the preparation of financial statements. Supplies on hand at the end of Year 2 by actual count were $300. Total Assets in the balance sheet are $6,205. Net Income is $1,883. Total Liabilities in the balance sheet are $895.

Journal entries to record items 1 through 13 from Year 2:
1. No journal entry needed on January 15, Year 2.
2. Debit Unearned Revenue and credit revenue for $500 each.
3. Debit Cash and credit Accounts Receivable for $1,200 each.
4. Debits to Cash for $3,500 and Accounts Receivable for $1,500. Credit Revenues for $5,000.
5. Debit Salaries expense for $37 and Salaries Payable for $38. Credit Cash for $75. This is the January 15, Year 2 payday journal entry. The other 11 paydays in Year 2 will all be identical and will have debits to Salaries Expense and credits to Cash for $190 each.
6. Debit Supplies Inventory and credit Accounts Payable for $800 each.
7. Debits to Office Rent Expense for $20, Office Rent Payable for $80 and Prepaid Office Rent for $140. Credit Cash for $240.
8. Debit Investments and credit Cash for $1,000 each.
9. Debits to Note Payable for $500, Interest Payable for $20 and Interest Expense for $40. Credit Cash for $560.
10. Debit Prepaid Office Rent $720 and credit Cash for the same amount. [It would be acceptable to expense the $140 that was in the Prepaid Office Rent from item #7 above. For consistency, we will wait and do that as part of the adjusting journal entries at the end of Year 2.]
11. Debit Prepaid Equipment Rental and credit Cash for $180 each. [For consistency, we will wait and adjust the Prepaid Equipment Rental account at the end of Year 2.]
12. Debit Cash and credit Dividend Revenue for $25 each.
13. Debits to Cash for $800 and to Loss on Sale of Investments $200. Credit Investments for $1,000.

Based upon the recording of the journal entries above, there are four adjusting journal entries required:
1. Debit Salaries Expense for $95 and credit Salaries Payable for the same amount
2. Debit Supplies Expense and credit Supplies Inventory for $600.
3. Debit Office Rent Expense and credit Prepaid Office Rental for $380 each.
4. Debit Equipment Rent Expense and credit Prepaid Equipment Rental for $180 each.

Total assets are $6,205. [Cash $3,805, Prepaid Equipment Rental $120, Supplies Inventory $300, Accounts Receivable $1,500 and Prepaid Office Rental $480.]

Accounting Cycle (continued): [1197a]
Total liabilities are $895. [Accounts Payable $800 and Salaries Payable $95.]

Owners' Equity totals $5,310. [Contributed Capital $900 and Retained Earnings $4,410]

Net Income is $1,883. [Sales Revenues of $5,500 and Dividend Revenue of $25. Expenses: Salaries $2,222, Interest $40, Supplies $600, Office Rent $400, Equipment Rent $180. Loss on sale of Investments $200.]

Which accounts require closing at the end of Year 2? [Sales Revenue, Dividend Revenue, Loss on Sale of Investments, Salaries Expense, Interest Expense, Equipment Rent Expense, Office Rent Expense and Supplies Expense.] The amount transferred to Retained Earnings has to equal Net Income.

Accounting Cycle: [1198a]

Entries to record items 1 through 14 in Year 1 are shown below:
1. Debit Cash for $60,000. Credits to Notes Payable and Owners Equity for $40,000.
2. No journal entry required. This arrangement is executory at this time.
3. Debits to Rental deposit for $15,000 and Prepaid Rent for $30,000. Credit Cash for $45,000.
4. Debit Supplies Inventory and credit Accounts Payable for $100,000 each
5. Debit Cash and credit Unearned Revenues for $400,000 each.
6. Debit Salaries Expense and credit Cash for $20,000.
7. Debit Prepaid Insurance $120,000 and credit cash for the same amount.
8. Debit Rent Expense for $150,000 and credit Cash for the same amount. Remember, this is for all of the lease payments in Year 1.
9. Debit Salaries Expense and credit Cash for $300,000 each. Remember, this is for all of the paydays in Year 1.
10. Debit Accounts Payable and credit Cash for $100,000.
11. Debits to Cash for $400,00, Unearned Revenues for $400,000 and Accounts Receivable for $200,000. Credit Revenues for $1,000,000.
12. Debit Cash for 600,000 and credit Unearned Revenues for the same amount
13. Debit Cash and credit Accounts Receivable for $200,000.
14. Debits to Cash for $1,000,000, Unearned Revenues for $600,000 and Accounts Receivable for $400,000. Credit to Revenues for $2,000,000.

The adjusting entries at the end of Year 1 include:
1. Debit Supplies Expense and credit Supplies Inventory both for $80,000.
2. Debit Salaries expense and credit Salaries Payable both for $10,000.
3. Debit Interest Expense and credit Interest Payable both for $2,000.
4. Debit Rent Expense and credit Prepaid Rent both for $15,000.
5. Debit Insurance Expense and credit Prepaid Insurance both for $50,000.

After the adjustments and closing entries, assets total $2,445,000. [Cash $1,925,000, Rental deposit $15,000, Prepaid Rent $15,000, Supplies Inventory $20,000, Accounts Receivable $400,000 and Prepaid Insurance $70,000.]

Liabilities are $32,000 [Notes Payable $20,000, Salaries Payable $10,000 and Interest Payable $2,000.]

Capital is $2,413,000 [contributed $40,000 and Retained Earnings of $2,373,000].

The firm's income for Year 1 was $2,373,000. The revenues were $3,000,000. The expenses totaled $627,000 [Insurance $50,000, Supplies $80,000, Interest $2,000, Rent $165,000 and Salaries $330,000].

What would the firm's Closing Journal Entry on December 31, Year 1 have looked like? [Debit to Revenues and credits to the Expenses. The number needed as a credit to balance the Closing Journal Entry (CJE) would be $2,373,000 and that would be a credit to Retained Earnings.]

Accounting Cycle (continued): [1198a]

The journal entries for Year 2 based on information in items 1 through 11 follow:
1. Debit to Rent Expense for $180,000 and credit to Cash for the same amount.
2. Debits to Salaries Expense for $20,000 and to Salaries Payable for $10,000. Credit Cash for $30,000.
3. Debit Cash and credit Accounts Receivable for $400,000.
4. Debit Salaries Expense for $330,000 and credit Cash for the same amount.
5. Debit Supplies Inventory for $200,000. Credits to Cash and Accounts Payable for $100,000 each.
6. Debit Cash and credit Unearned Revenue for $1,200,000.
7. Debit Investments and credit Cash both for $2,000,000.
8. Debit Accounts Payable and credit Supplies Inventory for $40,000 each.
9. Debit Accounts Payable and credit Cash for $60,000 each.
10. Debits to Unearned Revenues for $1,200,000 and Accounts Receivable for $800,000. Credit Revenues for $2,000,000.
11. Debit Cash and credit Unearned Revenues for $1,400,000 each.

Supplies on hand at December 31, Year 2 were $60,000. **Adjusting Journal Entries [AJE] are needed for Salaries, Supplies, Insurance, Interest Expense and Interest Revenue.** The Rent Expense account should contain $180,000 based on transaction #1 above.

Adjusting Entries at the end of Year 2 include:
1. Debit Salaries Expense for $10,000 and credit Salaries Payable for the same number. This will record salaries earned by employees since the last payday in December but not paid by the firm prior to the end of the year.
2. Debit Supplies Expense for $120,000 and credit Supplies Inventory for the same number. This will adjust the Supplies Inventory account from $180,000 down to $60,000. $60,000 of supplies were on hand at the end of the year.
3. Debit Insurance Expense for $60,000 and credit Prepaid Insurance for the same amount. This will reflect that $60,000 of insurance has expired in Year 2.
4. Debit Interest Expense and credit Interest Payable both for $2,000. The firm has to recognize the unpaid interest on the Note Payable and the expense associated with that note in Year 2.
5. Debit Interest Receivable for $75,000 and credit Interest Revenue for the same amount. This will recognize the interest earned on the certificate of deposit in Year 2 that remained unpaid at the end of Year 2.

The firm's income for Year 2 is $1,353,000. Revenues are $2,075,000. Total Expenses are $722,000. [Rent $180,000, Salaries, $360,000, Interest $2,000, Supplies $120,000 and Insurance $60,000]

The firm's Total Assets at December 31, Year 2 are $5,200,000 [Cash $2,225,000, Rent Deposit $15,000, Prepaid Rent $15,000, Supplies Inventory $60,000, Prepaid Insurance $10,000, Accounts Receivable $800,000, Investment $2,000,000, Interest Receivable $75,000]. The firm's Total Liabilities are $1,434,000 [Salaries Payable $10,000, Notes Payable $20,000, Interest Payable $4,000 and Unearned Revenues $1,400,000]. The firm's ending Capital is $3,766,000 [$40,000 invested by the owners and $3,726,000 earned by the firm and not paid out to the owners.]

The Trojan Company
Balance Sheet
December 31, Year 1

Cash	$1,925,000
Prepaid Rent	15,000
Rental Deposit	15,000
Prepaid Insurance	70,000
Supplies Inventory	20,000
Accounts Receivable	400,000
Total Assets	**$2,445,000**

Accounting Cycle (continued): [1198a]

Salaries Payable	$10,000
Notes Payable	20,000
Interest Payable	2,000
Total Liabilities	**$32,000**
Contributed Capital	$40,000
Retained Earnings	2,373,000
Total Owners' Equity	**$2,413,000**
Total Liab. & Owners' Equity	**$2,445,000**

The Trojan Company
Income Statement
For the Eleven Months Ended December 31, Year 1

Sales Revenue	**$3,000,000**
Expenses:	
Salaries	$330,000
Rent	165,000
Supplies	80,000
Insurance	50,000
Interest	2,000
Total Expenses	**$627,000**
Net Income	**$2,373,000**

The Trojan Company
Statement of Cash Flows
For the Eleven Months Ended December 31, Year 1

[Indirect Method]

Net Income	$2,373,000
Less increase in prepaid rent	-15,000
Less increase in rental deposit	-15,000
Less increase in supplies inventory	-20,000
Less increase in prepaid insurance	-70,000
Less increase in accounts receivable	-400,000
Plus increase in salaries payable	+10,000
Plus increase in interest payable	+2,000
Cash flow from operating activities	**$1,865,000**
Investment by owners	$40,000
Cash borrowed	20,000
Cash flow from financing activities	**$60,000**
Total cash flow	**$1,925,000**
Plus: beginning cash	-0-
Equals: ending cash	**$1,925,000**

Accounting Cycle (continued): [1198a]
[Operating cash flow using the direct method:]

Cash from clients	$2,600,000
Salaries paid	-320,000
Paid to suppliers	-100,000
Paid for rent	-195,000
Paid for insurance	-120,000
Operating cash flow	$1,865,000

The Trojan Company
Balance Sheet
December 31, Year 2

Cash	$2,225,000
Investment	2,000,000
Interest receivable	75,000
Prepaid Rent	15,000
Rental Deposit	15,000
Prepaid Insurance	10,000
Supplies Inventory	60,000
Accounts Receivable	800,000
Total Assets	$5,200,000
Unearned revenues	$1,400,000
Salaries Payable	10,000
Notes Payable	20,000
Interest Payable	4,000
Total Liabilities	$1,434,000
Contributed Capital	$40,000
Retained Earnings	3,726,000
Total Owners' Equity	$3,766,000
Total Liab. & Owners' Equity	$5,200,000

The Trojan Company
Income Statement
For the Year Ended December 31, Year 2

Sales Revenue	$2,000,000
Interest revenue	75,000
Total Revenues	$2,075,000
Expenses:	
Salaries	$360,000
Rent	180,000
Supplies	120,000
Insurance	60,000
Interest	2,000
Total Expenses	$722,000
Net Income	$1,353,000

Accounting Cycle (continued): [1198a]
The Trojan Company
Statement of Cash Flows
For the Year Ended December 31, Year 2

[Indirect Method]

Net Income	$1,353,000
Less increase in supplies inventory	-40,000
Plus decrease in prepaid insurance	+60,000
Less increase in accounts receivable	-400,000
Less increase in interest receivable	-75,000
Plus increase in interest payable	+2,000
Plus increase in unearned revenues	+1,400,000
Cash flow from operating activities	**$2,300,000**
Buy investments	-2,000,000
Cash flow from investing activities	**-$2,000,000**
Total cash flow	$300,000
Plus: beginning cash	1,925,000
Equals: ending cash	$2,225,000

[Operating cash flow using the direct method:]

Cash from clients	$3,000,000
Salaries paid	-360,000
Paid to suppliers	-160,000
Paid for rent	-180,000
Operating cash flow	$300,000

Accounting Cycle: [1199a]
The Merlin Company
Balance Sheet
December 31, Year 1

Cash	$348,800
Prepaid Rent	14,000
Prepaid Equipment Rent	5,700
Supplies Inventory	1,000
Accounts Receivable	260,000
Total Assets	**$629,500**
Notes Payable	$8,000
Interest Payable	375
Total Liabilities	**$8,375**
Contributed Capital	$90,000
Retained Earnings	531,125
Total Owners' Equity	**$621,125**
Total Liab. & Owners' Equity	**$629,500**

Accounting Cycle (continued): [1199a]
The Merlin Company
Income Statement
For the Five Months Ended December 31, Year 1

Sales Revenue	**$600,000**
Expenses:	
Salaries	$54,000
Rent	10,000
Supplies	3,000
Equipment Rental	1,500
Interest Expense	375
Net Income	**$531,125**

Statement of Cash Flows
Selected Requirements: [1200a]

1. Cash paid for salaries in Year 1.	$95,000
2. Payments for the purchase of Investments in Year 1.	$5,000
3. Notes Payable paid off in Year 1.	$21,000
4. Cash dividends paid in Year 1	$27,000
5. Cash received from the sale of Property, Plant and Equipment in Year 1	$80,000
6. Cash paid for Property, Plant & Equipment in Year 1	$80,000

Statement of Cash Flows: [1201a]

+Net Income	+$1,100	
+Loss on PPE	+500	
-Gain on Investments	-400	
-Increase in AR	-700	
+Decrease in Supplies Inv.	+100	
-Increase in Ppd. Rent	-400	
+Depreciation Expense	+400	
+Amortization Expense	+200	
+Increase in AP	+250	
+Increase in Tax Payable	+200	
-Decrease in Sal Payable	-300	
+Increase in Def. Tax Liability	+100	
Cash from Operations:		+$1,050
+Sale of PPE	+100	
+Sale of Investments	+900	
-Buy Patents	-700	
Cash from Investing:		+300
-Pay Dividends	-350	
Pay NP	-300	
Sell Capital Stock [incl. APIC]	+2,200	
-Buy Treasury Shares	-100	
Cash from Financing:		+1,450
= Net Increase in Cash:		$2,800

Statement of Cash Flows: [1202a]

+Net Income	+$1,000	
-Gain on PPE	-500	
+Loss on Investment	+400	
+Amortization Expense	+100	
+Depreciation Expense	+300	
+Decrease in AR	+200	
-Increase in Supplies Inventory	-100	
-Increase in Ppd. Rent	-100	
-Decrease in AP	-350	
+Increase in Tax Payable	+100	
+Increase in Salaries Payable	+100	
+Increase in Def. Tax Liability	+200	
Cash from Operations:		+ $1,350
+Sale of PPE	+800	
+Sale of Investments	+400	
-Buy Investments	-300	
Buy Patent	-200	
Cash from Investing:		$700
-Pay NP	-100	
Sell Shares [CS+APIC]	+2,100	
-Buy Treasury Shares	-300	
-Pay Dividends	-150	
Cash from Financing:		+$1,550
=Change in Cash: Increase of		+$3,600

Statement of Cash Flows: [1203a]

+Net Income	+$700	
+Loss on PPE	+300	
+Depreciation Expense	+300	
-Gain on Investment	-600	
-Increase in AR	-200	
+Decrease in Ppd. Rent	+400	
+Decrease in Ppd. Salaries	+200	
+Amortization Expense	+300	
+Increase in AP	+930	
+Increase in Interest Payable	+100	
+Increase in Unearned Rev.	+400	
+Increase in Rent Payable	+100	
-Increase in Supplies Inventory	-900	
Cash from Operations:		$2,030
+Sale of PPE	+1,200	
+Sale of Investments	+1,600	
-Buy Investments	-1,200	
-Buy PPE	-800	
-Buy Patents	-2,200	
Cash used in Investing:		-$1,400
-Pay Dividends	-130	
-Pay off NP	-1,900	
+Sell Capital [CS+APIC]	+1,500	
-Increase in Treasury Stock	-200	
Cash used in Financing:		-$730
= Net Decrease in Cash:		-$100

Statement of Cash Flows: [1204a]
Operations:
Net Income	+$60	
Depr. Exp.	+50	
Loss on PPE	+40	
Decrease in AR	+20	
Increase in Supplies	-10	
Increase in AP	+60	
Decrease in Sal. Pay.	-30	+$190

Investing:
Sell PPE	+20	
Buy PPE	-160	-140

Financing:
Issue Capital Stock	+40	
Pay Dividends	-70	
Increase in NP	+20	-10
Net change in cash:		**+$40**

Statement of Cash Flows: [1205a]
Operating Activities:
Net Income	+$60	
Depr. Expense	+40	
Gain on PPE	-100	
Decrease in AR	+30	
Increase in Ppd. Rent	-10	
Increase in AP	+30	
Decrease in Sal Pay.	-20	+30

Investing Activities:
Sell PPE	+120	
Buy PPE	-160	-40

Financing Activities:
Pay Dividends	-10	
Increase in NP	+30	
Issue Capital Stock	+30	+50
Total Increase in Cash		+$40

Statement of Cash Flows: [1206a]
Operating Activities:
Net Income	+$40	
Gain on PPE	-80	
Increase in AR	-90	
Decrease in Ppd. Rent	+10	
Depr. Expense	+50	
Decrease in AP	-30	
Salaries Payable	+20	-$80

Investing Activities:
Sell PPE	+120	
Buy PPE	-50	+70

Financing Activities:
Issue Capital Stock	+20	
Pay Dividends	-20	
Pay Notes Payable	-30	-30
Decrease in Cash		-$40

Statement of Cash Flows: [1207a]
Operating Activities:
Net Income	+$980	
Loss on Investments	+100	
Gain on PPE	-500	
Depreciation Expense	+300	
Amortization Expense	+100	
Decrease in AR	+200	
Increase in Prepaid Rent	-100	
Increase in Supplies Inventory	-100	
Decrease in Prepaid Salaries	+100	
Decrease in Interest Payable	-100	
Decrease in Unearned Revenues	-300	
Decrease in Rent Payable	-500	+$180 |//
Investing Activities
Buy Patents	-2,000	
Sell PPE	+1,200	
Sell Investments	+900	+100

Financing Activities:
Pay Notes Payable	-900	
Issue Capital Stock	+1,200	
Pay Cash Dividends	-380	
Buy Treasury Stock	-100	-180
Net Cash Provided		+$100
Add: Starting Cash		700
Equals: Ending Cash		$800

Statement of Cash Flows: [1208a]
Operating Activities:
Net Income	+$350	
Loss on PPE	+400	
Gain on Investments	-400	
Depreciation Expense	+200	
Increase in AR	-200	
Increase in Supp. Inv.	-200	
Amortization of Patents	+50	
Increase in Salaries Pay.	+300	+$500

Investing Activities:
Sell PPE	+600	
Sell Investments	+2,000	+2,600

Financing Activities:
Pay Cash Dividends	-350	
Pay Notes Payable	-100	
Issue Capital Stock	+1,000	+550
Net Cash Provided		+$3,650
Add: Starting Cash		100
Equals: Ending Cash		$3,750

Statement of Cash Flows: [1209a]
Net Income	+$4,500
+Loss on PPE	+1,000
-Gain on Investments	-6,000
+Depr. Expense	+3,000
-Increase in AR	-2,000
-Increase in Investments	-2,000
+Decrease in Ppd. Rent	+1,000

Statement of Cash Flows (continued): [1209a]

+Increase in AP	+4,000	
-Decrease in Int. Payable	-200	
-Decrease in Unearned Revenues	-1,000	
+Increase in Tax Payable	+2,000	
+Incerase in Sal. Payable	+3,000	
Cash from Operating Activities:		$7,300
+Sale of PPE	+1,000	
+Sale of Investments	+10,000	
-Buy PPE	-17,000	
Cash Used in Investing Activities:		-$6,000
-Pay Dividends	-2,500	
+Increase in LT NP	+10,000	
+Issue Capital Stock	+4,000	
Decrease in current NP	-500	
Cash from Financing Activities:		$11,000
=Net Cash Provided During the Year:		$12,300

Statement of Cash Flows: [1210a]

Net income	+$500
Gain on PPE	-600
Gain on investment	-100
Decrease in AR	+400
Increase Supplies inv	-100
Decrease in Ppd. Ins.	+100
Decrease in Ppd. Rent	+200
Increase in Ppd Sal.	-200
+Deprec. Exp	+100
Decrease in AP	-100
Decrease in Unearned Rev.	-160
Increase in Sal Pay.	+400
Cash from Operating Activities:	**+$440**
Sell PPE	+1,000
Sell Investments	+300
Buy Investments	-500
Buy PPE	-1,700
Cash from Investing Activities:	**-$900**
Pay Cash dividends	-200
Owners invest cash	+200
Cash from Financing Activities:	**-0-**
=Net Cash Used During the Year:	**-$460**

Articulation Exercise: [1211a]

1. Cash paid for salaries in Year 2. **[$150,000]** $_____

2. Payments for the purchase of Investments in Year 2. **[$105,000]** $_____

3. Notes Payable paid off in Year 2. **[$17,000]** $_____

4. Cash dividends paid in Year 2. **[$12,000]** $_____

5. Cash from the sale of Property, Plant and Equipment in Year 2 **[$31,000]** $_____

Articulation Exercise: [1212a]
1. Cash paid for salaries in Year 2. $ 115,000
2. Payments for the purchase of Investments in Year 2. $ 108,000
3. Notes Payable paid off in Year 2. $ 29,000
4. Cash dividends paid in Year 2 $ 38,000
5. Cash received from the sale of PP&E in Year 2 $ 81,000
6. Cash paid for Property, Plant & Equipment in Year 2 $ 160,000

Financial Statement Articulation: [1213a]
December, Year 1 Accounts Receivable	AA=	$600
December, Year 2 Accounts Receivable	BB=	$360
Year 2 Cash Paid for Salaries	CC=	$190
Year 1 Cash Paid for Salaries	DD=	$50
Year 2 Cash Paid for Utilities	EE=	$105
December, Year 2 Utilities Payable	FF=	$35
December, Year 2 Prepaid Insurance	GG=	$85
Year 2 Cash Paid for Insurance	HH=	$35
December, Year 2 Rent Payable	JJ =	$120
December, Year 2 Unearned Rent Revenue	KK=	$185
December, Year 2 Rent Receivable	LL=	$40

Statement of Cash Flows: [1214a]
1. Cash paid for salaries in Year 2 $ 130,000
2. Payments for the purchase of Investments in Year 2 $ 208,000
3. Notes payable paid off in Year 2 $ 13,000
4. Cash dividends paid in Year 2 $ 32,000
5. Cash received from the sale of Property, Plant and Equipment $ 42,000
6. Cash paid to acquire more Property, Plant and Equipment $ 84,000

Financial Statement Articulation: [1215a]
Year 2 Accounts Receivable	AA=	$100
Year 2 Consulting Revenues	BB=	$410
Year 3 Cash Paid for Salaries	CC=	$ 125
Year 2 Cash Paid for Salaries	DD=	$45
Year 2 Cash Paid for Utilities	EE=	$60
December, Year 2 Utilities Payable	FF=	$60
12/02 Prepaid Insurance	GG=	$-0-
December, Year 1 Prepaid Insurance	HH=	$5
December, Year 2 Rent Payable	JJ =	$15
Year 3 Rent Revenues	LL=	$95
Year 2 Cash Collected from Tenants	MM=	$75

Financial Statement Articulation: [1216a]
Year 2 Consulting Revenues	AA=	$240
Year 2 Cash Paid for Salaries	CC=	$ 50
December, Year 2 Utilities Payable	FF=	$30
December, Year 2 Prepaid Insurance	GG=	$15
December, Year 1 Rent Payable	JJ =	$00
Year 2 Rent Revenues	LL=	$80

Financial Statement Articulation: [1217a]

Year 3 Consulting Revenues	AA=_____ $240
Year 2 Consulting Revenues	BB=_____ $210
Year 3 Cash Paid for Salaries	CC=_____ $ 50
Year 2 Salaries Expense	DD=_____ $50
Year 2 Cash Paid for Utilities	EE=_____ $50
December, Year 3 Utilities Payable	FF=_____ $30
December, Year 3 Prepaid Insurance	GG=_____ $15
December, Year 1 Prepaid Insurance	HH=_____ $10
December, Year 2 Rent Payable	JJ =_____ $0
Year 3 Rent Revenues	LL=_____ $80
Year 2 Cash Collected from Tenants	MM=_____ $60

Articulation Exercise: [1218a]
1. Cash paid for salaries in Year 2. **[$124,000]** $_____
2. Payments for the purchase of Investments in Year 2. **[$71,000]** $_____
3. Notes Payable paid off in Year 2. **[$16,000]** $_____
4. Cash dividends paid in Year 2 **[$23,000]** $_____
5. Cash received from the sale of Property, Plant and Equipment in Year 2 **[$69,000]** $_____
6. Cash paid for Property, Plant & Equipment in Year 2 **[$95,000]** $_____

Articulation Exercise: [1219a]
1. Cash paid for salaries in Year 2. $___$145,000
2. **Payments for the purchase of Investments in Year 2.** $___197,000
3. Notes Payable paid off in Year 2. $___26,000
4. Cash dividends paid in Year 2. $___18,000
5. Cash from the sale of Property, Plant and Equipment in Year 2 $__53,000

Statement of Cash Flows: [1220a]
1. Cash paid for salaries in Year 2. $___150,000
2. Payments for the purchase of Investments in Year 2. $___105,000
3. Notes payable paid off in Year 2. $___17,000
4. Cash dividends paid in Year 2. $___12,000
5. Cash received from the sale of Property, Plant and Equipment, $___31,000

Statement of Cash Flows: [1221a]
1. Cash paid for salaries in Year 2. $125,000
2. Payments for the purchase of Investments in Year 2. $43,000
3. Notes Payable paid off in Year 2. $46,000
4. Cash dividends paid in Year 2 $29,000
5. Cash received from the sale of Property, Plant and Equipment in Year 2 $98,000
6. Cash paid for Property, Plant & Equipment in Year 2 $285,000

Statement of Cash Flows: [1222a]
1. Cash paid for salaries in Year 2. — $124,000
2. Payments for the purchase of Investments in Year 2. — $71,000
3. Notes Payable paid off in Year 2. — $16,000
4. Cash dividends paid in Year 2 — $23,000
5. Cash received from the sale of Property, Plant and Equipment in Year 2 — $69,000
6. Cash paid for Property, Plant & Equipment in Year 2 — $95,000

Statement of Cash Flows: [1223a]
1. Cash paid for salaries in Year 2. — $115,000
2. Payments for the purchase of Investments in Year 2. — $18,000
3. Notes Payable paid off in Year 2. — $41,000
4. Cash dividends paid in Year 2 — $38,000
5. Cash received from the sale of Property, Plant and Equipment in Year 2 — $80,000
6. Cash paid for Property, Plant & Equipment in Year 2 — $180,000

Accounting for Uncollectible Accounts Receivable: [1310a]

	Year 1	Year 2	Year 3	Year 4
Using the Percentage of Sales Method:				
Bad Debts Expense for the year	$60	$70	$120	$135
Carrying value of AR at December 31	140	350	500	625
AUA at December 31	10	30	120	155
Using the Aging Method:				
Bad Debts Expense for the year	$70	$70	$60	$110
Carrying Value of AR at December 31	130	340	550	700
AUA at December 31	20	40	70	80

Accounting for Uncollectible Accounts Receivable: [1311a]

	Year 1	Year 2	Year 3	Year 4
Using the Percentage of Sales Method:				
Bad Debts Expense for the year	$45	$40	$100	$110
Carrying value of AR at 12/31	250	300	380	140
AUA at December 31	20	-0-	40	50
Using the Aging Method:				
Bad Debts Expense for the year	$65	$40	$70	$130
Carrying Value of AR at 12/31	230	280	390	130
AUA at December 31	40	20	30	60

Accounting for Uncollectible Accounts Receivable: [1312a]

	Year 1	Year 2	Year 3	Year 4
Using the Percentage of Sales Method:				
Bad Debts Expense for the year	$38	$35	$80	$90
Carrying value of AR at December 31	197	455	665	855
AUA at December 31	13	15	25	25
Using the Aging Method:				
Bad Debts Expense for the year	$55	$28	$140	$55
Carrying Value of AR at December 31	180	445	595	820
AUA at December 31	30	25	95	60

Accounting for Uncollectible Accounts Receivable: [1313a]

	Year 1	Year 2	Year 3	Year 4
Percentage of Sales Method:				
Bad Debts Expense for the year	$60	$70	$120	$135
Carrying value of AR at December 31	140	350	500	625
AUA at December 31	10	30	120	155
Using the Aging Method:				
Bad Debts Expense for the year	$70	$70	$60	$110
Carrying Value of AR at December 31	130	340	550	700
AUA at December 31	20	40	70	80

Accounting for Purchases and Sales of Goods: [1466a]

a. Debit AR and credit Sales, both for $35,000. Decrease the physical count by $20,000.
b. Debit AP and credit Purchases by $50,000 each. Decrease the physical count by $50,000.
c. Debit Purchases and credit AP, both for $60,000. Increase the physical count by $60,000.

Accounting for Purchases and Sales of Goods: [1467a]

a. Debit Purchases and credit AP both for $40,000. Increase the physical count by $40,000.
b. Debit AR and credit Sales, both by $55,000. Decrease the physical count by $30,000.
c. Debit AP and credit Purchases by $70,000 each. Decrease the physical count by $70,000.

Accounting for Purchases and Sales of Goods: [1468a]

[Decrease Sales and AR by $15,000 for the information in 'a' above. The Sale really belongs to Year 2 based on the shipment date.]

[Item 'b' above was incorrectly recorded as a purchase in Year 1. The goods did not belong to Merlin until they were shipped on January 4, Year 2. Purchases and AP were both overstated by $30,000 because the journal entry had been recorded in the wrong year.]

[Item 'c' was correctly recorded in the firm's books on January 4, Year 2.]

[The firm's physical inventory should be reduced by $20,000 (net). Item 'a' should increase the physical inventory by $10,000 because the goods still belonged to Merlin. Item 'b' should reduce the physical count by $30,000 because these goods were erroneously included in the physical count. Merlin did not get title to these goods until the goods arrived on January 11, Year 2. Item 'c' should not be added to Merlin's inventory on December 31, Year 1 because the goods did not belong to Merlin on that date.]

Accounting for Purchase Discounts and Purchase Returns & Allowances: [1469a]

(a) Debit Purchases and credit Accounts Payable each for $1,000. To record the Return of Merchandise: Debit Accounts Payable and credit Purchases Returns each for $500.

(b) Debit Accounts Payable for $500. Credits to Cash for $490 and Purchase Discounts for $10.

(c) Debit Accounts Payable and credit Cash for $500 each.

The entries for the second set of circumstances.
(a) Debit Purchases and credit Accounts Payable both for $5,000. To record the price reduction: Debit Accounts Payable for credit Purchase Allowances for $500 each.

(b) Debit Accounts Payable for $4,500. Credits to Cash for $4,275 and Purchase Discounts for $225.

(c) Debit Accounts Payable for $4,500 and credit Cash for the same amount.

Inventory Methods: [1470a]

Ending Inventories:
1. Perpetual FIFO Year 1 $3,900
2. Perpetual Wtd. Average Year 1 $3,664
3. Perpetual LIFO Year 1 $3,000
4. Periodic FIFO Year 1 $3,900
5. Periodic Wtd. Ave. Year 1 $3,467
6. Periodic LIFO Year 1 $2,750
7. Perpetual FIFO Year 2 $1,350
8. Perpetual Wtd. Ave. Year 2 $1,290
9. Perpetual LIFO Year 2 $ 600
10. Periodic FIFO Year 2 $1,350
11. Periodic Wtd. Ave Year 2. $1,076
12. Periodic LIFO Year 2 $ 600
13. Perpetual FIFO Year 3 $7,300
14. Perpetual Wtd. Ave. Year 3 $6,916
15. Perpetual LIFO Year 3 $5,850
16. Periodic FIFO Year 3 $7,300
17. Periodic Wtd. Ave. Year 3 $6,648
18. Periodic LIFO Year 3 $5,850

Lower-of-Cost-or-Market for Inventories: [1471a]

	Year 1	Year 2
Cost Basis [Periodic FIFO]	$2,500	$18,000
Replacement Cost	$2,500	$18,000
Net Realizable Value [NRV]	$7,200	$28,800
NRV Less Normal Profit	$1,170	$9,360

Effects of Inventory Errors on the Financial Statements: [1472a]
A. [overstated by $15,000]

B. $_____ Year 2 [overstated by $130,000] $_____ Year 3 [understated by $80,000]

C. $_____ Year 2 gross profit [overstated by $180,000] $_____ Year 3 gross profit [understated by $40,000]

Inventories and Lower-of-Cost-or-Market:

A. [LCM is $12 per unit.]

B. [LCM is $129 per unit.]

C. [LCM is $220 per unit.]

Accounting for Inventory Transactions: [1473a]
a. Debit Purchases and credit Accounts Payable both for $25,000.
b. Debit Accounts Payable and credit Purchase Returns for $7,500 each.
c. Debit Accounts Payable and credit Purchases Allowances for $1,000 each.
d. Debit Accounts Payable for $16,500. Credits to Cash for $15,840 and Purchase Discounts for $660.

Other Issues: These three situations are independent from the others.
1. Yes, because freight costs are the ultimate responsibility of the seller when the goods are sold FOB destination.

Accounting for Inventory Transactions (continued): [1473a]
2. $50
3. Expense them immediately or add the labor to the cost of the inventory? Add to the inventory costs as being a necessary cost of making the inventory ready for sale. Add to the cost of inventory

Accounting for Inventories: [1474a]
1. [$297]
2. [$248]
3. [$339]
4. *[understated by $100]*
5. *[understated by $100]*
6. *[overstated by $500]*
7. *[understated by $600]*

Inventory Methods: [1475a]
1. **$1,480**: 10 units @ $8 and 100 units @ $14
2. Sales $20,300 – CGS $8,200 = **$12,100** Gross Margin [Ending inventory was $2,470 (130 units @ $19)]
3. **$6,350** [Ending inventory had been $1,170.]

Inventories and Lower-of-Cost-or-Market: [1476a]
$105 RC What is the 'market' value of each unit when implementing lower-of-cost-or-market procedures?

$110 _ What is the 'cost' of each unit when implementing lower-of-cost-or-market procedures?

$105 What value per unit represents the 'lower-of-cost-or-market' when implementing lower-of-cost-or-market procedures?

Larger or smaller? Without prejudice to your answers above, for the current year if the lower-of-cost-or-market is lower than cost and the ending inventory has to be 'written down', will the net income for the current year be made larger or <u>smaller?</u> Please circle the correct answer.

Larger or smaller? Without prejudice to your answers above, for the current year if the lower-of-cost-or-market is lower than cost and the ending inventory has to be 'written down', will the net income for the subsequent year be made <u>larger</u> or smaller? Please circle the correct answer.

Dollar Value LIFO: [1477a]
1. $670,000
2. $521,739
3. $897,822
4. $739,827
5. $461,538

Accounting for Inventories Using Dollar Value LIFO: [1478a]

Required: Determine the proper ending inventory value for each of the four years Year 2-Year 5 as it would appear in the firm's balance sheets.

December 31, Year 2.....$371,000
December 31, Year 3......434,637
December 31, Year 4......425,546
December 31, Year 5......543,728

LIFO Reserve: [1479a]
1. $1,900
2. $1,850
3. $1,900
4. $1,940

Accounting for Purchases and Sales of Goods: [1480a]

a. The physical inventory is correct and does not have to be adjusted. The goods still belonged to Christopher on December 31 and should be included in the ending inventory on December 31, Year 1. The sale should be recorded in Year 2 as is now the case in the accounting records of the firm for Year 2. Thus, no adjustment is required to either the physical count or to the accounting records for Year 1.

b. The purchased goods should be added to the physical count. These goods belonged to Christopher on December 31, Year 1 since they had been shipped to the firm before the end of the year. The accounting records of the firm also need to be adjusted since the purchase is now recorded in the books for Year 2 and it properly a purchase in Year 1.

c. The goods should be added to the physical count. These goods belonged to the firm and should be reflected in the firm's ending inventory. The purchase and the related Account Payable should be recorded in the books for Year 1.

Installment Sales Method: [1545a]

Gross Profit Recognized by Year:	Year 1	Year 2	Year 3
From Year 1 Sales	$6,000	$15,000	$6,900
From Year 2 Sales		6,000	12,000
From Year 3 Sales			12,000

Deferred Gross Profit At End of Each Year:	Year 1	Year 2	Year 3
From Year 1 Sales	$23,400	$7,200	$-0-
From Year 2 Sales		21,800	9,200
From Year 3 Sales			34,800

Accounting for Long-Term Construction Contracts: [1546a]

Revenues for Each Year	$1,215m	$810m	$675m
Expenses for Each Year	900m	600m	500m
Income for Each Year	315m	210m	175m
Balance in CIP at 12/31	1,215	2,025m	-0-
Balance in Progress Billings At December 31 of Each Year	1,000m	2,000m	-0-
Current Asset or (Current Liability) Amount at the December 31 of Each Year	215m	25m	N/A

Accounting for Long-Term Construction Contracts: [1547a]

Revenues for Each Year	$1,354m	$950m	$896m
Expenses for Each Year	1,100m	700m	900m
Income (Loss) for Each Year	254m	250m	(4m)
Balance in CIP at Dec. 31	1,354m	2,304m	-0-
Balance in Progress Billings At December 31 of Each Year	2,000m	3,000m	-0-
Current Asset or (Current Liability) Amount at the December 31 of Each Year	(646m)	(696m)	N/A

Interest on Self-Constructed Assets: [1548a]
Year 1: Capitalize $65,000 interest in the cost of the office building.
[$1,000,000 x 10% x 6/12] + [$600,000 x 10% x 3/12]

Year 2: Capitalize $134,167 interest in the cost of the office building.
[$2,300,000 x 10% x 7/12]

If the firm had not used funds from a construction loan and had, instead, used funds from operating activities, the interest rate would have been derived from the weighted-average cost of liabilities *unrelated* to the construction of this office building. [In this event, there is maximum amount of interest that can be capitalized. Interest capitalized cannot exceed the actual cost of interest during the period. This prevents firms from using an 'opportunity cost' type of calculation to *increase* their incomes as a result of using internally generated funds.]

Accounting for Long-Term Construction Contracts: [1549a]

	Year 1	Year 2	Year 3
Revenues for Each Year	933 million	614 million	553 million
Expenses for Each Year	800 million	600 million	300 billion
Income for Each Year	133 million	14 million	253 million
Balance in CIP at December 31	933 million	1,547 million	-0-
Balance in Progress Billings At December 31 of Each Year	1,000 million	2,000 million	-0-
Current Asset or (Current Liability) Amount at the December 31 of Each Year	(67 million)	(453 million)	-0-

Accounting for Long-Term Construction Contract Revenues: [1550a]
1. $40,000
2. $60,000
3. $100,000
4. $50,000

A Second Long-Term Construction Contract Example:
1. $1,250
2. $2,697
3. $1,053
4. $1,250

Tax Rates Handout: [1649a]
A MTR: _____ 20% ATR _____ 20%
B MTR: _____ 30% ATR _____ 24.3%
C MTR: _____ 40% ATR _____ 32.5%

If the individual decides to pursue the extra income, calculate the person's ATR *including* that extra income.

A MTR: _____ 21% ATR: _____ 20.5%
B MTR: _____ 35% ATR: _____ 26.7%
C MTR: _____ 40% ATR: _____ 33.3%

Tax Rates Handout: [1650a]
A MTR: _____ 25% ATR _____ 25%
B MTR: _____ 35% ATR _____ 29.3%
C MTR: _____ 30% ATR _____ 27.2%

Tax Rates Handout (continued): [1650a]
If the individual decides to pursue the extra income, calculate the person's new ATR *including* that extra income.

A MTR:	28%	ATR:	26.9%		
B MTR:	35%	ATR:	30.6%		
C MTR:	30%	ATR:	28.2%		

Tax Rates Handout: [1651a]

A MTR:	25%	ATR	15.6%	ATI	$13,500
B MTR:	25%	ATR	20.7%	ATI	$27,750
C MTR:	30%	ATR	26.5%	ATI	$73,500

If the individual decides to give up the extra income, calculate the person's new ATR *excluding* the income given up.

A ATDI	$8,400	MTR:	16%	ATR:	15%
B ATDI	$7,500	MTR:	25%	ATR:	19%
C ATDI	$7,000	MTR:	30%	ATR:	26.1%

Tax Rates Handout: [1652a]
A MTR: 0%   ATR 0%
B MTR 10%   ATR 6%
C MTR: 30%   ATR 18.75%

Each individual has an opportunity to earn an *extra* $10,000 of taxable income. Determine the MTR that is appropriate for each individual to use in making the decision whether or not to earn the extra income. If the individual decides to pursue the extra income, calculate the person's ATR *including* that extra income.

A MTR: 7%   ATR: 4.12%
B MTR: 15%   ATR: 8.57%
C MTR: 30%   ATR: 20%

Accounting for Deferred Taxes: [1653a]

	Year 1	Year 2	Year 3	Year 4
CTE (credit)	$60	$40	$114	$133
DTE (credit)	(20)	30	8	10
Net Income (Net Loss)	160	230	278	257

Accounting for Deferred Taxes: [1654a]

	Year 1	Year 2	Year 3	Year 4
CTE (credit)	$108	$72	$76	$84
DTE (credit)	12	(46)	(56)	21
Net Income (Net Loss)	280	124	80	395

Accounting for Deferred Taxes: [1655a]

	Year 1	Year 2	Year 3	Year 4
CTE (credit)	$40	$46	$96	$96
DTE (credit)	85	(33)	5	(55)
Net Income (Net Loss)	375	137	149	259

Accounting for Deferred Taxes: [1656a]

	Year 1	Year 2	Year 3	Year 4
CTE (credit)	$12	$90	$56	$45
DTE (credit)	48	9	(5)	68
Net Income (Net Loss)	240	151	299	287

Accounting for Deferred Taxes: [1657a]

	Year 1	Year 2	Year 3	Year 4
CTE (credit)	$12	$60	$36	($24)
DTE (credit)	48	(46)	40	(10)
Net Income (Net Loss)	140	136	174	(66)

Accounting for Deferred Taxes: [1658a]

	Year 1	Year 2	Year 3	Year 4
CTE (credit)	$36	$60	$70	($24)
DTE (credit)	18	(10)	7	3
Net Income (Net Loss)	306	170	223	(79)

Accounting for Deferred Taxes: [1659a]

	Year 1	Year 2	Year 3	Year 4
CTE (credit)	$34	$30	$36	($24)
DTE (credit)	16	(16)	39	(9)
Net Income (Net Loss)	200	206	175	(67)

Accounting for Deferred Taxes: [1660a]

Current Tax Expense for Year 1:	$30 debit
Deferred Tax Expense for Year 2:	$50 debit
Total Tax Expense for Year 3:	$100 debit
Deferred Tax Liability in the balance sheet Dated December 31, Year 3	$40 credit

Accounting for Deferred Taxes: [1661a]

Current Tax Expense for Year 1:	$30
Deferred Tax Expense for Year 2:	$50
Total Tax Expense for Year 3:	$100
[CTE=$120 debit, and DTE =$20 credit]	
Deferred Tax Liability in the balance sheet Dated December 31, Year 3 (credit balance)	$40

Taxes: Permanent and Temporary Differences: [1662a]
Year 1 Financial Accounting Income before tax $397,000
Year 1 CTE $60,000 debit
Year 1 DTE $7,000 debit

Year 2 CTE $126,600 debit
Year 2 DTE $10,000 credit

Taxes: Permanent and Temporary Differences: [1663a]
Year 1 CTE $351 debit
Year 1 DTE $81 credit

Year 2 CTE $294 debit
Year 2 DTE $43 debit

Taxes: Permanent and Temporary Differences: [1664a]
Year 1 CTE $6,000 debit
Year 1 DTE $30,000 debit

Year 2 CTE $66,500 debit
Year 2 DTE $8,500 debit

Taxes: Permanent and Temporary Differences: [1665a]
Year 1 CTE $14 debit
Year 1 DTE $26 debit

Year 2 CTE $123 debit
Year 2 DTE $7 debit

Temporary and Permanent Differences Between Tax and Financial Accounting: [1666a]
Year 1 CTE $96 debit
Year 1 DTE $37 debit

Year 2 CTE $40 debit
Year 2 DTE $67 debit

Taxes: Permanent and Temporary Differences: [1667a]
Year 1 CTE $16,500 debit
Year 1 DTE $21,000 debit

Year 2 CTE $96,400 debit
Year 2 DTE $23,000 debit

Deferred Taxes: Permanent and Temporary Differences: [1668a]
Year 1 CTE $155,750 debit
Year 1 DTE $10,500 debit

Year 2 CTE $112,000 debit
Year 2 DTE $24,500 debit

Taxes: Permanent and Temporary Differences: [1669a]
Year 1 CTE $40,800 debit
Year 1 DTE $3,000 debit

Year 2 CTE $86,100 debit
Year 2 DTE $4,500 debit

Taxes: Permanent and Temporary Differences: [1670a]
Year 1 CTE $39 debit
Year 1 DTE $42 debit
Year 1 Net Income $419

Year 2 CTE $164 debit
Year 2 DTE $6 debit
Year 2 Net Income $730

Acquisition Costs of Property, Plant and Equipment [PPE]: [1766a]

Discussion:
1. Capitalize all expenditures except the $22,000 on materials wasted in ordinary use by the firm. This should be expensed as a period cost.
2. Regardless of whether the invoice amount was paid within the discount period of 10 days, the firm should treat the purchase discount as having been taken for purposes of determining the correct cost basis of the this equipment. The extra $14,000 did not *have* to be paid if the firm had wanted to pay the lesser amount sooner. The $14,000 is really an interest expense.
3. The costs of renovating the building's wiring system requires some judgment as to the usefulness of the new wiring for purposes *other than*

Acquisition Costs of Property, Plant and Equipment [PPE] (continued): [1766a]
this particular equipment. The greater the usefulness for other purposes,
the weaker the argument for including the $20,000 as part of the cost basis
of this equipment.

The total capitalized cost should be $732,500.

Accounting for Depreciation: [1767a]
1. $1,333
2. $3,200
3. $15,467
4. (loss of $2,267)

Accounting for Property, Plant and Equipment: [1768a]

	Year 1	Year 2
Depreciation Expense: Straight-Line Method	$116,667	$175,000
Depreciation Expense: Sum-of-the-Years' Digits Method	215,385	305,128
Depreciation Expense: Double-Declining Balance Method	288,889	385,185
Modified Cost Recovery System (assume the printing press is in the 7-Year class)	371,429	636,735

Accounting for Depreciation and Changes of Estimates: [1769a]
1. $1,333
2. $3,200
3. $2,233

Accounting for Trade-Ins of Property, Plant and Equipment: [1770a]
1. Loss of $1,000. New asset at $8,000
2. Loss of $1,000. New asset at $8,000
3. Gain of $2,000] New asset at $7,000
4. Recognized Gain of $250 with $1,750 of deferred gain. New asset at $5,250
5. Recognized gain of –0– with $2,000 of deferred gain. New asset at $7,000

Accounting for Trade-Ins of Property, Plant and Equipment: [1771a]
1. Anderson recognizes a gain of $143 and defers a gain of $857. Anderson's new asset enters the accounting records at $5,143. Mark recognizes a loss of $2,000. Mark's new asset enters its accounting records at $7,000.

2. Anderson recognizes a gain of $1,000 and records its new asset at $6,000.. Mark recognizes a loss of $2,000 and its new asset enters its accounting records at $7,000.

3. Anderson recognizes a loss of $2,000 and records the new asset at $9,000 in its accounting records.. Mark recognizes a gain of $556 and defers a gain of $444. Mark records the new asset at $3,556 in its accounting records.

Accounting for Research and Development Costs and Related Issues: [1772a]
The $4,000,000 expenditure must be capitalized if it was successful and will produce future benefits to the firm through improved efficiency.

The $6,000,000 expenditure must be expensed because it represents a research and development activity to the firm. The expenditure must be expensed even if the results were successful in producing an idea that is commercially viable. This can result in a set of financial statements that are overly conservative. If there are future benefits resulting from the expenditure, the income statement will make it appear the expenditure was unsuccessful because the $6,000,000 will be shown as an expense. However, just because the firm has

Accounting for Research and Development Costs and Related Issues (continued): [1772a]
to expense the $6,000,000, that does not imply that management made a mistake in pursuing its attempt to diversify the firm's operations.

Accounting for Intangible Assets: [1773a]
Year 1: $30,000
Year 2: $40,000
Year 4: $188,333

Accounting for Goodwill: [1774a]
Year 1: $-0- Goodwill is no longer amortized starting in 2002.
Year 2: $-0- Goodwill is no longer amortized starting in 2002.

On January 1, Year 3, the implications for the $300,000 balance in the Goodwill account would involve writing off the entire balance as impaired. The supporting fair market values of the assets acquired earlier no longer justify having Goodwill in the balance sheet. Accordingly, the Goodwill would be written off due to the operations of impairment rules.

Accounting for Property, Plant and Equipment: [1775a]

	Financial Accounting Straight-Line Method	Tax Accounting Double-Declining Balance [Half Year Convention] 5 Year Recovery Period
Depreciation Expense for Year 1	$188,889	$780,000
Depreciation Expense for Year 2	$566,667	$1,248,000
Depreciation Expense for Year 3	$566,667	$748,800
Depreciation Expense for Year 4	$566,667	$449,280*
Depreciation Expense for Year 5	$566,667	$449,280**
Depreciation Expense for Year 6	$566,667	$224,640***
Depreciation Expense for Year 7	$377,778	$--------0
Depreciation Expense for Year 8	$-------0-	$--------0

*This value can be computed using DDB for tax (MACRS) or by doing the straight-line switchover for Year 4. The answer is $449,280 either way.

**This value must be computed using the straight-line switchover for Year 5.

***This value is for the remaining half year of the 5 year life for tax purposes (Cost Recovery Period).

Accounting for Property, Plant and Equipment: [1776a]

	Financial Accounting Straight-Line Method	**Tax Accounting** Double-Declining Balance [Half Year Convention] 3 Year Recovery Period
Depreciation Expense for Year 1	$583,333	$1,400,000
Depreciation Expense for Year 2	$875,000	$1,866,667
Depreciation Expense for Year 3	$875,000	$622,222*
Depreciation Expense for Year 4	$875,000	$311,111**
Depreciation Expense for Year 5	$291,667	$-------0-

*This number can be computed by switching over to straight-line or DDB for tax (MACRS).

**This number must be computed by switching over to straight-line for the last half-year for tax purposes.

Accounting for Property, Plant and Equipment: [1777a]
Financial Accounting
Straight-Line Method
Depreciation Expense for Year 1: **$72,917**
($600,000 - $100,000)/4 = $125,000
($125,000) (7/12) = $72,917

Depreciation Expense for Year 2: $125,000

Depreciation Expense for Year 3: $125,000

Depreciation Expense for Year 4: $125,000

Depreciation Expense for Year 5: $52,083 (not requested in this handout)

Tax Accounting
Double-Declining Balance [Half Year Convention] 3-Year Recovery Period
Depreciation Expense for Year 1: **$200,000**
($600,000 - $0) (2/3) (1/2) = $200,000

Depreciation Expense for Year 2: **$266,667**
($600,000 - $200,000) (2/3) = $266,667

Depreciation Expense for Year 3: **$88,889**
($600,000 - $466,667) (2/3) = $88,889

S.L. 'Switchover' for Year 3:
($600,000 - $466,667) / (3.0 - 1.5) = **$88,889** TIES WITH DDB TAX [we'll use S.L. in Year 4 for the final 'half-year']

S.L. Depreciation Expense in Year 4: **$44,444**
($600,000 - $466,667) / (3.0 - 1.5) = $88,889
$88,889 (1/2) = $44,444

Accounting for Property, Plant and Equipment (continued): [1777a]
Financial Accounting
Double-Declining Balance Method
Depreciation Expense for Year 1:
($600,000 - 0) (2/4)(7/12) = **$175,000**

Depreciation Expense for Year 2:
($600,000 - $175,000) (2/4) = **$212,500**

Depreciation Expense for Year 3:
($600,000 - $387,500) (2/4) = **$106,250**

Depreciation Expense for Year 4:
($600,000 - $493,750) (2/4) = **$6,250*** **FORCED** TO CAUSE THE C.V. TO EQUAL THE SALVAGE VALUE, $100,000.

Property, Plant and Equipment [Operating Assets]   [1778a]
1. $ 390,000

Without prejudice to your answer above, assume you have properly determined the machine's cost basis to have been $400,000. Use $400,000 as the cost basis in meeting the appropriate requirements below.

2. $16,603
3. $354,936
4. $57,143
5. $97,959
6. $32,383

Property, Plant and Equipment [Operating Assets]   [1779a]
7. $480,000

Without prejudice to your answer above, assume you have properly determined the machine's cost basis to have been $500,000. Use $500,000 as the cost basis in meeting the appropriate requirements below.

8. $13,988
9. $452,440
10. $71,429
11. $ 122,449
12. $ 38,026

Accounting for Contingent Liabilities: [1864a]
1. Disclose only
2. Accrue and disclose
3. Ignore or disclose
4. Disclose only

Accounting for Estimated Liabilities: [1865a]
1. Also determine the Estimated Warranty Liability at the ends of Year 1 and 2002. [$370,000 and $710,000, respectively.]
2. Determine the expense associated with this coupon program in Year 1 [$330,000] and the proper liability the firm should recognize at the end of Year 1 [$120,000].
3. Determine the amount of the manager's bonus for Year 1. [Bonus is $34,884]
4. Determine the manager's bonus for Year 1 based on these changed facts. [Bonus is $90,909.]

Accounting for Estimated Liabilities: [1866a]
1. Also determine the Estimated Warranty Liability at the ends of Year 2 and Year 3. [$2,720,000 and $4,260,000, respectively.]
2. Determine the expense associated with this coupon program in Year 2 [$1,100,000] and the proper liability the firm should recognize at the end of Year 2 [$410,000].
3. Determine the amount of the manager's bonus for Year 2. [Bonus is $120,192]
4. Determine the manager's bonus for Year 2 based on these changed facts. [Bonus is $357,142.]

Accounting for Liabilities: [1867a]
1. Determine the Interest Expense for Year 2 for each of the options under consideration.
$98,340.84 Interest Expense for Year 2 [from issuing bonds on December 31, Year 1]
$117,023.35 Interest Expense for Year 2 [from signing a Note Payable on December 31, Year 1]

2. Determine the Cash that would need to be paid out in Year 1 under both options.
$128,000 Cash payments in Year 3 from issuing Bonds Payable on December 31, Year 1.
$318,443.40 Cash payments in Year 3 from signing the Note Payable on December 31, Year 1.

3. Determine the carrying value on June 30, Year 6 [after the proper payment had been made and recorded on that date under both of the options] of the liability that would be created with each of the options.

$1,828,341.01 Carrying Value on June 30, Year 6 if the firm issues bonds on December 31, Year 1.
$991,996.24 Carrying Value on June 30, Year 6 if the firm borrows by signing a Note Payable on December 31, Year 1.

Accounting for Liabilities: [1868a]
1. Bonds would provide $5,486.11 cash and the note payable would provide $5,900.
2. Interest expense of $660.09 with the bonds and $469.52 with the note payable.
3. $600.00
4. $596.18
5. $5,488.19...the easy way to compute this is to recognize that the carrying value on December 31, Year 4 would be equal to the present value of the remaining 34 payments ($298.09 each) at 4% per six months....the PV Factor for an ordinary annuity is 18.411198....multiply the $298.09 times the factor and whoopee!!!!!!]

Accounting for Liabilities: [1869a]
1. How much cash would each alternative provide to the Miles Company on December 31, Year 1? [Bonds would provide $24,524.70 cash and the note payable would provide $25,000.]
2. What interest expense would the firm recognize in Year 2 under both alternatives? [Interest expense of $1,961.22 with the bonds and $1,495.40 with the note payable]
3. How much cash would the Miles Company have to pay out during Year 3 if it chose to issue the Bond Payable? [$2,000.00]
4. How much cash would the Miles Company have to pay out in Year 3 if it chose to borrow the money using the long-term Note Payable? [$1,806.65]
5. What would the carrying value of the Note Payable be on December 31, Year 6 after the tenth loan payment that would be made on that date? [$23,242.21...the easy way to compute this is to recognize that the carrying value on December 31, Year 6 would be equal to the present value of the remaining 50 payments ($903.32 each) at 3% per six months....the PV Factor for an ordinary annuity is 25.72976....multiply the $903.32 times the factor and whoopee!]

Accounting for Bonds Issued at a Premium: [1870a]
1. $22,477.33
2. Debit Cash for $22,477.33 and credits to Premium on Bonds Payable for $7,477.33 and to Bonds Payable for $15,000.00
3. Debits to Interest Expense for $1,123.87 and Premium on Bonds Payable for $226.13. Credit Cash for $1,350.00. New carrying value of $22,251.20
4. Debits to Interest Expense of $1,112.56 and to Premium on Bonds Payable for $237.44. Credit to Cash for $1,350.00
5. Debits to Interest Expense for $1,100.69 and to Premium on Bonds Payable for $249.31. Credit to Cash for $1,350.00
6. Debit to Interest Expense for $1,099.22 and to Premium on Bonds Payable for $261.78. Credit to Cash for $1,350.00
7. Debit Bonds Payable for $15,000 and credit to Cash for the same amount.

Accounting for Bonds Issued at a Discount: [1871a]
1. $17,980.18
2. Debits to Cash for $17,980.18 and to Discount on Bonds Payable for $2,019.82. Credit Bonds Payable for $20,000.00
3. AJE] at December 31, 2001: Debit Interest Expense for $719.21 and credits to Discount on Bonds Payable for $219.21 and to Cash for $500.00
4. Debit Interest Expense for $727.98. Credits to Discount on Bonds Payable for $227.98 and to Cash for $500.00
5. Debit Interest Expense for $737.09 and credits to Discount on Bonds Payable for $237.09 and to Cash for $500.00
6. Debit Interest Expense for $746.58 and credits to Discount on Bonds Payable for $246.58 and to Cash for $500.00.
7. Debit Bonds Payable for $20,000.00 and credit Cash for the same amount.

Accounting for Bonds Payable: [1872a]
1. $340.46
2. $56.66
3. $-0-
4. $463.19
5. Debit Bond Payable and credit Cash, both for $1,000.

Accounting for Bonds Payable: [1873a]
1. $1,597.11
2. Debit Cash for $1,597.11. Credit Bond Payable for $1,000 and Premium on Bonds Payable for $597.11
3. Debit Interest Expense for $47.91 and Premium on Bonds Payable for $52.09. Credit Cash for $100.00
4. $100.00 because there is only one interest payment date in that year.
5. $1,436.12

Accounting for Notes Payable: [1874a]
1. $1,144,571
2. Debit Interest Expense for $240,000 and Notes Payable for $904,571. Credit Cash for $1,144,571
3. Debit Interest Expense for $203,817 and Notes Payable for $940,754. Credit Cash for $1,144,571.
4. Debit Notes Payable and credit Cash both for $4,154,675

Accounting for Liabilities: [1875a]
1. The bonds would provide $9,409.10 cash and the note payable would provide $10,000.
2. Interest expense of $949.43 with the Bonds Payable and $792.87 with the Note Payable
3. $600.00
4. $1,156.60

Accounting for Liabilities (continued): [1875a]
5. $7,859.29...the easy way to compute this is to recognize that the carrying value on December 31, Year 6 would be equal to the present value of the remaining 20 payments ($578.30 each) at 4% per six months....the PV Factor for an ordinary annuity is 13.59033....multiply the $578.30 times the factor and whoopee!
6. $11,553.06...this is the present value of the remaining interest payments (30) and the present value of the face amount both for thirty 6-month periods.

Accounting for Bonds Payable: [1876a]
1. What is the issue price of the bond? **[$1,656.40]**
2. What is the journal entry made at the time the bond is issued? **[Debit Cash for $1,656.41. Credit Bonds Payable for $1,000.00 and Premium on Bonds Payable for $656.41.]**
3. What is the journal entry made at the time of the first interest payment on September 1, Year 1? **[Debit Interest Expense for $41.41 and debit Premium for $58.59. Credit Cash for $100.00.]**
4. How much cash will be paid out to the owners of the bond during Year 1? **[$100.00]**
5. What will be the carrying value of the bond on September 1, Year 2, after the interest payment on that date? **[$1,476.20]**

Accounting for Notes Payable and Bonds Payable: [1877a]
1. What would be the carrying value of the note payable on December 31, Year 2 after the payment for that day had been properly recorded? $_____ [$9,718.33]
2. How much interest expense would Thind Company recognize during Year 3 as a result of issuing the note payable? $_____ [$971.83]
3. How much interest expense would Thind Company recognize during Year 2 if it chooses to issue the ten bonds payable? $_____ [$924.36]
4. What would be the carrying value of the ten bonds payable in the books of the Thind Company on December 31, Year 2 after the interest payment for that day had been properly recorded? $_____ [$11,346.55]

Accounting for Notes Payable and Bonds Payable: [1878a]
1. What would be the carrying value of the note payable on December 31, Year 2 after the payment for that day had been properly recorded? $_____ [$7,185.61]
2. How much interest expense would Thind Company recognize during Year 3 as a result of issuing the note payable? $_____ [$862.27]
3. How much interest expense would Thind Company recognize during Year 2 if it chooses to issue the ten bonds payable? $_____ [$1,030.06]
4. What would be the carrying value of the ten bonds payable in the books of the Thind Company on December 31, Year 2 after the interest payment for that day had been properly recorded? $_____ [$8,758.04]

Accounting for Liabilities: [1879a]

1. Which alternative would provide *more* cash to the Vacation Company on December 31, Year 1? Circle one: Bond Payable or ***Note Payable***?
2. Which alternative would produce the *smallest* Interest Expense during Year 2? Circle One: ***Bond Payable*** or Note Payable
3. How much *cash* would the Vacation Company have to pay out during Year 2 if it chose to issue the Bond Payable? $_____ [$240.00]
4. How much *cash* would the Vacation Company have to pay out in Year 2 if it chose to borrow the money using the long-term Note Payable? $_____ [$300.87]
5. What would the *carrying value* of the Note Payable be on December 31, Year 2 after the first loan payment that would be made on that date? $_____ [$1,603.11]]

Constructing An Amortization Table for a Note Payable: [1880a]

Date	Payment	Interest Expense	Principal Reduction	Carrying Value
May, 1 Year 1				$600,000
November, 1 Year 1	$92,833	$30,000	$62,833	537,167
May, 1 Year 2	92,833	26,858	65,974	471,192
November 1, Year 2	92,833	23,560	69,273	401,919
May, 1 Year 3	92,833	20,096	72,737	329,182
November Year 3	92,833	16,459	76,374	252,808
May, 1 Year 4	92,833	12,640	80,193	172,615
November, 1 Year 5	92,833	8,631	84,202	88,413
May, 1 Year 5	92,833	4,421	88,413*	-0-

*Rounded up by $1.

Constructing An Amortization Table for a Note Payable: [1881a]

Date	Payment	Interest Expense	Principal Change	Carrying Value
April, 1 Year 1				$1,000,000
July, 1 Year 1	-0-	$20,000	+20,000	$1,020,000
October, 1 Year 1	-0-	20,400	+20,400	1,040,400
January, 1 Year 2	-0-	20,808	+20,808	1,061,208
April, 1 Year 2	-0-	21,224	+21,224	1,082,432
July, 1 Year 2	$147,763	21,649	-126,114	956,318
October, 1 Year 2	147,763	19,126	-128,637	827,681
January, 1 Year 3	147,763	16,554	-131,209	696,472
April, 1 Year 3	147,763	13,929	-133,834	562,638
July, 1 Year 3	147,763	11,253	-136,510	426,128
October, 1 Year 3	147,763	8,523	-139,240	286,888
January, 1 Year 4	147,763	5,738	-142,025	144,862
April, 1 Year 4	147,763	*2,901	-144,866	-0-

*adjusted to cause a zero balance after the last payment.

Accounting for Notes Payable: [1882a]
1. $1,672
2. $3,964
3. $13,121

Accounting for Bonds Payable: [1883a]
AAA = $95
BBB = $99
CCC = $3,099
DDD = $22,429
EEE = 6%
FFF = 8%

Accounting for Bonds Issued at a Discount: [1884a]
1. $930.70
2. Debit Cash for $930.70 and Discount on Bonds Payable for $69.30. Credit Bonds Payable for $1,000.00
3. Debit Interest Expense for $55.84. Credit Discount on Bonds Payable for $15.84 and credit Cash for $40.00. The new carrying value is $946.54.
4. Debit Interest Expense for $56.79. Credit Discount on Bonds Payable for $16.79 and to Cash for $40.00. The new carrying value is $963.33.
5. Debit Interest Expense for $57.80. Credit Discount on Bonds Payable for $17.80 and Cash for $40.00. The new carrying value is $981.13.
6. Debit Interest Expense for $58.87. Credit Discount on Bonds Payable for $18.87 and Cash for $40.000. The new carrying value is $1,000.00.
7. Debit Bonds Payable and credit Cash, both for $1,000.00

Accounting for Bonds Issued at a Premium: [1885a]
1. $1,036.30
2. Debit Cash for $1,036.30. Credit Bonds Payable for $1,000.000 and Premium on Bonds Payable for $36.30.
3. Debit Interest Expense for $41.45 and debit Premium on Bonds Payable for $8.55. Credit Cash for $50. The new carrying value is $1,027.75.
4. Debit Interest Expense for $41.11 and Premium on Bonds Payable for $8.89. Credit Cash for $50.00. The new carrying value is $1,018.86.
5. Debit Interest Expense for $40.75 and debit Premium on Bonds Payable for $9.25. Credit Cash for $50.00. The new carrying value is $1,009.61.
6. Debit Interest Expense for $40.38 and debit Premium on Bonds Payable for $9.62. Credit Cash for $50.00. The new carrying value is $1,000.00*. In practice the carrying value is adjusted to equal the face value by adjusting the Interest Expense figure and, in this example, the debit to the Premium on Bonds Payable.
7. Debit Bonds Payable and credit Cash, both for $1,000.00.

Accounting for Interest Payable and Simple Interest: [1886a]
Interest Expense for Year 1:	$83,333
Interest Expense for Year 2:	$50,000
Interest Payable at December 31, Year 1:	$83,333

Simple Interest Examples: [1887a]
1. What Interest Revenue would the firm recognize for each of the four years? [Interest Revenue of $50 for each of the four years]
2. How large a liability must the firm record on December 31 of Year 1? [$826,446]
  How much Interest Expense will the firm recognize in the second year? [$57,851]
3. What will be the size of the monthly car payments? [$725.00 per month]

Compound Interest Examples: [1888a]
1. What Interest Revenue would the firm recognize for each of the four years? **Interest Revenue of $50.00 in Year 1, $52.50 in Year 2, $55.13 in Year 3 and $57.88 in Year 4]**
What amount would be received at maturity? **$1,215.51**

2. How large a liability must the firm record on December 31 of Year 1? **$816,298**
How much Interest Expense will the firm recognize in the second year? **$61,141**

3. How much Interest Expense will the firm recognize over the four-year life of this Note Payable? **$7,874**
How large will be the maturity amount on the Note Payable? **$37,874**
How much Interest Expense will be recognized in Year 4? **$1,908**

4. **$3,756,574**

Accounting for Annuities with Compound Interest: [1889a]
1a. What will be the size of each payment? **$2,716,235**
1b. How much Interest Revenue will the firm recognize during Year 2? **$186,667 in the first four months and $258,334 in the last eight months**
1c. How large will be the carrying value of the investment on April 30, Year 2 after the first annual payment has been received and properly recorded? **$4,843,766**
2a. How large will each of the quarterly payments be? Assume quarterly compounding. $321,479
2b. How much Interest Expense will the firm recognize in the three months ended April 30, Year 2? **$82,268**
2c. What will be the carrying value of the Note Payable on July 31, Year 2, after the payment on that date has been made and properly recorded? **$2,256,681**
3. What is the present value of this series of payments? **$7,435,987**
Would the firm recognize Interest Expense or Interest Revenue each year during the 14 years? **Interest Revenue**

Accounting for Liabilities: [1890a]
Required:
1. $1,135.90
2. $90.69
3. $60.00
4. $100.00
5. $222.79
6. $808.70
7. $1,093.85

Accounting for Liabilities: [1896a]
Required:
1. $1,135.90
2. $90.69
3. $60.00
4. $100.00
5. $222.79
6. $808.70
7. $1,093.85

Accounting for Bonds Payable: [1897a]
Coupon Rate: FFF 7%
Market Rate: GGG 6%
AAA = $ 165
BBB = $ 7,675
CCC = $ 2,630
DDD = $ 170

Accounting for Bonds Payable (continued): [1897a]
EEE = $_____ 7,505
FFF = _____ % 7%
GGG = _____ % 6%

Accounting for Bonds Payable: [1898a]
AAA = $_____ 391
BBB = $_____ 25,967
CCC = $_____ 2,399
DDD = $_____ 401
EEE = $_____ 25,566
FFF = _____ % 8%
GGG= _____ % 5%

Accounting for Treasury Shares: [1931a]
In April Year 2, the Schaefer Company sold 250 treasury shares for $80 per share.
Credit Contributed Capital from T/S transactions, $6,500.

In July Year 2, the Schaefer Company sold 100 of the remaining treasury shares for $50 per share.
Debit Contributed Capital from T/S transactions, $400.

Required:
Determine the proper ending balance in the firm's Contributed Capital account from Treasury Share Transactions on December 31, Year 2. *$6,100*

Accounting for Various Stockholders' Equity Topics: [1932a]
Required:
1. Determine the proper ending balance in the firm's Retained Earnings account at the end of Year 2. **$390,000**
   $500,000 - $40,000 -$170,000 - $200,000 + $300,000]

2. Determine the proper ending balance in the Contributed Capital from Common Stock account at the end of Year 2 resulting from the transactions described.
   $490,000 = $120,000 + $170,000 + $200,000

Calulating Return on Equity: [1933a]
#1 ROE= 35.4%
#2 ROE= 47.1%
#3 ROE= 37.1%
#4 ROE= 38.8%

Accounting for Various Stockholders' Equity Topics: [1934a]
Required:
3. Determine the proper ending balance in the firm's Retained Earnings account at the end of Year 4.
   $600,000 - $30,000 - $170,000 - $300,000 + $750,000 = **$850,000**

4. Determine the proper ending balance in the Contributed Capital from Common Stock account at the end of Year 4 resulting from the transactions described.
   $120,000 + $170,000 + $300,000 = **$590,000**

Accounting for Treasury Shares: [1935a]
Required:
Determine the proper ending balance in the firm's Contributed Capital account from Treasury Share Transactions on December 31, Year 2. **$100**

Various Topics Related to Common and Preferred Shares: [1936a]
Required: Show the journal entry to record the issuance of these shares.
Debit Cash for $600,000 and credit Common Stock contributed Capital for the same amount.
Debit Land for $73,333 and credit Building for $146,667. Credit Preferred Stock Contributed Capital for $220,000

1. In Year 1, The Adrian Company had Net Income of $550,000c. Early in Year 2, the firm decided to issue a 30% common stock dividend when the shares had a fair market value of $20 per share. The board of directors properly determined the Contributed Capital associated with this stock dividend to be $100,000d. No cash dividends were paid in Year 2. During Year 2, the firm had Net Income of $400,000e.

Required: Determine the firm's ending Retained Earnings balance at December 31, Year 2, as a result of this information. Also determine the ending balance for the Contributed Capital from Common Stock account on December 31, Year 2.

December 31, Year 2 Ending RE: $550,000c - $100,000d + $400,000e = $850,000.

December 31, Year 2 Ending Balance for Contributed Capital from Common Stock account: $600,000f + $100,000d = $700,000.

2. Early in Year 3, the firm decided to distribute a 10% common stock dividend when the fair market value of the common shares was $30g each. Net Income in Year 3 was $500,000j. The firm declared and distributed a cash dividend in November Year 3 in the amount of $100,000h.

Required: Determine the firm's ending Retained Earnings balance at December 31, Year 3 as a result of this information.

December 31, Year 3 Retained Earnings balance $850,000 -$136,500g -$100,000h + $500,000j = $1,113,500

3. Early in Year 4, the firm declared and distributed a '2 for 1' stock split when the fair market value of each common share was $120. Cash dividends declared and distributed late in Year 4 amounted to $120,000k. Net Income for Year 4 was $300,000l.

Required: Determine the firm's Ending Retained Earnings balance at December 31, Year 4 as a result of this information.

December 31, Year 4 Retained Earnings balance $1,113,500 - $120,000k = $300,000l = $1,293,500

Accounting for Preferred Share Dividends: [1937a]
Required: Determine the amounts that would be paid to the preferred and common shareholders out of the $470,000 dividend.

Preferred shareholders would get $200,000 x 6% x 3 = $36,000 for dividends in arrears. For the current year preferred shareholders would get $12,000. In total, preferred shareholders would get $48,000.

Common shareholders would get the remainder, or $422,000.

Required: Determine the amounts that would be paid to the preferred shareholders and to the common shareholders out of the $470,000 dividend.

Preferred shareholders would get $200,000 x 6% x 3 = $36,000 for dividends in arrears. For the current year preferred shareholders would get $12,000. Then, the preferred shareholders would get another $60,333A from their 'participation' in the large dividend declared by the board. In total, preferred shareholders would get $108,333.

Various Topics Related to Common and Preferred Shares: [1936a cont.]
Common shareholders would get $60,000B and $301,667 from the allocation of the 'excess' as described in the paragraph below for a total distribution of $361,667.

A: $470,000 – $48,000 to preferred shareholders for three years in arrears and current year - $60,000B to common shareholders [$1,000,000 x 6%] leaves an 'excess' to be allocated of $362,000. Allocate the $362,00 as follows: 10/12 to common and 2/12 to preferred. These are the ratios of the Contributed Capital attributable to common and preferred shareholders, respectively.

Accounting for Treasury Shares: [1938a]
Required: Show the proper journal entries to record each of these treasury share transactions.

1. The journal entry to record the purchase of 1,000 treasury shares.
Debit Treasury Shares for $37,000 and credit Cash for the same amount.

2. The journal entry to record the sale of 400 of the treasury shares at $30 per share.
Debit Cash for $12,000. Debit Retained Earnings for $2,800. Credit Treasury Shares for $14,800.

3. The journal entry to record the sale of 300 of the treasury shares at $60 per share.
Debit Cash for $18,000. Credit Contributed Capital from Treasury Share Transactions for $6,900. Credit Treasury Shares for $11,100.

4. On a related note, what would be the balance in the treasury stock account after all three of the above transactions had been properly recorded? **$11,100.**

Financial Risk: [1939a]
ROE for firm X under these two scenarios are 31.8% and 3.8%. ROE for firm Y under these two scenarios are 67.5% and –2.5%.

Interest Rate Risk:
Solution: the new payment size after making four payments under the initial rate is $34,026.35. The initial payment size is $39,233.05 and four payments in this amount are made. These four payments result in a new principal amount of $396,485.09 that needs to be amortized over the remaining 8 years (two payments per year) using the new interest rate of 8%. Thus, the new payment size is $34,026.35

Foreign Currency Risk:
AR: $70,000
Year 1: $17,500 gain
Year 2: $29,167 loss

Interest Rate Risk: [1940a]
1. $848,633.99.....Divide the amount borrow ($8,000,000) by an Ordinary Annuity Factor (n=30 I=10%: 9.42691) to get the original payment amount.
2. $735,871.98......First, calculate the carrying value after ten payments have been recorded. You can do this the long way by recording ten journal entries. Alternatively, you can calculate the present value of the *remaining* 20 payments at the original interest rate of 10%. Either way, the carrying value on December 1, Year 11 after the payment for that date has been recorded will be $7,24,899.55. Then divide this amount by an Ordinary Annuity Factor (n=20 and I=8%: 9.81815) and you obtain the *new payment size* shown earlier.

Calculating Return on Equity: [1941a]
Alternative #1: 35.43%
Alternative #2: 47.14%
Alternative #3: 37.14%
Alternative #4: 38.78%

Calculating Return on Equity: [1942a]
Alternative #1: 14.6667%
Alternative #2: 44.6667%
Alternative #3: 33.333%
Alternative #4: 36.29%

Interest Rate Risk: [1943a]
1. $627,878.18.....Divide the amount borrow ($5,000,000) by an Ordinary Annuity Factor (n=20 I=11%: 7.96333) to get the original payment amount.
2. $554,532.74......First, calculate the carrying value after three payments have been recorded. You can do this the long way by recording three journal entries. Alternatively, you can calculate the present value of the remaining 17 payments at the original interest rate of 11%. Either way, the carrying value on May 1, Year 4 after the payment for that date has been recorded will be $4,739,723.29. Then divide this amount by an Ordinary Annuity Factor (n=17 and I=9%: 8.54363) and you obtain the ***new payment size*** shown earlier.

Interest Rate Risk: [1944a]
1. $1,174,596.25......Dividing a factor from the ordinary annuity tables (n=20 and I=10%) into the amount borrowed ($10,000,000) you get this payment size.
2. $1,311,738.40....First, get the carrying value of note on May 1, 2006 after the 5t^h payment is recorded on that date ($8,934,072.47). This number can be obtained the 'long way' by recording five journal entries on the payment dates. Alternatively, this carrying value will be equal to present value of the remaining 15 payments using the original interest rate. ($1,174,596.25 times Annuity Factor [n=15 and I=10%: 7.60608]. Second, calculate the ***new payment size*** by dividing this carrying value by an Annuity Factor [n=15 and I=12%: 6.81086

Financial Risk: [1945a]
Required: Calculate the returns on equity [ROE] to these two firms under two different scenarios: one, the firms earn 30% on their assets and, two, the firms earn 5% on their assets. **[ROE for firm A under these two scenarios are 35% and 3.75%. ROE for firm B under these two scenarios are 110% and -15%.]**

Interest Rate Risk:
Required: Calculate the *new* payment size if, after making two payments to the lender, the new interest rate is adjusted to 8%. **[Solution: the new payment size after making two payments under the initial rate is $37,047.98. The initial payment size is $40,121.29 and two payments in this amount are made. These two payments result in a new principal amount of $469,001.35 that needs to be amortized over the remaining 9 years (two payments per year) using the new interest rate of 8%. Thus, the new payment size is $37,047.98.]**

Foreign Currency Risk:
Required: What is the cost of the truck as it would be recorded in the books of Acme on December 1, Year 1? [$1,429]
What is the gain/loss that the Acme Company must show in its Year 1 income statement given the facts as presented here? [Loss of $238]
What would be the gain/loss that would be reported in its Year 2 income statement based on the facts? [Gain of $417]

Accounting for Treasury Shares: [1946a]
1. The journal entry to record the purchase of 1,000 treasury shares.
Debit Treasury Shares for $35,000 and credit Cash for the same amount.

2. The journal entry to record the sale of 400 of the treasury shares at $50 per share.
Debit Cash for $20,000. Credits to Contributed Capital from Treasury Share Transactions and to Treasury Shares for $6,000 and $14,000, respectively.

Accounting for Treasury Shares (continued): [1946a]
   3. The journal entry to record the sale of 300 of the treasury shares at $32 per share.
for $9,600. Debit Contributed Capital from Treasury Share Transactions for $900. Credit Treasury Shares for $10,500.

   4. On a related note, what would be the balance in the Treasury Stock account after all three of the above transactions had been properly recorded? **$10,500**

Accounting for Preferred Share Dividends: [1947a]
Required: Determine the amounts that would be paid to the preferred and common shareholders out of the $170,000 dividend.

Preferred shareholders would get a total of $48,000. [$200,000 x 8% x 2 = $32,000 for the arrears. $16,000 for the current year.]

Common shareholders would get $122,000. [$170,000 - $48,000]

Assume all of the facts above and that the preferred shares were participating as well as cumulative.
Required: Determine the amounts that would be paid to the preferred shareholders and to the common shareholders out of the $170,000 dividend.
Preferred shareholders would get a total of $71,429. [$200,000 x 8% x 2 = $32,000 for the arrears. $16,000 for the current year. Plus, 2/7 of the 'excess' dividend of $106,000 = $23,429.
Common shareholders would get $98,571. [$40,000 + 5/7 of the 'excess' dividend of $82,000 = $58,571]

Assume all of the facts above *except* that the preferred shares are only participating.
Required: Determine the amounts that will be paid to the preferred shareholders and to the common shareholders out of the $170,000 dividend.
P/S: $16,000 + (2/7)($114,000) = $48,570.
C/S: $40,000 + (5/7)($114,00) = $121,430.

Various Topics Related to Common and Preferred Shares: [1948a]
Required: Show the journal entry to record the issuance of these shares.
Debit Cash and credit Contributed Capital for Common Shares both for $500,000.

Debit Land for $40,000 and Building for $80,000. Credit Contributed Capital for Preferred Shares for $120,000.

   1. In Year 1, The Orion Company had Net Income of $300,000A. Early in Year 2, the firm decided to issue a 50% common stock dividend when the shares had a fair market value of $120 per share. The board of directors determined that these shares warrant a Contributed Capital valuation of $250,000B. No cash dividends were paid in Year 2. During Year 2, the firm had Net Income of $400,000C.
Required: Determine the firm's ending Retained Earnings balance at December 31, Year 2, as a result of this information.

Ending Retained Earnings at December 31, Year 2: $300,000A - $250,000B + $400,000C = $450,000.

   2. Early in Year 3, the firm decided to distribute a 20% common stock dividend when the fair market value of the common shares was $130D each. Net Income in Year 3 was $500,000F. The firm declared and distributed a cash dividend in November Year 3 in the amount of $100,000E.
Required: Determine the firm's ending Retained Earnings balance at December 31, Year 3 as a result of this information.
Ending Retained Earnings at December 31, Year 3: $450,000 - $195,000D - $100,000E + $500,000F = $655,000.

Various Topics Related to Common and Preferred Shares (continued): [1948a]
   3. Early in Year 4, the firm declared and distributed a '4 for 1' stock split when the fair market value of each common share was $120. Cash dividends declared and distributed late in Year 4 amounted to $120,000G. Net Income for Year 4 was $300,000H.

Required: Determine the firm's Ending Retained Earnings balance at December 31, Year 4 as a result of this information.

Ending Retained Earnings at December 31, Year 4: $655,000 - $120,000G + $300,000H = $835,000.

Selected Accounting Topics: [1949a]
   1. $_____ What would be the correct ending balance in the firm's Retained Earnings account on December 31, Year 4?
   $400,000 from the net incomes in of the four years reduced by $3,500 by the treasury share sale in Year 4 = $396,500.

   2. $_____ What would be the correct ending balance in the firm's Treasury Stock account on December 31, Year 4?
   $35,000 = 700 shares still owned times their $50 per share cost basis.
   3. **22.4%.**
   4. **4.4%**
   5. **Gain $10,714**
   6. **$45,000 loss**

Accounting for Owners' Equity: [1950a]
   1. **$70,000** How much money would the common shareholders receive from the cash dividend declared and paid on December 31, Year 2?

   The preferred shareholders would get $10,000 for 'arrears' dividends and $10,000 for the current year. Then the common shareholders would get $35,000 [10% of $350,000]. The 'excess' dividends are $45,000. Common shareholders would get 35/45 of this amount, or $35,000. Total distributions to the common shareholders would be $70,000

   2. **The increase in RE would be $425,000 [$500,000 less $75,000]**
   3. **$31,839 [$20,000 + $11,839]**
   The preferred shareholders would get $20,000 initially [$10,000 for arrears from Year 3 and $10,000 for Year 4]. Common shareholders would then get $77,000, 10% of their Contributed Capital account balance ($770,000A) as adjusted since the start of the firm. The initial distributions to both preferred and common shareholders would be $97,000. The excess dividend to be allocated would be $103,000. $100,000/$870,000 of this excess would go to preferred shareholders ($11,839). $770,000/$870,000 of this excess would go to common shareholders ($91,161). [A: Contributed Capital for common shareholders: $350,000 + $75,000 + $345,000 = $770,000.]

Accounting for Marketable Securities: [2121a]
11. Trading securities: $4,000 realized gain and $23,000 unrealized gain
12. AFS $nothing…..
13. $6,000 unrealized gain [from AFS]
14. Trading securities: $13,000 realized loss and $5,000 unrealized loss
15. AFS $nothing……
16. $1,000 unrealized loss [from AFS]

Accounting for Marketable Securities: [2122a]
11. Trading securities: $2,000 realized gain and $25,000 unrealized gain
12. AFS $nothing.....
13. $4,000 unrealized gain
14. Trading securities: $11,000 realized loss and $9,000 unrealized loss
15. AFS $nothing
16. $3,000 unrealized loss

Accounting for Marketable Securities: [2123a]
Based on the information given, what items would appear in the income statement of the Hopkins Company for the year ended **December 31, Year 2**?

Trading securities:
    $1,750 realized gain
    $1,000 unrealized loss

AFS:
    Realized gain/loss (if any) NONE
    Unrealized gain/loss (if any) NONE

Based on the information given, what items would appear in the income statement of the Hopkins Company for the year ended **December 31, Year 3**?

Trading securities:
    $2,250 realized loss
    $1,500 unrealized gain

AFS:
    $5,000 realized gain
    Unrealized gain/loss (if any) NONE

Accounting for Marketable Securities: [2124a]
Trading securities:
    $750 realized gain

    Unrealized gain/loss (if any) NONE   [By chance, the Valuation Allowance balance does not have to be adjusted.]

AFS:
    Realized gain/loss (if any) NONE

    Unrealized gain/loss (if any) NONE

Based on the information given, what items would appear in the income statement of the Hopkins Company for the year ended **December 31, Year 3**?

Trading securities:
    $4,500 realized gain
    $5,250 unrealized loss

AFS:
    $1,000 realized gain
    Unrealized gain/loss (if any) NONE

Accounting for Trading Securities: [2125a]
What would appear in the USC Company's income statement for the year ended December 31, Year 2 and related to the *trading securities portfolio?*?
Unrealized Loss of $2,000 and Dividend Revenue of $1,200

What accounts and balances would appear in the USC Company's balance sheet dated December 31, Year 2 related to the *trading securities portfolio?*
Trading Securities at cost = $28,000 and a credit balance in the Valuation Allowance for $2,000. The fair market value of this portfolio is $26,000 on this date.

Accounting for Marketable Securities: [2126a]
Based on the information given, what items would appear in the income statement of the Hopkins Company for the year ended December 31, Year 2?
Debt Securities HTM: *Only Interest Revenue which cannot be determined from this data.*
Trading securities   **Realized Gain of $2,000 and Unrealized Gain of $5,000**
AFS: *Nothing would appear in the income statement for the AFS portfolio*
[For the AFS (Available for Sale Portfolio), there would be $2,000 and $3,000 Unrealized Gains in the stockholders' equity section of the balance sheets at December 31, Year 1 and December 31, Year 2, respectively.]

Accounting for Marketable Securities: [2127a]
Debt Securities HTM: $1,600 Realized Gain and Interest Revenue that cannot be determined from this data.
Trading securities: $3,000 Realized Loss and $2,000 Unrealized Loss
AFS $nothing......

Based on the information given and for the following portfolios, what items would appear in the balance sheet of the Wayne Company for the year ended December 31, Year 2?

Debt Securities HTM: $10,000 would be the value for this portfolio in the balance sheet.
Trading securities: at cost of $28,000 and a credit balance in the Valuation Allowance of $1,000, yielding a fair market value of $27,000.

Accounting for Marketable Securities: [2128a]
Based on the information given, what items would appear in the income statement of the Wayne Company for the year ended December 31, Year 2?
Debt Securities HTM: Interest revenue only
Trading securities   Unrealized Loss $3,000
                      Realized Gain of $2,000
AFS   Nothing

[For the AFS (Available for Sale Portfolio), there would be $3,000 Unrealized Gain in the stockholders' equity section of the balance sheet at December 31, Year 2.]

Accounting for Available for Sale Securities: [2129a]
What would appear in the USC Company's Income Statement for the year ended December 31, Year 2? [Dividend Revenue of $800. Interest Revenue of $8,622. Amortization of the premium on the Bonds Investment was $1,378.]

What accounts and balances would appear in the USC Company's balance sheet dated December 31, Year 2? [*Available for Sale Securities* $113,790 (fair market value). The cost basis of these securities is $122,733* and the balance in the Valuation Account is a credit balance of $8,943. *In the stockholders' equity section there would be an Unrealized Loss for $8,943 (debit balance).* *Assumes amortization of the premium on the Investment in Bonds was $1,378 in Year 2.]

Accounting for Available for Sale Securities (continued): [2129a]

During Year 3, the firm purchased 500 shares of Acme Corporation for $60 per share. USC also sold all 400 Orion shares for $30 per share before USC received any dividends in the year. USC Company continued to hold the bonds throughout Year 3 because it expected interest rates to rise.

What journal entry would be made at the time of the sale of the Orion shares? [Debit Cash for $12,000 and debit Realized Loss for $4,000. Credit *Available for Sale Securities* for $16,000.]

At December 31, Year 3, the fair market value of all 100 bonds was $105,242. [The effective rate had fallen back to 8%.] The fair market value of all 500 Acme shares at December 31, Year 3 was $31,000.

What would appear in the USC Company's income statement for the year ended December 31, Year 3? [Realized Loss of $4,000. Interest Revenue of $8,509.39*. (*Premium amortization of $1,490.61.)]

What would appear in the USC Company balance sheet at December 31, Year 3?

Available for Sale Securities at fair market value of $136,242. (The cost basis of these securities would be $135,242 and there is a $1,000 debit balance in the Valuation Account. There is an Unrealized Gain on Available for Sale Securities of $1,000 in the stockholders' equity section. This account has a credit balance.)

Accounting for Investments Using the Equity Method: [2143a]

Required: Prepare journal entries recording this information in the books of the Orion Company for Year 1:

Investment		$8,000,000	
Cash			$8,000,000
Investment		600,000	
Equity in Earnings of Mark			600,000
Cash		150,000	
Investment			150,000
Equity in Earnings of Mark		160,000	
Investment			160,000
Equity in Earnings of Mark		880,000	
Investment			880,000

In Year 2, Mark reported earnings of $4,000,000. Mark declared and paid dividends of $200,000 in Year 2.

Orion did not change its ownership interest over Mark during Year 2.

Required: Prepare proper journal entries recording this information in the books of Orion for Year 2.

Investment		$1,200,000	
Equity in Earnings of Mark			$1,200,000
Cash		60,000	
Investment			60,000

Accounting for Investments Using the Equity Method (continued): [2143a]

Equity in Earnings of Mark	160,000	
Investment		160,000
Equity in Earnings of Mark	880,000	
Investment		880,000

Accounting for Investments Using the Equity Method: [2144a]

Required: Prepare journal entries recording this information in the books of the Michigan Company for Year 1:

Investment	$5,000,000	
Cash		$5,000,000
Investment	400,000	
Equity in Earnings of UCLA		400,000
Cash	40,000	
Investment		40,000
Equity in Earnings of UCLA	80,000	
Investment		80,000
Equity in Earnings of UCLA	100,000	
Investment		100,000

In Year 2, UCLA reported earnings of $2,000,000. UCLA declared and paid dividends of $150,000 in Year 2.
MICHIGAN did not change its ownership interest over UCLA during Year 2.

Required: **Prepare proper journal entries recording this information in the books of MICHIGAN for Year 2.**

Investment	$800,000	
Equity in Earnings of UCLA		$800,000
Cash	60,000	
Investment		60,000
Equity in Earnings of UCLA	80,000	
Investment		80,000
Equity in Earnings of UCLA	100,000	
Investment		100,000

Accounting for Non-Marketable Investments Using the Cost Method: [2145a]

Required: Prepare journal entries to record this information in the financial records of the Merle Company.

Yr. 1	Investment	$1,800,000	
	Cash		$1,800,000

Recognizes having paid $60 per share for 30,000 shares of Courtney.

Accounting for Non-Marketable Investments Using the Cost Method (continued): [2145a]

Yr. 1	Dividend Receivable	100,000	
	Dividend Revenue		100,000

Recognizes Merle's 5% of Courtney's declared dividend of $2,000,000 in Year 1.

Yr. 2	Cash	103,000	
	Dividend Receivable	2,000	
	Dividend Receivable		100,000
	Dividend Revenue		5,000

To recognize receipt of $100,000 from the Year 1 dividend *and* $3,000 of the dividend declared in Year 2 and paid in Year 2. 40% of the $100,000 Year 2 dividend will not be paid until January Year 3. Merle's share is 5% or $2,000 and this becomes a Dividend Receivable. The credit to Dividends Receivable is for the $100,000 received from the Year 1 dividend. Dividend Revenue is from the accrual basis and recognizes 5% of the dividend declared in Year 2 [$100,000 x 5%].

Yr. 3	Cash	2,000	
	Dividend Receivable		2,000

Records the receipt of $2,000 dividends declared in Year 2 payable in Year 3.

Yr. 3	Dividend Receivable	2,500	
	Dividend Revenue		2,500

Records Merle's share of Courtney's dividend declared in Year 3, but payable in Year 4.

Yr. 4	Impairment Loss	900,000	
	Investment		900,000

Records Merle's impairment loss in Year 4 related to the investment in Courtney. The investment is being written down to $900,000.

	Cash	2,500	
	Dividend Receivable		2,500

Records Merle's share of Courtney's dividends declared in Year 3, but paid to Merle in Year 4.

Accounting for Non-Marketable Investments Using the Cost Method: [2146a]

Required: Prepare journal entries to record this information in the financial records of the Brian Company.

Yr. 1	Investment	$4,000,000	
	Cash		$4,000,000
	Dividend Receivable	1,000	
	Dividend Revenue		1,000
Yr. 2	Dividend receivable	10,000	
	Cash	31,000	
	Dividend Receivable		1,000
	Dividend Revenue		40,000
Yr. 3	Cash	10,000	
	Dividend receivable	4,000	
	Dividend Receivable		10,000
	Dividend Revenue		4,000
Yr. 4	Impairment Loss	3,890,000	
	Investment		3,890,000
	Cash	4,000	
	Dividend receivable		4,000

Consolidated Financial Statements: [2147a]

	Stephen	Jasmine	Consolidated
Cash	$100	$150	$250
Accounts Receivable	200	350	500
Investment in Jasmine	500	---	-0-
PPE (net)	600	400	1,000
Total Assets	$1,400	$900	$1,750
Accounts Payable	$200	$350	$500
Mortgage Payable	300	50	350
Capital	600	200	600
Retained Earnings	300	300	300
Total Liab. & Owners' Equity	$1,400	$900	$1,750

Consolidated Financial Statements: [2148a]

The Alicia Company has 70% ownership interest in Brian Company. The separate financial statements of the Alicia Company and Brian Company are shown below.

	Alicia	Brian	Consolidated
Cash	$200	$400	$600
Accounts Receivable	300	600	800
Investment in Brian	700	---	-0-
PPE (net)	800	500	1,300
Total Assets	$2,000	$1,500	$2,700
Accounts Payable	$100	$300	$300
Mortgage Payable	400	200	600
Minority Interest	-0-	-0-	300
Capital	900	600	900
Retained Earnings	600	400	600
Total Liab. & Owners' Equity	$2,000	$1,500	$2,700

Consolidated Financial Statements (continued): [2148a]

Brian owes $100 to Alicia [AR/AP]. There were no inter-company transactions in the current year. The book values of Brian's assets and liabilities equal their fair market values.

Prepare a consolidated balance sheet for the Alicia Company.

Consolidated Financial Statements: [2149a]

	Liz	Jess	Consolidated
Cash	$700	$400	$ 1,100
Accounts Receivable	400	600	700
Investment in Jess	960	---	-0-
PPE (net)	800	1,100	1,900
Total Assets	$2,860	$2,100	$ 3,700
Accounts Payable	$160	$500	$ 360
Mortgage Payable	1,000	400	1,400
Capital	800	700	800
Minority Interest (20%)			240
Retained Earnings	900	500	900
Total Liab. & Owners' Equity	$2,860	$2,100	$ 3,700

Consolidated Financial Statements: [2150a]

	Kyle	**Bonita**	**Consolidated**
Cash	$300	$500	$ 800
Accounts Receivable	400	300	650
Investment in Bonita	900	---	-0-
PPE (net)	800	900	1,700
Total Assets	$2,400	$1,700	$ 3,150
Accounts Payable	$300	$450	$ 700
Mortgage Payable	500	350	850
Capital	600	300	600
Retained Earnings	1,000	600	1,000
Total Liab. & Owners' Equity	$2,400	$1,700	$ 3,150